CHRISTIAN ORIGINS IN
EPHESUS AND ASIA MINOR

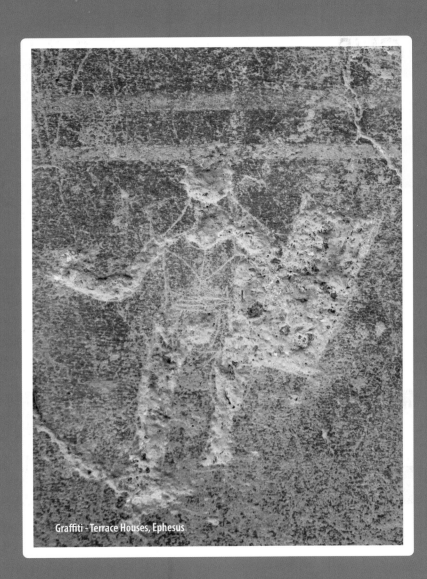
Graffiti - Terrace Houses, Ephesus

CHRISTIAN ORIGINS IN
EPHESUS AND
ASIA MINOR

Mark R. Fairchild, Ph.D.
Luke J. Peters Professor of Biblical Studies
Huntington University

HIERAPOLIS • ALEXANDRIAN TROAS • MILETUS
NICAEA • LAODICEA • COLOSSAE • ASSOS
NICOMEDIA • METROPOLIS • NYSA • PHILADELPHIA
EPHESUS • THYATIRA • SARDIS • PERGAMON
MAGNESIA • TRALLES • SMYRNA • APHRODISIAS

Christian Origins in
Ephesus and Asia Minor

Author
Mark R. Fairchild

Photos
All photos copyright by Mark R. Fairchild

Layout
Cüneyt Oral, Tutku Tours

Cover Design and Maps
Sinan Özşahinler, Tutku Tours

Publisher Company
Arkeoloji ve Sanat Yayınları Tur. San. Tic. Ltd. Şti.
Hayriye Cad. Cezayir Sok. No.5/2 Beyoğlu-İstanbul

Printing Company
İnkılap Kitabevi Baskı Tesisleri
Printing Certificate No: 10614
Çobançeşme Mah. Altay Sk. No: 8
Yenibosna – Bahçelievler / İstanbul

ISBN: 978-605-396-333-2
Certificate No: 10479

Bookstores:

arkeo_pera_
Yeniçarşı Cad. No: 66/A
34433, Galatasaray
Beyoğlu-İstanbul
Tel.: 0212 249 92 26

arkeo_ege_
Kıbrıs Şehitleri Caddesi
1479 Sok. No: 10/A
Alsancak-Konak-İzmir
Tel.: 0232 422 36 38

www.arkeolojisanat.com / info@arkeolojisanat.com

Contents

Chapter 3

Chapter 4

Chapter 5

Chapter 6

In memory of

Donald Gerald (Ike) Fairchild

May 11, 1931 – August 28, 2004

and

Robert Leroy Marsh

January 19, 1924 – August 2, 2010

Εὐχαριστῶ τῷ θεῷ μου ἐπὶ πάσῃ τῇ μνείᾳ ὑμῶν.

Philippians 1:3

Acknowledgments

The process of writing this book has involved many years of travel in Turkey and the opportunity to meet hundreds of wonderful and gracious Turkish people who have assisted me in my research. There are far too many people to mention by name, but the hospitality that I have received from numerous strangers in this land has overwhelmed me time and time again. As I have traveled to remote sites throughout Anatolia, I have often stopped at cafes to ask for directions. On many occasions the local residents have hopped into my vehicle and have accompanied me to sites where they have spent several hours with me in the field. As a stranger, I have been taken into a number of Turkish homes where I have been introduced to families and have been fed meals and have been given gifts. I am embarrassed to say that I have seldom been as gracious and hospitable as my Turkish friends. I do not know how to express my gratitude to them except to put it in print.

Foremost among my Turkish friends, I must mention Levent Oral, the owner and president of Tutku Tours. Without his friendship and benefactions none of this would be possible. Additionally, I wish to thank the staff at Tutku Tours who have made numerous arrangements for my complicated itineraries throughout Turkey. Their flawless precision has made my journeys more productive and enjoyable. I also want to thank Sinan Özşahin for his work on the maps in this volume and Cuneyt Oral for his tireless work on the layout of the book.

Huntington University has honored me with the Luke J. Peters Chair of Biblical Studies and the university graciously awarded me a sabbatical leave for the writing of this book. The assistance and support of the university and my colleagues has meant a great deal to me. I have been truly blessed to work at Huntington University.

Finally and most profoundly, I want to thank my wife Darlene for her patience and support, particularly during the weeks and months that I have been away from home on my travels. Together, we have raised four wonderful children, Peter, Hannah, Ennea and Malina and words cannot express how proud I am of each of them. Most of the credit for their upbringing is due to Darlene who has provided the parental care necessary during my travels.

Pontus Euxinus

Propontis

Nicomedia

Chalcedon

Pythia Therma

Nicaea

Parium

Cyzicus

Caesarea Germanice

Cius

Apamea Myrlea

Lampsacus

Apollonia ad Rhynadacum

Prusa ad Olympum

Abydus

Miletopolis

Dardanus

Hadriani

Ilium

Scepsis

Pionia

Dorylaeum

Midaeum

Alexandria Troas

Antandrus

Hadrianutherae

Hadrianeia

Accilaeum

Gargara

Assos

Adramyttium

Cotiaeum

Nacoleia

Perperene

Ancyra

Aezani

Mirus

LESBOS

Pergamum

Stratonicea (Hadrianopolis)

F. Caecus

Synaus

Cadi

Appia

Aquae

Attaea

Nacrasa

Alia

Cidyessus

Pitane

Thyatira

Iulia Gordus

Temenothyrae (Flaviopolis)

Dioclea

Prymne

Myrina

Aegae

Tomaris

Silandus

Acmonia

Bruzus

Palaeobeudus

Cyme

Hierocaesarea

Bagis

Eucarpeia

Phocea

Magnesia ad Sipylum

Daldis (Flaviopolis)

Thermae Theseos

Sebaste

Hierapolis

Tabala

Bria

Erythrae

Smyrna

Sardis

Philadelphia

Eumeneia

Stectorium

Metropolis

Clazomenae

Blaundus

Teos

Hypaepa

Apollonierum

Apamea

Lebedus

Metropolis

Colophon

Antiochia ad Maeandrum

Hierapolis

Notium

Laodicea

Ephesus

Nysa

Mastaura

Harpasa

Colossae

Sanaus

Magnesia

Tralles

Orthosia

Aphrodisias

Lysinia

SAMOS

Priene

Heraclea Salbace

Sagalassus

Miletus

Alabanda

Neapolis ad Harpasum

Apollonia Salbace

Hadriani

Alinda

Heraclia ad Latmum

Sebastopolis

Colonia Olbasa

Euromos

Labranda

Cys

Tabae

Cidramus

Andeda

Iasus

Mylasa

Stratonicea

Pogla

PATMOS

Bargylia

Cibyra

Laghe

Verbe

Myndus

Halicarnassus

Ceramus

Bubon

Balbura

Bargasa

Termessus Minor

COS

Oenoanda

Caunus

Cadyanda

Calynda

Telmessus

Tlos

Choma

Pinara

Arneae

Arycanda

Sidyma

Candyba

Limyra

Xanthus

Myra

RHODES

Patara

Phellus

Cyaneae

Antiphellus

Aperlae

Aegean Sea

CHIOS

1st Century Asia Minor

Design by TUTKU TOURS

Red = Paul's First Mission
Blue = Paul's Second Mission

Green = Paul's Third Mission

Ephesus Celsus Library

Introduction

Scholars today believe that Ephesus was one of the five largest cities in the Mediterranean region during the first century. A visit to the archaeological site today confirms that the ancient city was indeed large. The apostle Paul visited Ephesus on his third missionary journey and spent more time at Ephesus than he did at any other location on his journeys. Due to its size and strategic location, Ephesus was an important city. After Paul's death, his disciple Timothy spent a considerable amount of time in Ephesus. Then in the last decades of the first century, the apostle John made his home in Ephesus, where early church traditions claim he was buried. Even in the early years of the second century we have evidence of a flourishing Christian church in Ephesus and the surrounding region.

In time, Ephesus became the center of Christian ministries in Asia Minor. While in Ephesus, Paul established the School of Tyrannos (Acts 19:9). The school was probably no more than a lecture hall that a patron, Tyrannos, provided for Paul's use. Here Paul trained disciples for two years, teaching them the basics of the faith and strategies for evangelism. In time he sent them out to dozens of other locations in Asia Minor where they shared the gospel and established churches. As a result, Luke could make the exaggerated claim that "all who lived in Asia heard the word of the Lord" (Acts 19:10).

At some point in the latter half of the first century, the apostle John moved to Ephesus. During John's ministry at Ephesus, he was recognized as the "elder," the patriarch and leader of the Christian community in Asia Minor. In a similar way to what Paul was doing, John also sent several of his students (disciples) to the surrounding cities and churches. The largest of these congregations were mentioned in the seven letters found at the beginning of the book of Revelation. These churches were having difficulties integrating their Christian faith and practices with the imperial demands of Domitian near the end of the first century. By this time Christianity had spread throughout Asia Minor, Phrygia, Mysia and Bithynia and the Christian populations in

Fig. 1 Ephesus Scholasticia Baths
*These baths were constructed in the 2nd century around the temple of Hadrian,
on the north side.*

the cities were faced with some tough decisions. Should they submit to the demands of emperor worship, or stubbornly resist and face the ridicule, harassment and persecutions that would surely follow?

The writings of the early Christians tell us a great deal of what happened when the Christian faith first burst upon the scene in Ephesus and the surrounding territory. But, there was much more that the Scriptures did not record. Paul, John and their disciples visited many cities and towns throughout the region as they carried the gospel message to the people of Asia Minor. Luke, the author of the Acts of the Apostles went so far as to say that all of Asia Minor heard the Christian message (Acts 19:10). Recent archaeological work and research at Ephesus have added many insights to our understanding of early Christianity at Ephesus. This book will describe recent discoveries at Ephesus and their bearing upon the origin of Christianity in the city. We will also look at the impact of Paul's ministry not only in Ephesus, but also in the surrounding cities and villages of Asia Minor. Additionally, we will explore the extension of Paul's ministry through his disciples who ministered in Ephesus and beyond. Thus, we will explain the history and archaeology of other significant cities in Asia Minor, including cities not mentioned in the N.T., but cities where Christianity most probably was established in the first century.

In time, the apostle John migrated to western Anatolia and Ephesus. Thus, we will also examine John's ministry in Ephesus and Asia Minor. Finally, we will examine the writings of Ignatius, a Christian bishop who wrote letters to several churches in western Anatolia as he was taken to Rome to be executed for his faith. At about the same time in the first decade of the second century, the governor of Bithynia, Pliny the Younger, wrote a letter to the Roman emperor Trajan regarding the recrimination of Christians in the province. These letters offer us insights into the evolving plight of Christians short-ly after the apostolic period and lead us into the fluctuating fortunes of the Anatolian Christian community during the later imperial period.

Any attempt to synthesize the letters attributed to Paul in the New Testament with the Acts of the Apostles, the Johannine writings, the book of Revelation, Ignatius' writ-ings and Pliny's correspondence will risk criticism from many quarters. Some scholars will question the historicity of some of the sources. Others will question the dating

Fig. 2 Ephesus Reused Sarcophagus with Alpha Omega and Chi Rho

This sarcophagus was reused during the Byzantine period. The original in-scription on the side has been largely chiseled out. The lid displays two com-mon Christian symbols: a Chi-Rho (the first two letters of Christos), flanked by an Alpha and Omega. In Rev 22:13 Jesus said "I am the Alpha and the Omega, the first and the last, the beginning and the end."

and / or authenticity of the sources. There are numerous issues that this volume cannot address without detracting from its primary purpose. Indeed, no single approach to the issues could be concocted that would satisfy all parties. Many people reading this are aware of the historical issues surrounding the Acts, particularly regarding Luke's recollection of the speeches. Others will point to the letters attributed to Paul. Some scholars do not accept that Paul wrote letters to the Ephesians or the Colossians and many scholars do not subscribe to the Pastoral Epistles as Pauline epistles. Since there was probably more than one Christian leader in Asia Minor named John, many scholars believe that John's gospel, epistles and apocalypse were written by different people. Additionally, the dating of all these documents is yet another complicating factor that is greatly disputed among scholars. I do not want to give the impression that New Testament studies are mired in intractable disputes and controversies. In fact, recent research has greatly advanced our understanding of the ancient world and the Bible. However, I do want to illustrate the impossibility of writing a volume that will satisfy all readers. Consequently, the present volume will express the common traditional understanding of the issues. That is to say that the early Christian community generally believed that Paul authored these letters, that John the apostle authored three letters and the apocalypse and that Luke's Acts gives reliable information. I assume that readers will be able to modify the data that I present here according to their own perspectives. For those who wish to date Paul's Letters later in the first century (Ephesians & Colossians to the 70's and the Pastoral Epistles to 80's) the sequencing of these books in this volume still holds true. Those who wish to investigate the issues more thoroughly should consult the commentaries that I have listed in the bibliography. These commentaries are recognized as some of the top commentaries and they represent all of the positions on the topics that I've just discussed.

There are several technical terms that are used throughout this volume. Most of these terms are explained when they are first used. However, I have provided a glossary at the end of the book for reference. Additionally, I have supplied two charts that are appended to the volume. The first is a chart of the various archaeological periods with dates and a brief description of the period. The second chart is a timeline of Asia Minor that integrates important historical events that have impacted Asia Minor along with a listing of the Roman emperors and significant biblical events that were related to Asia Minor.

Chapter 1

Ephesus: The Proud City of Artemis

The cult site at Ephesus established for the worship of the Anatolian mother goddess may be one of the oldest sanctuaries in Anatolia. The beginning of the cult is enshrouded in the vague stories of myth and history. Pindar (according to Pausanias) claimed that the cult originated with the Amazon women who established a place for the worship of the mother goddess at Ephesus. Callimachus likewise supports this version asserting that the Amazons set up a cult statue of the goddess beneath an oak tree and danced around it in their armor. Pausanias however, claimed that the sanctuary was established earlier. Instead, Pausanias asserted that Coresus, a son of the earth and Ephesus, a son of the river god Cayster founded the cult site. Although the issue is debated, this early cult site was probably dedicated to Cybele the indigenous Anatolian mother god. When the Greeks colonized the area, they co-opted the sacred site and transformed the cult into their virgin goddess Artemis. Although Cybele was a fertility goddess, Artemis was not. The cult statues of Artemis found at Ephesus have numerous lobes that some scholars have thought were multiple breasts (fig. 26). It is possible that these were a remnant vestige of Cybele. But, there is no evidence to indicate that the worship of Artemis at Ephesus was related to fertility. In fact, it seems that women associated with Artemis were ascetic in their sexual behavior and the so-called breasts are understood by scholars in a variety of ways.

It is impossible to determine the dimensions or appearance of the Amazon cult site under the oak tree or whether these early stories were etiologies to explain the unknown origins of the site. However, it is clear that a sanctuary of some sort predated the arrival of the Ionian colonists at Ephesus. Pottery found at the site indicates that the site was occupied as early as the Bronze Age. Archaeological work at the site has indicated that a peripteral temple was constructed in the last half of the eighth century. This temple was destroyed in a flood in the seventh century. In the middle of the sixth century after the Lydians seized the city, King Croesus built a huge temple dedicated to Artemis measuring 115 meters by 46 meters with 127 Ionic columns 13 meters in height. This temple, known as the Artemision was destroyed by fire in 356 B.C., but it was later rebuilt near the end of the fourth century on an even larger scale: 137 meters in length by 69 meters in width with columns 18 meters in height. In A.D. 268 this temple was destroyed by the Goths. It seems that the temple was never rebuilt after this and the architectural pieces were scavenged in the years thereafter for other building projects.

In Acts 19:35-36 the clerk who tried to quell the crowd in the theater of Ephesus referred to Artemis and "the undeniable fact" of "the image that fell from heaven." The ancient historian Appian reported that an image of the mother goddess (Cybele) fell from heaven at the Phyrgian city of Pessinos in 204 B.C. This tradition was also later reported by Herodian. It is possible that the story was fabricated to reinforce the position of Cybele in the Anatolian religion. However, it is equally possible that a meteorite landed at Pessinos and that the object was taken as the goddess having fallen from heaven. A few ancient statues of Artemis used black stone or dark wood to portray the goddess. A blackened iron-nickel meteorite could pass as the head of the goddess. The image of Artemis played an important role in the cult from as early as the seventh century B.C. An altar preceded the great temple in Ephesus and sources seem to indicate that the cult statue was brought out of the Artemision and placed on a base in front of the altar to observe the sacrifices.

The temple of Artemis was a place of asylum for anyone fleeing from harm. The temple precincts protected anyone who sought safety and security. When Croesus attacked the city in the sixth century the Ephesians stretched ropes from the temple columns of the Artemision to the city in an attempt to expand the temple precinct and to protect the city from Croesus' troops. Later in 46 B.C. Arsinoe IV the teenage Egyptian sister of Cleopatra was consigned to the protection of the Artemision by Julius Caesar. After Caesar's assassination, Cleopatra and Marc Antony ordered Arsinoe's execution. The slaughter of Arsinoe in 41 B.C. was a shocking and egregious violation of the temple's sanctity.

Although all ancient cities had patron deities, the fame of the cult at Ephesus was world famous. This was reflected in the comments of the clerk of Acts 19 who, according to Luke's account, stated "who is there after all who does not know that the city of the Ephesians is guardian of the temple of the great Artemis?" Likewise, Demetrius the silversmith who stirred up the riot referred to Artemis as "she whom all of Asia and the world worship." The temple of Artemis at Ephesus was described by Herodotus and the ancient authors as one of the seven wonders of the ancient world. An inscription dated to A.D. 44 referred to the Artemision as an "ornament of the entire province" and Pausanius asserted that all cities worshipped the Ephesian Artemis and honored her above all other gods. The city was so possessive of the temple that when Alexander the Great offered to pay for the reconstruction of the temple after the 356 B.C. destruction, the residents of the city refused the offer, probably because they wanted no outside authority providing patronage for the sanctuary. The economic benefits, notoriety and influence that the city gained from its association with the Artemision made the temple the preeminent source of pride in the city.

When a growing and expanding Christian community cropped up in Ephesus, it is not surprising that many within the city were disturbed and rose in opposition against Paul and his followers. Demetrius the silversmith was economically driven. Fewer people were buying the small votive shrines that he and his fellow craftsmen manufactured and sold to the pilgrims who came to the Artemision to pay homage to the goddess. He stirred up the crowds of the city by appealing to the pride and prestige that Ephesus enjoyed through their association with the Artemision. According to Luke, the charge against the Christians in the city was that they disrespected the goddess and deemed the temple as worthless (Acts 19:26-27). From the outset, the church and the temple were on a collision course.

The Ancient History and Archaeology of Ephesus (Selçuk)

The Ancient History of Ephesus

Pausanias, working from earlier sources, reported that when an Ionian colony led by Androclus arrived at Mt. Pion (Panayır Dağ - one of two mountains surrounding Ephesus) the local people had already established a sanctuary to the ancient mother god at the site. The Ionian settlement was founded around 1000 B.C. and the ancient sanctuary was probably a site for the worship of the Anatolian Cybele. An ancient sanctuary to Cybele has been found on the northeast base of Mt. Pion, about 600 meters from where the Artemision was later built. A number of other Cybele cult sites have been located in the area. The Ionians built a sanctuary to Artemis, known as the Artemision sometime in the eighth century B.C. This sanctuary superseded the earlier shrine dedicated to Cybele. In 560 B.C. the Lydian King Croesus invaded Ephesus and the Ionian cities. When a treaty was established with the Lydians, the city of Ephesus was moved off Mt. Pion to level ground next to the Artemision. At that time the Artemision was replaced with a new temple of enormous size, underwritten in large part by Croesus. When the Lydians were crushed by the Persians in 546 B.C. Ephesus survived and thrived. The Persians built a new road, the Royal Road, linking the Persian capital Susa with Sardis and Ephesus. Ephesus became the chief

Fig. 3 Ephesus Artemision

Ephesus' most famous landmark was the Artemision, the largest temple in the ancient world and one of the seven wonders of the world. The temple, dedicated to the goddess Artemis, was the pride of the city (Acts 19:27) and was 115 meters long, by 55 meters wide and 18 meters in height when constructed in the seventh century B.C. The temple contained 127 columns. The temple was destroyed and rebuilt several times (Strabon claimed it was destroyed and rebuilt seven times) and today has little more than the foundation and portions of two columns.

Fig. 4 Ephesus - The Foundations of the Artemision

When Paul wrote to the Ephesians he declared that the church was the temple of God, built upon the foundation of the apostles and prophets with Jesus Christ as the chief corner stone (Eph 2:19-22). This was the temple that would have been foremost on the minds of the Ephesians.

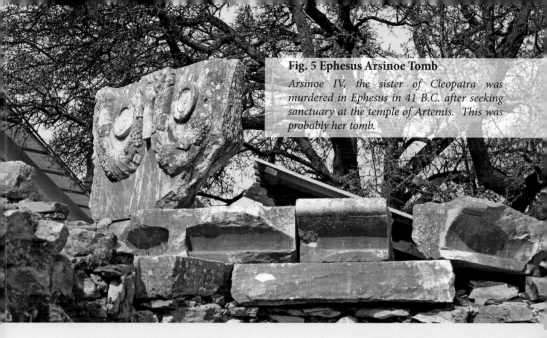

Fig. 5 Ephesus Arsinoe Tomb

Arsinoe IV, the sister of Cleopatra was murdered in Ephesus in 41 B.C. after seeking sanctuary at the temple of Artemis. This was probably her tomb.

port on the Aegean Sea and prospered greatly. The Artemision was destroyed by fire in 356 B.C. and was rebuilt near the middle of the third century B.C. The new temple was considered one of the seven wonders of the ancient world (figs. 3 and 4).

Alexander swept through Asia Minor in 334 B.C. breaking Persian control of the area. Following his death, Lysimachus relocated Ephesus to the foot of Mt. Pion, encircled it with a wall ten kilometers in circumference, and dredged out the Cayster River to create a new harbor. In the struggles following Alexander's death, Ephesus was controlled by several of the Diodochoi as they struggled for power in Asia Minor. In time, Lysimachus and the Macedonians were tossed out of Asia Minor and for a while the Ptolemies and Seleucids struggled for control of the region. The Seleucids eventually prevailed, but when they were defeated by the Romans and Pergamenes at the battle of Magnesia in 189 B.C., Ephesus and Asia Minor were given to the Pergamene rulers. When the Pergamene Kingdom was dissolved in 133 B.C., Ephesus was incorporated into a new Roman province (Asia Minor), created in 129 B.C., and was made the capital of the province. In 88 B.C. Ephesus and most of Asia Minor were taken by Mithridates VI of Pontus. In one night, Mithridates' forces sur-

reptitiously massacred 80,000 Romans and Italians living in the cities of Asia Minor. This action brought about the First Mithridatic War which concluded in 84 B.C. when Sulla recaptured the city and region. In 41 B.C. Arsinoe IV, an Egyptian princess, was murdered at the Artemis Temple by Cleopatra and Marc Antony. Arsinoe, probably only a teenager at this point, had sought sanctuary at the Artemision. Her murder, in gross violation of the sanctity of the temple was an outrage to those in Ephesus and Rome (fig. 5).

Ephesus reached its peak during the early imperial period. At that time the city was the largest port on the Aegean and was the commercial and financial center of Asia Minor. Ephesus had the largest population in the region (estimated between 300,000 and 400,000 people) and was named Neokoros (guardian of the imperial temple) four times. The city was sacked by the Ostrogoths in A.D. 262 and the temple of Artemis was looted and burned. However, the silting of the Cayster River led to the ultimate decline of the ancient city. The river was frequently dredged in order to keep the channel open to the Aegean Sea, but the silting continued and eventually the city was abandoned. Today, the ancient city lies eight kilometers from the Sea (fig. 6).

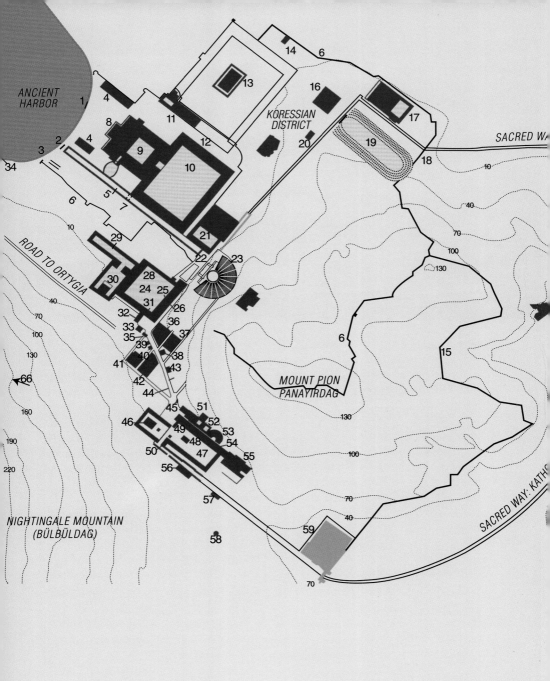

ANCIENT
HARBOR

KORESSIAN
DISTRICT

SACRED WA

ROAD TO ORTYGIA

MOUNT PION
PANAYIRDAG

NIGHTINGALE MOUNTAIN
(BÜLBÜLDAG)

SACRED WAY: KATHO

10

40

70

100

130

100

70

40

70

1
4
8
2
4
3
34
9
11
12
10
5
6
7
13
14
6
16
17
19
20
18
21
29
22
23
30
28
24
25
31
26
32
36
33
37
35
39
38
40
41
43
42
44
45
46
50
49
48
47
51
52
53
54
55
56
57
58
59
66
15
6
160
190
220

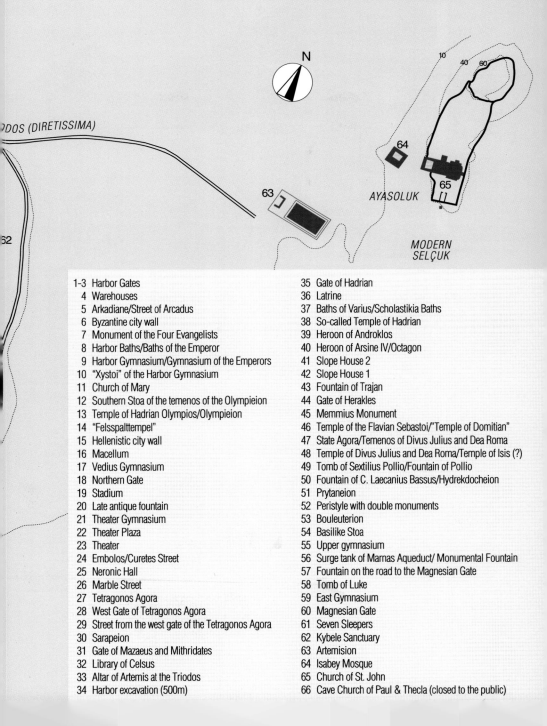

N

ODOS (DIRETISSIMA)

64

63

AYASOLUK

65

62

MODERN
SELÇUK

10 40 60

Fig. 6 Ephesus Harbor

The harbor at Ephesus was the lifeblood of the city. Ephesus had the largest Anatolian port on the Aegean Sea and was located at the mouth of the Cayster River, a major artery leading to the interior of Asia Minor. Various scholars estimate that the city had a population between 250,000 and 500,000 during the first century. However, the slow movement of silt down the Cayster River eventually filled the Ephesian harbor and moved the Aegean shoreline about five miles from the ancient city. The harbor was heavily silted during Paul's days and the Romans attempted to dredge the harbor to keep the harbor open. However, the silt eventually won and ancient Ephesus was largely abandoned by the eleventh century. Today, the ancient harbor is a swamp.

The Current Remains at Ephesus

Ephesus is the largest archaeological site in Turkey and this account will only summarize some of the more important remains. At the southeast corner of the site a road from the Magnesia Gate led to Magnesia ad Maeandrum. Further west beyond the modern entrance to the site, there was a bath and gymnasium complex built around A.D. 150, the Upper Baths. These were joined on the west to the State Agora. The State Agora, built during the first century B.C. and supplemented during the Roman period, was the political and administrative center for the city. The agora was 175 meters long and 60 meters wide. On the south side there was a double colonnade with a large water tower and a decorative nymphaeum (fountain) midway down the agora (fig. 7). This was built during the first century A.D. Further to the southwest an-

other nymphaeum built in A.D. 80 had statues, columns and niches in its two story façade. On the north side of the agora a three aisled colonnaded basilica used for administrative purposes was built in A.D. 11. This ran the length of the north side of the agora. Beyond the basilica to the northeast there was a roofed Odeon (for musical performances) or Bouleuterion (for meetings of the town council) constructed around A.D. 150 (fig. 8). This Bouleuterion could seat 1,500 people. The Prytaneion was positioned to the west of the Bouleuterion. The Prytaneion was the most important political building in the city. It housed the ever burning fire of Hestia Boulaia and was where political business was conducted. On the far west side of the State Agora, Domitian built his temple. The temple was constructed upon vaulted chambers to

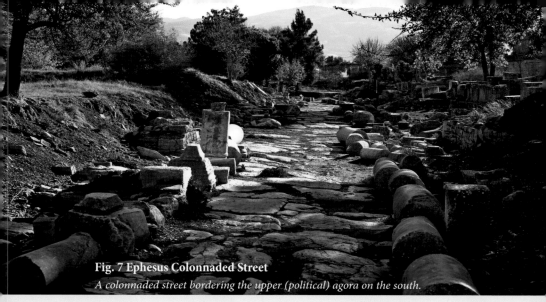

Fig. 7 Ephesus Colonnaded Street

A colonnaded street bordering the upper (political) agora on the south.

bring that area of the city up to the height of the State Agora (fig. 9). The chambers today are loaded with important inscriptions found at Ephesus to protect them from the weather. The Museum of Inscriptions is only open by special appointment. Domitian's temple built near the end of the first century A.D. was almost as big as the Artemision, measuring 110 meters by 55 meters. It contained a colossal statue of Domitian more than eight meters tall, portions of which are in the Ephesus Museum along with the altar of Domitian (figs. 10 and 11).

Fig.8 Ephesus Bouleuterion

The town council (the boule) met here to discuss civic issues. The bouleuterion borders the upper (political) agora on the north.

Fig. 9 Ephesus Domitian Temple Vaulted Foundation

Domitian's temple was constructed at the high point of the city, bordering the west side of the political agora. The platform for the temple was raised with barrel vaulted substructures.

Fig. 10 Ephesus Domitian Colossus

The forearm and head of a colossus statue of Domitian from Domitian's temple. The colossus was probably 23 feet in height.

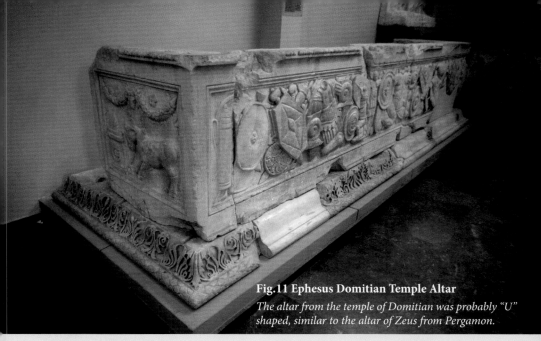

Fig.11 Ephesus Domitian Temple Altar

The altar from the temple of Domitian was probably "U" shaped, similar to the altar of Zeus from Pergamon.

In front of the Temple of Domitian there was a fountain and a monumental street (Curetes Street) heading northwest (fig. 12). Curetes Street was the main street of Ephesus leading from the upper political center of the city to the lower commercial center of the city. It was colonnaded and was lined with shops, important monuments, inscriptions, statues, a fountain and a temple terminating at the Celsus Library. The most important of these structures are the fountain of Trajan (A.D. 103), (fig. 13) the baths of Varius (late 1st A.D.), the Temple of Hadrian (early 2nd A.D.) (fig. 14) and the public latrines (late 1st A.D.). On the south side of the street, the terrace

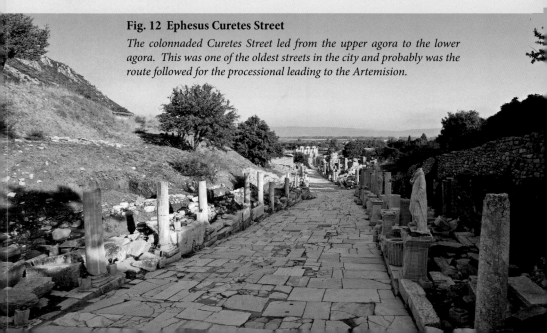

Fig. 12 Ephesus Curetes Street

The colonnaded Curetes Street led from the upper agora to the lower agora. This was one of the oldest streets in the city and probably was the route followed for the processional leading to the Artemision.

Fig. 13 Ephesus Trajan Fountain

The two story Trajan Fountain was completed around 113 A.D. and was dedicated to the emperor Trajan.

Fig. 14 Ephesus Hadrian Temple

The small temple dedicated to Hadrian during the second century used a portion of the baths of Scholasticia and faced Curetes Street on the north.

houses of the wealthy citizens of Ephesus had been covered with mud for centuries. These have been excavated and are now open to the public (figs. 15, 16 and 17). These homes are the equal of those in Pompeii. Dating back to the first century B.C. and later, these homes have mosaic floors, marbled walls, frescoed walls, peristyle courtyards, columns, impluviums (miniature pools), personal baths, and aediculated shrines. These were the homes of the wealthy and powerful residents of Ephesus. Scholars estimate that over ninety-five percent of the population lived in poverty. The general population could only dream of living like this. The wealthy upper class constituted less than a tenth of one percent of the overall population in the ancient Mediterranean world .

At the bottom of the hill, on the south side of Curetes Street, the memorial tomb of Arsinoe IV was found. Curetes Street terminates at a plaza in front of the Library of Celsus. The façade of the early second century A.D. library has been reconstructed to its full two story height (fig. 18). Inside, the original library had three floors. As one of the largest libraries in the ancient world, the library held 12,000 volumes. Northeast of the library stood the main gate to the lower Commercial Agora (fig. 19). The gate was built in 4 B.C. by Mazaeus and Mithridates, two freedmen of the imperial family, in honor of Augustus. The Commercial Agora was 123 meters square with a two story double colonnaded portico surrounding the agora (fig. 20). Shops surrounded the agora on the outside of

Fig. 15 Ephesus Terrace Houses

The recently excavated Ephesian Terrace Houses illustrate aristocratic life in ancient Ephesus. These homes were lavishly decorated with beautiful mosaic floors, frescoed walls, marble facing, peristyle courtyards, and accoutrements that only the wealthy could afford.

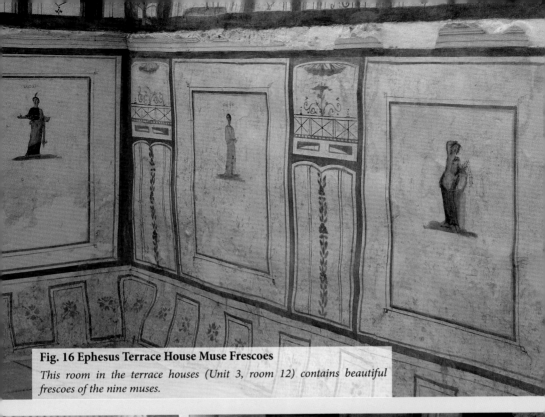

Fig. 16 Ephesus Terrace House Muse Frescoes

This room in the terrace houses (Unit 3, room 12) contains beautiful frescoes of the nine muses.

Fig.17 Ephesus Terrace House Poseidon Mosaic

On the perimeter of a peristyle courtyard one of the terrace houses has this floor mosaic depicting the triumph of Poseidon and Amphitrite. The mosaic is flanked by additional geometric mosaics and walls with marble facing. Less than one percent of the population could afford such domestic surroundings. Scholars estimate that approximately ninety five percent of the general population in the Mediterranean world lived in poverty.

Fig. 18 Ephesus Celsus Library

The library was erected as a heroon (an honorific tomb) for T. Julius Celsus Polemaeanus in the early second century A.D. The two story façade is punctuated with four aediculae on the lower story and three on the top. The niches on the bottom contained statues that represented the virtues: wisdom, moral excellence, contemplation and understanding.

Fig. 19 Ephesus Mazaeus and Mithridates Gate

This gate was erected at the southeast entrance to the commercial agora by two freedmen, Mazaeus and Mithridates. The gate was built in 3 B.C. to honor Caesar Augustus.

Fig. 20 Ephesus Commercial Agora

The squared commercial agora was surrounded by a double colonnade with shops on the periphery. The agora was first constructed in the 3rd century B.C. and was enlarged and rebuilt during the 1st century B.C. Demetrius stirred up the guild of silversmiths at Ephesus in opposition to Paul and his followers (Acts 19:23-41). The shops of these artisans probably came from this agora.

Fig.21 Ephesus St. Paul Cave Mosaic of Paul and Thecla

A cave on Bülbül Dağ above the Serapeion contains several frescoes and graffiti including this frescoe of Paul and Thecla, dated to the early Byzantine period.

Fig. 22 Ephesus Theater

The theater at Ephesus was originally constructed in the late second century B.C. and was enlarged to its present capacity of 25,000 people during the first century A.D. Further construction continued into the second and perhaps the third century.

Fig. 23 Ephesus Stadium

An early stadium, probably earthen, existed at this site during the Hellenistic period. The present stadium was likely constructed during the reign of Nero in the middle of the first century. In the late Roman period the eastern portion of the stadium was sealed off, probably for gladiatorial games and public executions.

the portico. A basilica, dedicated to Nero ran the length of the east side of the agora. On the southwest side of the agora a second or third century A.D. temple to Serapis was built. Behind the Serapion about 100 meters up the slope of Mt. Bülbül a rock cut cave was found that contained a number of Christian frescoes and graffiti. Some of the graffiti contained Christian prayers and a few of the frescoes illustrated the story of Paul and Thecla (fig. 21). Thecla was a woman from Iconium who converted to Christianity when Paul preached in the city. The story is relayed in the apocryphal *Acts of Paul and Thecla*, an early 2nd century Christian writing. With a date in the early Byzantine period, this fresco may be the earliest depiction of Paul ever found.

Northeast of the Commercial Agora was the theater mentioned in the Acts of the Apostles (fig. 22). This was originally built in the second century B.C. and was expanded in the first and third centuries A.D. in order to increase its capacity to 25,000 people. The stage building was also enlarged to create a three storied façade. The theater is still in excellent shape. Northwest of the theater was the Theater Gymnasium (2nd A.D.) with a palaestra (a colonnaded courtyard for exercise) and baths. West of this complex another palaestra and gymnasium complex was constructed on a much larger scale earlier during Domitian's reign. This palaestra, was surrounded by the Halls of Verulanus, named after an Ephesian priest of the imperial cult. It measured 215 meters by 260 meters and was

Fig. 24 Ephesus Mary Basilica

The second ecumenical council met at Ephesus in 431 A.D. However, the church of Mary was not constructed until around 500 A.D. The church was constructed by enclosing a colonnaded stoa within the walls of the church. It is possible that the council met in this colonnaded stoa.

Fig. 25 Ephesus Museum
Artemis Altar or Statue Base

It is not clear if this cylindrical object was an altar to Artemis or a statue base. The inscription states that a woman named Cominia Junia set up this (or another) altar to keep a vow to Artemis. The relief depicts a veiled woman praying before an incense altar while a flutist stands nearby. The object dates to the second century AD and was found in the agora.

Fig. 26 Ephesus Artemis Statue

The large 9 ½ foot high Artemis statue was found in the Prytaneion along with two smaller statues of Artemis. The Great Artemis statue has been dated to the time of Trajan. The headdress (polos) emulates the crown of Cybele and the lobes have been interpreted as breasts, eggs or testicles.

surrounded by a triple colonnade. Attached to this on the west, the Harbor Gymnasium had a smaller palaestra surrounded by rooms. Further to the west were the Harbor baths. This entire complex leading all the way to the harbor was built during the end of the first century or the beginning of the second century A.D. Running along the south side of all these gymnasiums and baths was the Harbor Street (Street of Arcadius), originally constructed during the Hellenistic period, leading from the theater to the ancient harbor.

Marble Street ran south to north beginning at the east end of the Celsus Library plaza, passing the theater on the west and terminating at the north end of the city. This passed the east side of the Theater bath complex and passed a Byzantine Palace that may originally have been yet another first century bath complex. The street continued north to the city limits and passed the stadium (originally built during the Hellenistic period, fig. 23) and yet another gymnasium and bath complex. The Vedius Gymnasium and bath complex was constructed in the middle of the second century A.D.

On the northwest side of the city, near the ancient harbor, a large complex exists called the Church of Mary (fig. 24). This may have been the spot for the third ecumenical council in Ephesus in A.D. 431. This was a fifth or sixth century church that was constructed by modifying a large stoa from an earlier (early 2nd A.D.) Olympieion. The massive Olympieion was built around A.D. 130 and dedicated to Hadrian as Zeus Olympieion. This was the second imperial cult temple constructed in Ephesus. It lies in the northwest corner of the city.

Fig. 27 Ephesus St. John Basilica & Tomb of John

A fifth century church was built over the traditional tomb of John the apostle. In the sixth century Justinian erected a massive crucifix shaped basilica at the site.

Not far from the main archaeological site, there are three important locations that require less time to investigate. Foremost among these is the Ephesus Museum (fig. 25). This is an excellent museum that exhibits the most important finds from the archaeological site. Not far away is the site of the Artemision (figs. 3 and 4). The rebuilt temple from the first century measured 125 by 61 meters and had three rows of eight columns on the front, three rows of nine columns on the back and three rows of twenty-one columns on the sides. Each column was about 20 meters in height. Aside from one column, a few architectural pieces and a foundation wall, little remains today at the ancient site. The nearby Church of St. John is a sixth century basilica that replaced a fourth century church on the site. The basilica is shaped like a cross and John is purportedly buried under the marble floor in the center of the church (fig.27). It is believed that many architectural pieces from the Artemision and the stadium were reused in the construction of the basilica.

Chapter 2

Christian Origins in Ephesus

The ancient city of Ephesus provides us with a unique opportunity to see the origin, growth, development and maturation of the Christian faith within a first century city. At no other city do we have such abundant testimony of Christians over the formative years of the church. From the establishment of the Christian faith in Ephesus around A.D. 52 to the end of the first century and the first years of the second century, we have no less than seven sources to document the progress of the church.

Luke, the author of the third gospel, wrote the Acts of the Apostles around A.D. 80. However, Acts provides us with much earlier information regarding the progress of the Christian church. Luke's account began with events following the crucifixion of Jesus (around A.D. 30) and continued up to the imprisonment of Paul in Rome around A.D. 62. The account of ministry at Ephesus that we find in Acts gives us information that we can find nowhere else. Paul's letters to the Corinthians, written from Ephesus during Paul's third mission, offer scant (but helpful) information about Ephesus. Naturally 1 & 2 Corinthians deal primarily with issues at Corinth. However, these letters shed valuable light upon Paul's ministry at Ephesus. When Paul arrived in Jerusalem after the third mission, he was arrested and spent two years in prison in Caesarea. Later he was shipped to Rome where he spent additional time incarcerated in a Roman jail. During that time he wrote four "Prison Epistles." One of them, to the Ephesians, was written anywhere between A.D. 60-62. The New Testament contains another two letters attributed to Paul that were written to his disciple Timothy (1 & 2 Timothy) who was instructed to remain in Ephesus in order to resolve certain problems in the church at that city. The dating of these letters is disputed, but it is quite likely that they were written after the prison epistles and before John's writings. Sometime in the latter half of the first century, the apostle John moved to Ephesus and became the respected elder (leader) of the churches in Asia Minor. During this time John wrote 1, 2 & 3 John. These letters address problems and issues that were relevant to not only the church at Ephesus, but also concerns of churches throughout the area of Asia Minor. The last book of the New Testament, Revelation, was certainly the NT's most unusual. Written during the reign of Domitian (probably around A.D. 90-95), Revelation begins with seven small letters written to churches in Asia Minor. One of these letters was written to the church at Ephesus offering advice as to how to deal with persecutions levied against the church during that time. The six other letters were written to churches in Asia Minor that were facing similar problems. The churches in each location dealt with the issues somewhat differently and the letters to each of these churches provides us with insights into the complexity of the problems and the manner in which each church tried to deal with it. Finally, about a decade after the last book of the New Testament, we have a collection of letters from an early church father, Ignatius, who wrote seven letters to various churches as he was being hauled from Antioch to Rome for martyrdom. One of these letters was written to the church at Ephesus around A.D. 109. Three others were written to nearby churches in Smyrna, Tralles and Magnesia. Together they provide additional information regarding the travails of the church in Asia Minor.

With all of these sources, we are able to piece together a fairly good idea of the earliest history of the church at Ephesus and Asia Minor extending from its establishment for the next sixty years into the early second century. No other church provides us with the opportunity to examine the development of a church in such detail.

Chronology:

A.D. 48 Paul attempts to visit Ephesus (2nd mission), but is prevented from doing so (Acts 16:6).

A.D. 52 Paul, Aquila & Priscilla arrive at Ephesus (end of 2nd mission), but Paul does not stay.

A.D. 53-55 Paul finally arrives at Ephesus (3rd mission). Paul writes 1 & 2 Corinthians.

A.D. 58 Paul returns at the end of 3rd mission, meets Ephesian elders at Miletus (Acts 20).

A.D. 60-62 Paul writes to the Ephesians from Roman jail (Ephesians).

A.D. 64 Paul writes to Timothy at Ephesus (1 & 2 Timothy).

A.D. 85-90 John's ministry in Ephesus & Asia Minor (1,2,3 John).

A.D. 90-95 John writes to seven churches including Ephesus (Revelation 2).

A.D. 109 Ignatius writes letter to Ephesians.

We cannot forget that the early churches had very little guidance in the Christian faith. The Christian Scriptures were being written throughout the first century and nobody at that time had a copy of the New Testament as we have it today. Near the end of the first century, a few churches had a letter or two from apostles, but even these letters were not immediately recognized as Scripture. The Gospels were not written until the last three decades of the first century and the traditions of Jesus were generally passed down from generation to generation orally. There may have been small written traditions regarding Jesus in some locations, but an in-depth understanding of Jesus was rare among the churches. Moreover, most churches throughout the Mediterranean had no local pastor and seminaries to train pastors were nonexistent. The earliest churches had to rely upon a system of itinerate evangelists, teachers, prophets and ministers who traveled from one location to another to teach and supply the ministerial needs of the local congregations.

Thus, with little or no Scripture and with infrequent contact with knowledgeable Christian workers, most churches struggled as they tried to cobble together an understanding of the Christian faith. Misunderstandings of Jesus, Paul, Peter and other Christian leaders were common. Dynamic and persuasive individuals arose within many of these congregations to supply leadership for the church. Some of these leaders, no doubt, were capable ministers who faithfully communicated the gospel. Others, however, misled their churches intentionally or unintentionally through a misunderstanding of the faith or for personal gain. False teachers, false prophets or faulty understandings of the gospel were the reason why most of the New Testament letters were written. The New Testament letters were written to resolve problems caused by the theological ignorance common within the churches of the first century.

Acts 18 – Aquila and Priscilla at Ephesus

Early church testimony is consistent in its description of Luke as a traveling companion of Paul. The so-called "we" sections of Acts appear to be instances when Luke used terms like "we" and "us" to indicate his personal participation in the events that he narrated. The "we" sections are found in Acts 16, 20, 21, 27 & 28. At other times Luke utilized a variety of sources for the information he recorded in Acts. Luke used a similar process in the composition of his gospel. In Luke 1:1-4 the writer described the exacting process he utilized in researching the story of Jesus. Luke claimed that he strove to consult the primary sources (v.2), thoroughly investigated everything (v.3) and pursued accurate information (v.4). We can assume that Luke researched his sources similarly when he wrote Acts. Luke's writings (Luke and Acts) only go as far as his sources take him. Even though Acts is known as the "Acts of the Apostles," in fact

Luke records almost nothing about most of the apostles. Early church sources and Apocryphal Acts of the Apostles offer hints regarding the ministries of many of these apostles. But Luke either was unable to acquire reliable information on these ministries or he felt that pursuing these storylines would detract from his purposes in writing his Acts. Thus, Luke's account of the early history of the church is not comprehensive. There is much that Luke leaves out. Any reconstruction of these early years must weave together the information gleaned from sources along with a measure of plausible speculation. Nevertheless, Luke's account in Acts is a good starting point. Without the information found in Acts it would be impossible to reconstruct the ministries of Paul.

The first hint of ministry to the city of Ephesus occurred during the second mission in Acts 16:6. Luke explained that Paul and his companions "passed through the Phrygian and Galatian regions after being prevented by the Holy Spirit to speak the word in Asia Minor." The route of Paul's travel was not well designated. Phrygia and Galatia were both east of Asia Minor and Paul first traveled through Galatia in order

Fig. 28 Ephesus Menorah

According to Acts 19:8, Paul shared the Gospel for three months at the synagogue in Ephesus. To date no synagogue has been found in the excavations of the city. This is not surprising since only about twenty percent of ancient Ephesus has been uncovered by archaeologists. Nevertheless, in a city the size of Ephesus, a large Jewish population probably existed during the first century. Evidence of a Jewish community in Ephesus is established by an image of a menorah inscribed on the steps to the Celsus Library.

to approach the borders of Asia Minor. Phrygia bordered Asia Minor on the northeast. Did Paul enter Asia Minor and retreat back northeast into Phrygia and Galatia? Next, Luke narrated that Paul made his way to Mysia, a northern region of Asia Minor and he tried unsuccessfully to enter Bithynia, northeast of Mysia. No specific cities were mentioned along the route until Paul arrived in Alexandrian Troas. Whatever the route, the section in Acts indicates that Paul wanted to preach in Asia Minor – most likely Ephesus. It may be implied that Paul even attempted to penetrate the province before he was directed elsewhere. What prevented Paul from ministering in Asia Minor? Was this a physical barrier, a threat or perhaps a strong sense of apprehension from the Holy Spirit?

Later on during the second missionary journey Paul traveled to Corinth where he met Aquila and Priscilla, Christians who had been driven out of Rome following an edict issued by the emperor Claudius (Acts 18:2). This edict was also mentioned by the Roman historian Suetonius and can be dated to A.D. 49. After eighteen months, Paul

Fig. 29 Corinth Apollo Temple
The temple of Apollo at Corinth dates to 540 B.C. and was a peripteral temple with six Doric columns along the front and fifteen columns along the sides.

departed from Corinth with Aquila and Priscilla. They put into port at Ephesus and Paul entered the synagogue and briefly shared the gospel (Acts 18:19). Although the Ephesians requested that Paul stay longer, the apostle had other plans and he continued his journey to Syrian Antioch. However, Aquila and Priscilla remained in Ephesus where they continued their ministry.

Shortly thereafter, a Jew named Apollos arrived at Ephesus from Alexandria. Alexandria was a well known intellectual center and it had a large Jewish population. Luke describes him as a dynamic and eloquent man who was well versed in the Hebrew Scriptures (18:24-25). He also noted that Apollos was teaching the way of the Lord. However, Apollos was not familiar with the ministry of Jesus. Apollos was somewhat aware of John the Baptist's ministry, but it is not clear what exactly Apollos knew beyond John's proclamation of the coming kingdom.

When Aquila and Priscilla encountered Apollos, they took him aside and instructed him regarding the ministry and teachings of Jesus. Later Apollos wanted to minister in Corinth and with the support of the Ephesian church he traversed the Aegean Sea and engaged in a prominent ministry in Achaia. Paul arrived in Ephesus while Apollos was in Corinth and thus he had no contact with Apollos prior to or during Apollos' Corinthian ministry. This is important to note, since as we will shortly see, Apollos' Corinthian ministry created problems.

1 & 2 Corinthians – Apollos at Ephesus and Corinth

Paul arrived in Ephesus on his third mission. Sometime during Paul's ministry in Ephesus, word reached the apostle that there were troubles across the Aegean Sea in the Corinthian church. Chloe, a woman from the Corinthian church, sent messengers to Paul informing him that the Corinthian church had become seriously fractured (1 Cor 1:11). Squabbles and divisions arose within the church over a host of issues. At the center of the trouble was Apollos. It does not seem to have been his intention, but Apollos' enthusiasm and dynamic personality caused many of the Corinthians to cling to his teaching to the exclusion of other Christian leaders. They seem to have established a circle of followers who elevated Apollos and his beliefs above those of Paul, Peter and even Christ. The movement was akin to the philosophic schools where philosophers debated among themselves and competed for adherents. Corinth was located close to Athens where it was common for influential teachers to establish philosophic schools and personality cults. Rhetoric (the art of persuasive speech) was a powerful tool used by philosophers, orators, military officials and politicians to influence people with their speeches. The Corinthians failed to realize that Christianity was not a competition pitting one preacher against another.

Perhaps Apollos contributed to this. From Luke's description Apollos was eloquent and charismatic. Perhaps he got caught up in the excitement of ministry and did not realize where the Corinthians were taking this. Perhaps Apollos' inexperience and lack of knowledge created some misunderstandings. Remember, only months earlier Aquila and Priscilla had to take him aside to teach him the basics of the new Christian faith. Apollos was not theologically sophisticated at that point in his ministry and neither were the Corinthians. There were no Christian scriptures at that time, no theology books and no one to guide the church following Paul's departure from Corinth. When the problems arose at Corinth, Paul wrote 1 Corinthians from Ephesus, attempting to unravel several issues, such as immorality within the church, the problem of eating meat offered to idols, problems regarding the observance of the Lord's supper, misuse of the gifts of the spirit, issues concerning the role of women in the church and mis-understandings of the resurrection. Some of these problems may be traced back to Apollos' ministry and teaching.

What do 1 & 2 Corinthians tell us about Paul's ministry in Ephesus from approxi-mately A.D. 53-55? Three things: First, 1 Cor 16:8-9 tells us that Paul was in Ephesus when he wrote these letters in an attempt to resolve the problems across the sea in Corinth. Second, the letters to the Corinthians corroborate and expand upon what we learned in Acts regarding the ministry of Apollos. Third, the Corinthian correspon-dence tells us that Paul was mobile during this period at Ephesus. He freely moved around addressing problems and engaged in evangelistic and ministerial work during these three years. At some point during that period Paul evidently met with Apollos and talked about what Apollos had done and said in Corinth (1 Cor 16:10-12). Moreover, Paul encouraged Apollos to return to Corinth to correct some of their errant practices and to let them know that Paul and Apollos were of one accord. Since Paul also men-tioned his impending third visit to Corinth (2 Cor 13:1-2), it is clear that the apostle made a trip to Corinth during his ministry in Ephesus. This trip was never mentioned by Luke in his account of Acts.

Acts 19 – The Third Mission and Paul's Work at Ephesus

After coming to Ephesus, Paul spent almost three years ministering to Jews and Gentiles alike. This was the longest period of time that Paul spent at any of his mission churches. Shortly after Paul's arrival in Ephesus, the apostle encountered twelve men who, similarly to Apollos, were only acquainted with the ministry of John the Baptist. The account of Paul's ministry to these men (Acts 19:1-7) immediately followed Luke's discussion of Apollos' actions (18:24-19:1a). These men were described as "disciples," but Luke probably had in mind Apollos' disciples. It would be a remarkable coincidence for Luke to include two encounters with persons who only knew of John the Baptist's work, if they were not connected to one another. All four gospels indicate that John the Baptist had a profound impact upon the Jewish community in Palestine. In addition, the Baptist's influence expanded to the Jewish community in Alexandria from where Apollos had come and beyond. Paul communicated the gospel to these men and they were baptized.

Paul's strategy during his missions was to visit cities that included a Jewish population. Even though Paul realized that God entrusted him with a ministry to the Gentiles (Gal 2:7-8), he still recognized the importance and priority of ministry to the Jews. When Paul later wrote to the Romans, he acknowledged that the gospel was the power of God for salvation to everyone who believed, to the Jew first and secondarily to the Gentiles (Rom 1:16, similar to Paul's speech in Acts 13:46). The narratives in Acts generally follow this pattern. When Paul entered a new city he began his ministry not in the gymnasium, forum or agora. Rather with few exceptions, Paul began his ministry in the synagogue. As a traveling Jew, Paul would be afforded hospitality, food and shelter, with other Jews. Moreover, Paul was given an opportunity to address the gathering of Jews at the synagogue. Paul always used these opportunities to share the good news of the gospel. In addition to the Jews, the congregation of the synagogue typically included monotheistic Gentiles (non-Jews) who abstained from idol worship and more or less followed the Jewish teachings of Sabbath observance, purity and dietary restrictions. These Gentiles were not circumcised and thus were not considered Jewish, even though they largely practiced the Jewish faith. These monotheistic Gentiles were known as God Fearers and were mentioned several times in Acts (13:16, 26; 17:4, 17; 18:7).

Paul taught at the synagogue in Ephesus for three months until opposition arose against the Christians. No evidence of a Jewish synagogue has been found to date in the excavations at Ephesus. However, an inscribed menorah has been discovered on the steps leading up to the Library of Celsus. Another menorah may have been etched upon the side of the southern gate, the Gate of Mazeus and Mithridates (fig. 30). The menorah was a seven branched candlestick that was present in the temple in Jerusalem. The menorah became the most distinctive symbol of a Jewish presence throughout the Mediterranean world. Further evidence of a Jewish presence in Ephesus was found in seven inscriptions found at the site that refer to cultic associations linked to the Jewish God.

When trouble arose in the synagogue, Paul departed from the synagogue and began teaching at the school of Tyrannus. The term "school" can be understood as a "lecture hall" rather than a school as we would understand it today. Education for the youth generally took place in the gymnasium, where school teachers taught their

48

Fig. 30 Ephesus Menorah

The menorah was a seven branched candlestick located in the temple in Jerusalem. The menorah became the distinctive symbol of Judaism. This menorah was found inscribed at the entrance to the agora.

students. Philosophers, however, taught in various places such as stoas and lecture halls. It makes more sense to imagine that Paul was teaching adults and evangelizing in a manner similar to the way philosophers attempted to persuade audiences. Thus, it seems that Paul was teaching at the lecture hall of Tyrannus.

In recent years a large stele (stone inscription) was found in the harbor at Ephesus (fig. 31). The inscription is an honorific inscription honoring a number of individuals who contributed funds for the construction of harbor buildings and works. In two places on the inscription the family of Tyrannos is mentioned. Tyrannos is not a common name and it is probably a reference to the family that provided Paul a place to teach the Christian faith in a lecture hall owned by Tyrannos. The inscription, currently in the Ephesus Museum, is important not only because it affirms the existence of the Tyrannos family at Ephesus, but also because the inscription identifies Tyrannos as a benefactor or patron. Many of Paul's wealthy converts became patrons of the apostle and the local church.

Recently uncovered in archaeological excavations are the spectacular slope houses, also known as the terrace houses (fig. 32). These excavations have revealed the residences of Ephesus' most important and wealthy citizens. Many of the homes were supplied with running water, and were laid out with decorative mosaic floors and frescoed

Fig. 31 Ephesus Tyrannos Inscription

When Paul withdrew from the synagogue in Ephesus, he began teaching the disciples at the school of Tyrannus (Acts 19:9). Excavations at harbor in Ephesus turned up this large inscription honoring the many citizens of Ephesus who contributed sums of money for the construction of the harbor and harbor buildings. Among those who contributed for the construction, the inscription mentions one (possibly two) person(s) by the name of Tyrannos. This may very well be a reference to the person who provided Paul with quarters for the training of his disciples.

Fig. 32 Ephesus Terrace Houses

The school of Tyrannus was a building where Paul trained disciples for a period of two years (Acts 19:10). Nothing is known about the accommodations provided for Paul, but it can be assumed that the owner of the structure was wealthy. This is suggested not only by the fact that Tyrannus owned such a building, but also by the previously mentioned donor inscription.

walls. They included homes with open air atriums, columns, impluviums and marble faced floors and walls (fig. 33). Lecture halls have also been located among these homes. Since the wealthy tended to occupy the same areas within a city, it is logical to assume that the Tyrannos family lived in this area and it is possible that the lecture hall of Tyrannos was located here as well. These homes were occupied from the first to the seventh century A.D. and they were modified and rebuilt several times over that period.

Another interesting discovery is a cave that is located some distance up Bülbül Dağ (Nightingale Mountain) behind the Serapeum that is located near the lower agora. The cave was a Christian sacred site from as early as the first or second century. Over 500 inscriptions and graffiti have been found in the cave dating back as early as the fifth

Fig. 33 Ephesus Terrace Houses

Tyrannus seemed to have functioned as Paul's patron in Ephesus. Since the wealthy generally lived in the same neighborhoods, it seems likely that Tyrannus lived in or around the terrace houses. It is also possible that the school of Tyrannus was located in or near the home of Tyrannus. Shops fronted the terrace houses facing Curetes Street and one of these could have been used for the school.

century. Additionally, the cave contains several layers of plaster and frescoes dating back as early as the fifth century. One of the frescoes depicts Paul and Thecla (fig. 21, mentioned earlier). This is the only image of Paul ever found at Ephesus and one of the earliest depictions of Paul anywhere, dating to the 6th century. Thecla was a disciple of Paul's who was never cited in the New Testament, but whose story was detailed in the second century writing *The Acts of Paul and Thecla*.

The cave clearly marked a Christian tradition at this spot in Ephesus. The cave is isolated on the mountainside away from the center of the ancient city. Why did this cave become a sacred site? Could this have been the site of Paul's residence at Ephesus during his prolonged stay during the third mission? Perhaps the site marked the spot of John's home. As we will soon see, John came to Ephesus sometime after Paul and ministered here until his death. Another possibility is that the place was an early church at Ephesus. In a city the size of Ephesus, there must have been dozens of churches and this cave could scarcely have held more than two dozen people. We may never know the significance of this sacred cave, but the early Christian community at Ephesus considered it important.

The conclusion of Paul's stay in Ephesus was marred by a disturbance instigated by an individual named Demetrius who stirred up tradesmen from the commercial agora. As Luke tells it, Demetrius was a silversmith who produced small votive statuettes of Artemis which he sold to pilgrims who came to Ephesus in order to worship the goddess at the Artemision. Due to the Christian ministry in Ephesus and Asia Minor, Demetrius believed that fewer people were honoring Artemis and that his business was threatened. He called together the guild of artisans who made the votive statuettes and together they incited a riot against Paul and his followers. The mob seized Gaius and Aristarchus, two of Paul's helpers and hauled them into the theater where tensions escalated as many of the people of Ephesus joined in the bullying. When Paul became aware of what was happening, he attempted to enter the theater, but was prevented by friends (including some powerful Asiarchs) who feared for his life. Although no harm came to Gaius and Aristarchus, Paul took this as a sign that it was time to move on. Shortly thereafter, Paul left for Macedonia.

Numerous terracotta statuettes have been found at the temple of Artemis along with a smaller number of silver ones. The Ephesus Museum displays a small gold statuette from the 7th century B.C. (fig. 34). These were the kinds of shrines that Demetrius and the artisans from the guild made and sold to pilgrims attending the

Fig. 34 Ephesus Votive Statue

This gold votive statue was found among the remains of the Artemision and dates to the seventh century B.C. Votive offerings of various sorts were common offerings given to deities, were produced by local artisans and were sold to worshippers visiting the sanctuary. The end of Paul's ministry in Ephesus came about through a riot instigated by silversmiths from Ephesus who made such votive offerings. According to Acts 19:23-41, the silversmith Demetrius stirred up trouble for Paul by gathering together other craftsmen in opposition to Paul's ministry in Ephesus. Utilizing the charge that Paul was undermining their business and that he was disgracing the goddess Artemis (and thereby the great temple), the artisans initiated a riot that resulted in Paul leaving town.

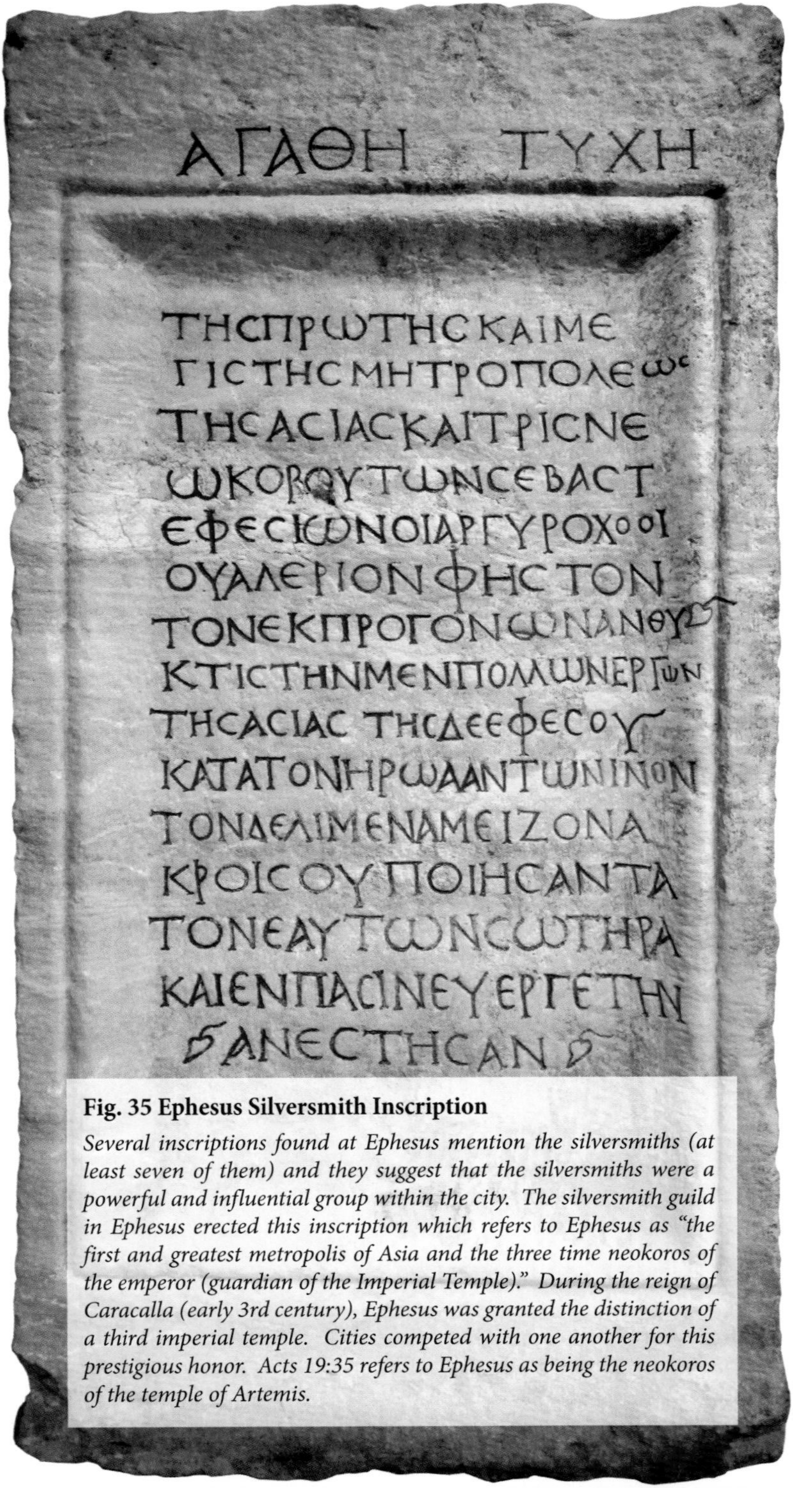

ΑΓΑΘΗ   ΤΥΧΗ

ΤΗΣΠΡΩΤΗΣΚΑΙΜΕ
ΓΙΣΤΗΣΜΗΤΡΟΠΟΛΕΩ
ΤΗΣΑΣΙΑΣΚΑΙΤΡΙΣΝΕ
ΩΚΟΡΟΥΤΩΝΣΕΒΑΣΤ
ΕΦΕΣΙΩΝΟΙΑΡΓΥΡΟΧΟΟΙ
ΟΥΑΛΕΡΙΟΝ ΦΗΣΤΟΝ
ΤΟΝΕΚΠΡΟΓΟΝΩΝΑΝΘΥ
ΚΤΙΣΤΗΝΜΕΝΠΟΛΛΩΝΕΡΓΩΝ
ΤΗΣΑΣΙΑΣ ΤΗΣΔΕΕΦΕΣΟΥ
ΚΑΤΑΤΟΝΗΡΩΑΑΝΤΩΝΙΝΟΝ
ΤΟΝΔΕΛΙΜΕΝΑΜΕΙΖΟΝΑ
ΚΡΟΙΣΟΥ ΠΟΙΗΣΑΝΤΑ
ΤΟΝΕΑΥΤΩΝΣΩΤΗΡΑ
ΚΑΙΕΝΠΑΣΙΝΕΥΕΡΓΕΤΗΝ
ΑΝΕΣΤΗΣΑΝ

Fig. 35 Ephesus Silversmith Inscription

Several inscriptions found at Ephesus mention the silversmiths (at least seven of them) and they suggest that the silversmiths were a powerful and influential group within the city. The silversmith guild in Ephesus erected this inscription which refers to Ephesus as "the first and greatest metropolis of Asia and the three time neokoros of the emperor (guardian of the Imperial Temple)." During the reign of Caracalla (early 3rd century), Ephesus was granted the distinction of a third imperial temple. Cities competed with one another for this prestigious honor. Acts 19:35 refers to Ephesus as being the neokoros of the temple of Artemis.

temple. At least seven inscriptions have been found at Ephesus that mention the trade guild of the silversmiths. One of these is displayed at the Ephesus Museum and is an honorific inscription that refers to the guild of the silversmiths at Ephesus (fig. 35). The inscription proudly begins with the words: "The Silversmiths of the first and greatest metropolis of Asia and the three time Neokoros of the emperor [keeper of the imperial temple] Ephesus honor Velerius Festus . . ." The inscription recognized Velerius Festus for benefactions done to the city during the third century A.D. Another inscription found at Ephesus is likely dated to the first century and referred to an individual named Demetrius who was described as a "neopoios" (temple warden). Some have thought that this referred to Demetrius the silversmith, mentioned in Acts. However, the name of Demetrius was common at this time and the identification of this person with the person mentioned in Acts 19 is far from certain.

The first-century theater at Ephesus remains in an excellent state of preservation (fig. 36). Originally built in the second century B.C., the theater was rebuilt and expanded in the first and third centuries A.D. to enlarge the seating capacity to 25,000

Fig. 36 Ephesus Theater
Paul was forced to leave Ephesus following a disturbance led by the silversmith Demetrius that culminated in a riot in the theater (Acts 19).

people. This theater was the largest theater in all of Anatolia, which is not surprising given the size of the ancient city. Ephesus was the largest city in Anatolia, due in large part to its harbor, one of the chief ports on the Aegean Sea.

Acts 20 – Paul's Farewell Address to the Ephesians

Ephesus' harbor had been silting up during the Hellenistic period and by the time of Paul's visit, the harbor could no longer accommodate the largest ships sailing the Aegean Sea. The harbor was originally about 5 meters deep, but the slow, steady silting of the Cayster River resulted in a shoreline that steadily moved further to the west. The Aegean Sea is currently seven kilometers further to the west. Inscriptions indicate that the Romans tried dredging the harbor to keep it open, but these efforts had limited success. Since the city was economically dependent upon access to the sea, the city was abandoned when the harbor was eventually closed.

Upon Paul's return to Asia at the conclusion of the third mission, Acts reports that Paul's ship put into port at Miletus. From there, Paul called the elders of Ephesus to say his last goodbyes. The text of Acts states that "Paul had decided to sail past Ephesus in order that he might not have to spend time in Asia; for he was hurrying to be in Jerusalem, if possible, on the day of Pentecost" (Acts 20:16). Passenger ships did not

exist in Paul's time, and passengers usually traveled on cargo ships destined for specific ports. Paul probably made this choice when he chose a ship at Assos (20:14). Many ships would put into port at Ephesus, since this was the largest city on the Aegean Sea and was a primary center for imports and exports. However, since Ephesus' port was silting up at this time, the largest cargo ships could not harbor at Ephesus. Miletus, with four harbors, was fast becoming an alternate choice for sailors.

At the end of the third mission, Paul was traveling with many of his disciples to Jerusalem. These disciples were representatives from the various Gentile churches throughout Galatia, Phrygia, Asia Minor, Macedonia and Achaia. They accompanied Paul back to Jerusalem with gifts for the Jerusalem church in order to show their solidarity with the Jewish Jerusalem church.

Paul's mission to the Gentiles was criticized by Jewish Christians who did not believe that God was embracing the Gentile people and allowing them to enter into the covenant community. The testimony of Paul's traveling companions was proof of what

Fig. 37 Miletus Theater

Miletus was a major seaport during the first century situated on a peninsula with four harbors. Over the years the Maeander River has filled the bay between Mt. Mycale and Mt. Latmos with soil, pushing the shoreline about five miles to the west of Miletus. One of the western harbors was here in the foreground below the theater.

God was doing among the Gentiles. As Paul revisited the churches in the cities of Anatolia, Macedonia and Greece, he took up a collection for the Jewish Christian church in Jerusalem and selected representatives who would accompany him to Jerusalem (1 Cor 16:1-5). If representatives from all of Paul's churches accompanied him on this journey, we can imagine as many as twenty people traveling with Paul at this time. Some of these companions were mentioned in Paul's letters and Acts.

Alternate readings of many of the ancient biblical manuscripts (known as the Western and Byzantine texts) have a longer reading at this place in the journey. This reading found its way into the King James Version which asserts that Paul's journey went from Assos to Mitylene to a point opposite Chios, to Samos, to Trogyllium and finally to Miletus (Acts 20:14-15). The oldest and most accurate manuscripts of Acts leave out the reference to Trogyllium. However, this alternate reading may preserve a tradition that was lost after Acts was written.

If Paul was in a hurry to reach Jerusalem, the decision to choose a ship destined for Miletus and then calling the elders from Ephesus to meet him in Miletus would not make much sense (Acts 20:17). Messengers sent from Miletus to Ephesus would have to make their way around the bay of Miletus and the massive swamps created by the silting of the Maeander River before arriving at Ephesus. The return journey to Miletus by the Ephesian elders would take the same amount of time. The longer reading of the Western texts, stating that the ship stopped at Trogyllium, makes better sense of the narrative. Trogyllium was located on a mainland promontory north of the bay of Miletus and just east of the island of Samos. At this point Paul could have sent one or two of his traveling companions north to Ephesus, instructing the elders to meet Paul in Miletus. The strait between Samos and Trogyllium was only about a mile wide and these messengers could have been quickly dropped off on the coast with a dinghy. This would have shaved two days off from the journey. The messengers would have followed the coast north, past the Panionium (the political and religious center of the defunct Panionian League), and on to Ephesus. They would have rejoined Paul when they led the Ephesian elders to Miletus.

Miletus was a sizeable city in its own right, estimated to be around 75,000 people during the Roman period. Miletus was the oldest city of the Ionian League, which had been obsolete for some time at the time of Paul's arrival. However, Miletus was still one of the most important cities of Asia Minor chiefly due to their excellent harbors. Just as the Cayster River was silting up the harbor at Ephesus, so also the Maeander River was pouring its alluvial deposits into the large bay between Mount Mycale and Mount Latmos. The Miletians likewise resorted to dredging to keep their harbors open. But today, the sea is nowhere to be found (fig. 37).

58

The Ancient History and Archaeology of Miletus (near Balat)

The Ancient History of Miletus

Miletus was the oldest city among the settlements of the Ionian League and along with Ephesus, it was one of the most powerful members of the league. Archaeological investigations have shown that Miletus was first settled in the sixteenth century B.C. by Minoan colonists from Crete. Strabo adds that Sarpedon fled Crete after he was defeated by his brother Minos and founded the city of Miletus. Around 1400 B.C. the Mycenaeans gained control of Miletus. Located on a peninsula near the Meander River, the city was ideally located and had four harbors. The site probably functioned as a trading post at this time and was mentioned in the Hittite records. The Ionians arrived around 1000 B.C., and as Herodotus explained, they killed all the male residents, and established their colony. The city became very prosperous and powerful and by the eighth century B.C. Miletus had established a number of its own colonies, particularly in the Sea of Marmara, the Black Sea and Egypt. Pliny stated thatt Miletus had established about ninety colonies throughout the Mediterranean.

In 546 B.C. the Persians gained control of Anatolia's west coast and Miletus was under their dominion. However, Miletus took a leading role in the Panionian revolt against the Persians in 499 B.C. and after the Persians wiped out the Ionian fleet off the coast of Lade (near the harbor of Miletus), Miletus was destroyed and its citizens were enslaved. Afterwards Miletus was rebuilt and by the middle of the fifth century B.C. the city was once again a prosperous port. Nevertheless, Miletus never regained its former glory and it was eventually eclipsed by Ephesus as the preeminent city of the region.

In 334 B.C. Alexander broke the power of the Persians in the area and following Alexander's death Miletus was taken by Lysimachus, who contributed a great deal to the city's development. Later however, when Lysimachus was defeated, Miletus and all of Asia Minor were taken by the Seleucids who controlled the region until their defeat by the Romans in 189 B.C. At that time, the Romans gave Asia Minor into the hands of the Pergamene Kingdom, and when the Pergamene Kingdom dissolved in 133 B.C. the Romans assumed control of the territory and soon created the Roman province of Asia Minor. Miletus continued to prosper under the Romans and the city's population during that time was about 75,000 people. However in the late Roman Imperial period the silt from the Meander River filled the harbors and reduced the viability of Miletus' economy. The city began its final decline. In the late Byzantine period the city was forced to dredge the river to keep its lifeline open, but eventually the Meander River won out. Today, the coastline is eight kilometers away and the four harbors of the ancient seaport hub are now swamps.

Christian Beginnings at Miletus

According to Acts 20:15-16, Paul came to Miletus at the end of his third mission, as he was heading to Jerusalem. Rather than stopping at Ephesus, where Paul felt he would be detained too long by friends and associates (Paul was more than two years in Ephesus earlier on the third mission), he instead put in at the larger harbor at Miletus. There Paul called the elders of the Ephesian church and upon their arrival at Miletus, Paul delivered his farewell address. The only other reference to Miletus in the New Testament is in 2 Tim 4:20, an enigmatic passage at the end of the letter that states that Paul left Trophimus sick in Miletus. There is no indication in either of these references that a church had been established at Miletus. But, given the proximity of Miletus to Ephesus, it is certain that the city was evangelized. The reference to the convalescence of Trophimus at Miletus may imply that he found hospice in the home of a Christian caretaker.

Fig. 38 Miletus Theater God Fearer Inscription

A Jewish community is evident from inscriptions found on the seats of the theater. This inscription reads: "Place of the Jews and the God Fearers."

Fig. 39 Miletus Theater

The theater at Miletus was originally constructed in the middle of the third century B.C. and was reconstructed later during the Hellenistic period and again during the first century A.D. The theater could hold 17,000 people.

Fig. 40 Miletus Lion Harbor

The northwest harbor was protected by a chain that extended across the entrance from one lion statue to another on the opposite side. These marble lions were installed in the third century B.C.

Fig. 41 Miletus North Agora Stoa

As a major seaport, Miletus had several agoras for commercial imports and exports. Although the harbors have silted up, the high water table still retains a great deal of rainwater.

61

There is clear evidence of a sizeable Jewish community at Miletus. A synagogue has been located near the northwest harbor. Also, one of the rows in the theater contains an inscription translated 'Place of the Jews and the God Fearers' (fig. 38). This rare inscription gives evidence not only to a Jewish community in Miletus, but also to a group of Gentiles who associated with the synagogues. Paul almost always preached at synagogues in new cities and found converts not only from among the Jews but also among the God Fearing Gentiles (Acts 17:4 & 17).

The Current Remains at Miletus

Located on a peninsula jutting into the Aegean Sea, Miletus had three harbors on its west side and another one on the east. A large theater sat along the west coast of Miletus overlooking the central western harbor (fig. 39). The theater was originally built at the beginning of the fourth century B.C. and was modified in the Hellenistic period and in the Roman period. The theater's capacity was 15,000 people and is still in excellent shape. Higher on the hill to the northeast of the theater there is a Hellenistic heroon (an honorific tomb). Down the slope on the other side of the hill, there are two Hellenistic period Lion statues mired in the mud that once guarded the entrance to the northwest harbor (fig. 40). Deeper into the harbor to the southeast, there was a synagogue dated to the Roman period. Further still, there were two harbor monuments. One of the monuments was 7.5 meters high and was built upon a round stepped pedestal eleven meters in diameter. The monument was triangular, decorated with ships' prows, tritons and dolphins and at the top there was a cauldron resting upon a tripod. An inscription suggests that it was built in the first century B.C. The second monument was smaller and was dedicated during the reign of Vespasian at the end of the first century A.D.

A Doric Stoa from the Hellenistic period wrapped around two sides of the monuments, roughly following the contour of the harbor (fig. 41). This stoa extended for 165 meters along the northern harbor and contained more than thirty shops. Behind the stoa, the North Agora was constructed in three separate sections from the fifth century B.C. to the Hellenistic period. East of the agora, bordering on the harbor stood the Delphinion. This temple, dedicated to Apollo Delphinios the protector of seamen and ships, was the oldest and most important temple in the city and dates back to the sixth century B.C.

In addition to the North Agora, two other agoras existed in Miletus during the first century. The South Agora, built in the second century B.C., was a massive 164 meters by 196 meters, one of the largest in the ancient world. This agora was surrounded on all four sides by stoas and shops. An Ionic Stoa with an additional nineteen shops led from the South Agora north to the Lion Harbor. The northern gate of the agora leading to the Ionic Stoa was the impressive Miletus Market gate (2nd century A.D.) that was removed from the site and now stands in Berlin. The West Agora, likewise dating to the Hellenistic period, was by comparison a mere 79 meters by 191 meters. This agora is presently unexcavated. The number and size of Miletus' agoras is testimony to the economic and commercial power that the city possessed. East of the West Agora, bordering on the Theater Harbor is the stadium. This too is unexcavated, but the stadium can be dated to the second century B.C. East of the stadium are the well preserved Baths of Faustina and accompanying Palaestra, built in the latter half of the second century A.D.

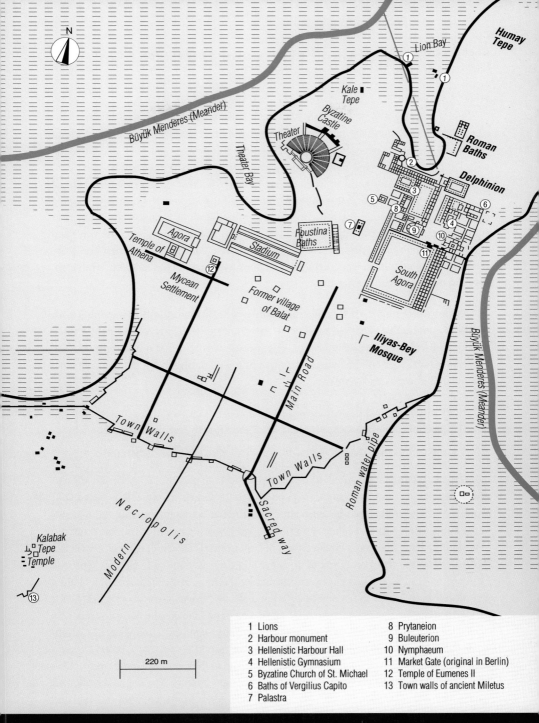

N

Büyük Menderes (Meander)

Humay Tepe

Lion Bay

1

1

Kale Tepe

Byzatine Castle

Theater

Theater Bay

Roman Baths

2

Delphinion

6

5

8

3

Poustina Baths

7

4

9

10

Agora

Stadium

Temple of Athena

11

Mycean Settlement

12

Former village of Balat

South Agora

Iliyas-Bey Mosque

Main Road

Town Walls

Town Walls

Roman water pipe

Necropolis

Sacred way

Modern

Kalabak Tepe Temple

13

Büyük Menderes (Meander)

220 m

1	Lions	
2	Harbour monument	
3	Hellenistic Harbour Hall	
4	Hellenistic Gymnasium	
5	Byzantine Church of St. Michael	
6	Baths of Vergilius Capito	
7	Palastra	
8	Prytaneion	
9	Buleuterion	
10	Nymphaeum	
11	Market Gate (original in Berlin)	
12	Temple of Eumenes II	
13	Town walls of ancient Miletus	

MILETUS

Design by **TUTKU TOURS**

Paul, God Fearers and Judaizers

Paul's ministry was not always embraced by fellow Jews in the cities that he visited. On many occasions, the gospel was more readily received by the God Fearers who associated with the synagogues. God Fearers were frequently mentioned in connection with Paul's ministry. God Fearers were Gentile (non-Jewish) people who had abandoned polytheism and became monotheists. Many of these God Fearers associated with the Jews in cities and towns throughout the Mediterranean world and adopted several Jewish practices. The Jews provided accommodations for these God Fearers to attend the synagogue (probably physically separated from the Jews in some way) and embraced them in fellowship. The God Fearers seem to have been somewhat Torah observant, complied with Jewish dietary restrictions and honored the Sabbath. However, they did not practice circumcision.

The Jews provided these God fearing Gentiles with an opportunity to join the Jewish covenant community. That required strict observance of the Torah over a two or three year period followed by circumcision. The process was a bit too much for most God Fearers (in particular circumcision), but some followed through with the requirements. They were known as Proselytes.

Paul's missionary strategy involved going to cities that included a Jewish population. Paul believed that the Gospel should be offered first to Jews who would then function as priests to the rest of the world. This was a scriptural notion extending back to the Old Testament call of Israel. Paul specifically referred to this view when he wrote to the Romans: "I am not ashamed of the Gospel for it is the power of God for salvation to everyone who believes, to the Jew first and also to the Greek" (Rom 1:16). Since Paul himself was Jewish the apostle could anticipate finding hospitality among fellow Jews in the cities and towns he visited. Food and lodging was a concern of anyone traveling in antiquity. Paul's message however was not always well received, even among Jews. In those instances, Paul often found an eager audience among the Gentiles. This was reflected in Act 13:46 when Paul was rejected by the Jews in Pisidian Antioch. Paul's response was to appeal to the non-Jewish population: "It was necessary that the word of God should be spoken to you first; since you repudiate it, and judge yourselves unworthy of eternal life, behold, we are turning to the Gentiles." Likewise, at Corinth when Paul was rejected by his Jewish listeners, his response was "Your blood be upon your own heads. I am clean. From now on, I shall go to the Gentiles" (Acts 18:6). This non-Jewish population primarily consisted of the God Fearers who eagerly embraced the Gospel. Paul included them in his message at Pisidian Antioch: "Men of Israel and you who fear God" (13:16) and "sons of Abraham's family and those among you who fear God" (13:26). Elsewhere in Paul's ministry, we see more God Fearers converted to the faith in Thessalonica (Acts 17:4), Corinth (18:7) and perhaps in Athens (17:17).

Perhaps one of the reasons why Paul's message was so well received by these God Fearers was because Paul declared that salvation was not dependent upon circumcision. Naturally, the prospect of entering God's kingdom without circumcision was appealing to men who were uncircumcised. On the other hand, this issue was one of the chief reasons why many of the Jews rejected Paul's message. The concept of a circumcision-free covenant with God was foreign and repulsive to many Jews. This seemed to run contrary to long established Jewish traditions and to cheapen the covenant with God. The Jews insisted that circumcision was necessary for anyone to enter into God's covenant community. For some of these Jews, it was not enough to be a God Fearer. One needed to complete the process with circumcision. Proselytes were "in," but God Fearers were out. Paul, however, argued that circumcision was unnecessary.

After his first mission, Paul returned to the Gentile church at Syrian Antioch only to discover that Jewish Christians from Jerusalem had come to Antioch claiming that circumcision and Torah observance were necessary to complete their salvation (Acts 15:1-2). Paul and Barnabas strenuously argued with these Jewish Christians (commonly referred to as "Judaizers"). They traveled to Jerusalem to meet with the leaders of the Jerusalem church in order to resolve the problem. After much discussion, a compromise solution was agreed upon. Jewish Christians would continue the practice of circumcision. However, Gentiles who converted to the faith would be not be burdened with the practice.

It seems that these Judaizers had also carried their demands to Paul's churches in Galatia. Consequently, Paul addressed this issue as the central concern in his letter to the Galatians. In this letter Paul strongly denounced this teaching, claiming that those who spread this message were "distorting the Gospel" (1:7) and were trying to "bewitch" the Galatians (2:1). Those who chose to receive circumcision "have been severed from Christ" (5:4). As Paul said: "neither circumcision nor uncircumcision mean anything to God" (6:15).

After the elders from Ephesus arrived in Miletus, Paul shared with them a parting message while realizing that he would never see them again. These were disciples that Paul had trained during the three years he had spent with them earlier, so the moment was emotional for both the apostle as well as for the Ephesians. If Luke's recollection of the speech is accurate, Paul shared with these leaders a message of caution. Paul was convinced that trouble would soon descend upon the church at Ephesus and he warned them of persuasive men who would arise and spread false teaching within the congregation. Paul's foresight was correct. In the years to come, up through the end of the first century, Ephesus was beleaguered with individuals who set the church on a course through troubled waters.

Paul's Letter to the Ephesians – Paul's Continued Ministry to Ephesus

Paul was more than just an evangelist who established churches and invited people to follow Christ. With his letters, Paul continued to minister to all of his churches even in his absence. The postal system in the first century was nowhere close to what we enjoy today and of course telephones and email where beyond the imagination of anyone who lived back then. Nevertheless, Paul continued to maintain contact with his churches and attempted to resolve problems in his congregations when issues arose. The use of letters was terribly inefficient, since it would take weeks or months before messengers from the congregations would travel to Paul with news of the problems. In turn, it would take an equal amount of time for the apostle to return a message to the congregation. By then, the problem could be much worse or additional problems could arise and complicate the issue. As a result, Paul wrote dozens of letters or small notes to the churches. Many of these letters have been preserved in the New Testament, but it is also important to note that many of his letters have been lost. Of those that have been lost, we know that Paul wrote a letter to the Laodiceans (mentioned in Colossians 4:16) that has never been recovered. Likewise Paul wrote at least two letters to the Corinthians (mentioned in 1 Cor 5:9 and 2 Cor 2:4), aside from First and Second Corinthians.

Thus, it should not be a surprise if Paul wrote more than one letter to the Ephesians. In Ephesians 3:3-4 Paul mentioned a brief letter that he had previously written to the church at Ephesus. This letter had to do with "the mystery of Christ." The specifics of this letter cannot be known, since it has never been found. However, the letter evidently pertained to some of the issues related to what Paul wrote in the canonical letter to the Ephesians. In Eph 3:4 Paul asked the Ephesians to re-read the earlier letter in order to better understand the revelation that God had given to Paul on the mystery of Christ.

The issue or issues behind the canonical letter to the Ephesians are not easy to determine. Of all Paul's letters, scholars are more puzzled regarding the purpose of

Ephesians than any other. One thing is clear, however. Paul did not write casual letters simply to pass on greetings or to give personal updates. Rather, all of Paul's letters were written to address problems in the churches that were addressed. The letter to the Ephesians was written from a prison and was one of the apostle's so-called Prision Epistles. Paul wrote four letters from prison (Ephesians, Colossians, Philippians and Philemon) and it is not certain where the apostle was when these letters were written. Some scholars believe Paul was at Caesarea in Palestine at the time when these were written, since he was imprisoned there for two years. However, most scholars believe that he was in Rome when they were penned. If so, this would seem to be the time of Paul's imprisonment mentioned in Acts 28 and this would date the letters to somewhere between 60-62 A.D.

One of the chief concerns of Paul's as he wrote this letter was to emphasize the fact that Gentiles who had placed their trust in Christ were incorporated into God's covenant community along with believing Jews. Thus, in 2:11-22 Paul stressed that "you, the Gentiles in the flesh who are called 'uncircumcised' by the so-called 'circumcised' . . . were at that time separate from Christ, excluded from the commonwealth of Israel, and strangers to the covenants of promise, having no hope and without God in the world. But now in Christ Jesus you who formerly were far off have been brought near by the blood of Christ. For He Himself is our peace, who made both groups into one, and broke down the barrier of the dividing wall. . . . in order that He might reconcile them both in one body to God through the cross . . . for in Him we both have our access in one Spirit to the Father. So then you are no longer strangers and aliens, but you are fellow citizens with the saints and are of God's household." The issue was taken up again in chapter 3. Thus it is safe to surmise that the issue was a contentious issue at Ephesus. In light of the above discussion regarding Paul, the God Fearers and Judaizers, this problem was a significant issue to resolve if Paul was going to forge a composite Jewish and Gentile church.

However, there was another issue that concerned Paul as he wrote this letter. This is clear from Paul's words in chapter four. Here Paul discussed the role of church leaders whose purpose was to equip the saints and build up the body of Christ (4:11-12). Paul continued: "until we all attain to the unity of the faith, and of the knowledge of the Son of God, to a mature man, to the measure of the stature which belongs to the fullness of Christ. As a result, we are no longer to be children, tossed here and there by waves, and carried about by every wind of doctrine, by the trickery of men, by craftiness in deceitful scheming, but speaking the truth in love, we are to grow up in all aspects unto Him, who is the head, even Christ" (4:13-14). The reference to the "mature man" and the exhortation to "no longer be children" suggests that the Ephesians had not grown in the faith as Paul would have liked. Moreover, Paul followed these words with a caution not

Fig. 42 Ephesus Celsus Library Sophia Statue

The proud philosophic traditions greatly influenced cities on both sides of the Aegean Sea. The acquisition of knowledge and wisdom (here personified by the statue "wisdom of Celsus") was paramount for many of those who lived in Ephesus.

ΣΟΦΙΑ
ΚΕΛΣΟΥ

to be manipulated by the various doctrines and teachings of crafty and deceitful frauds. Thus, it appears that false teachers had emerged in Ephesus who were misleading the Christian community in the city.

What was the nature of this false teaching? The next several verses (4:17-24) provide the answers. When Paul states that "you should no longer walk as the Gentiles walk" (17), he is referring to behaviors that the Ephesian Christians have adopted that are contrary to the faith. Likewise, when he states "but you did not learn Christ in this way" (20), he is rebuking the Ephesians for departing from the teachings that he (Paul) had taught earlier during his three year ministry with them. In between these verses Paul reprimanded the Christian community for "the futility of their mind," for "being darkened in their understanding," for "the ignorance that is in them" and the "hardness of their heart" (17-18). Consequently, they have "become callous," "have given themselves over to sensuality" and were practicing "every kind of impurity with greediness" (19).

Throughout the book there is a frequent reference to terms such as "knowledge," "insight," "understanding," "wisdom" and the "mind" along with contrasting terms like "ignorance," "futility of the mind," "darkened in understanding," "unwise" and "foolish." One of the themes in Ephesians is Paul's emphasis upon how the knowledge and wisdom of God triumph over ignorance, the trickery of men and deceitful teaching (fig. 42).

Philosophy had made a powerful impact upon the Aegean world for hundreds of years before the time of Paul. Paul himself argued with the Stoic and Epicurean philosophers in Athens (Acts 17:18) and no doubt argued with other philosophers on numerous other occasions during his missions. Philosophic schools flourished throughout the Mediterranean region and these philosophies eroded beliefs in the traditional gods and became a substitute for religion for many people. It was natural for people to co-opt philosophic beliefs and combine them together with their new faith in Christ. This process is known as syncretism and the practice was common in the past as well as in the present. For early Christians who had no Bible as we know it today and who had no theological training, it was difficult to sort things out and to determine God's truth. Even though Paul visited and revisited his churches and sent his disciples to discuss these theological matters, misunderstandings persisted and false teaching grew alongside the truth. Here in Ephesus, Paul patiently and tactfully corrected misunderstandings of the Gospel. Perhaps the reason why scholars have had problems of precisely determining the purpose of Paul's letter to the Ephesians is because Paul is too amicable in the manner that he approached the problems. Instead of naming the false teachers and repetitiously bashing their teachings, Paul firmly underscored his understanding of the gospel and resolutely denounced the ignorance that led his disciples astray.

Fig. 43 Ephesus Celsus Library

Ephesus possessed one of the largest libraries in the ancient world, containing more than 12,000 volumes.

Magic and witchcraft were commonly practiced throughout the Mediterranean world and Ephesus was no exception. The well known *Ephesia Grammata* were six magical words that were inscribed upon the cult image of Artemis in the Artemision. From as early as the fifth or fourth century B.C., these words were commonly invoked throughout the Mediterranean world for protection from evil powers and they were often inscribed upon amulets. These were meaningless words whose power resided in the correct pronunciation of the words. Additionally, inscriptions have been found

70

at Ephesus that invoke curses as well as other inscriptions that refer to the rituals of divination. Yet another inscription refers to a magician. Furthermore, magical dice (*astragalos*) where found at Ephesus. These were used for discerning the future and for obtaining answers to questions asked of deities (fig. 43).

Magical practices at Ephesus were also mentioned in the New Testament. At the time of Paul's arrival in the city, there were Jewish exorcists who were using the name of Jesus to cast out evil spirits (19:13-17). Similar to the use of the *Ephesia Grammata*, these exorcists attempted to use the name of Jesus as a magic word to expel demons. Though their efforts were unsuccessful, the story illustrates the practice of magic words to manipulate evil spirits. The narrative in Acts continued to describe vast numbers of magicians who converted to the faith and abandoned these magic practices (19:18-20). "Many of those who practiced magic brought their books together and began burning them in the sight of all; and they counted up the price of them and found it fifty thousand pieces of silver" (19:19). The pieces of silver were either drachmas or denarii, both of which were approximately one day's wage. While the price of a magic book probably exceeded the price of other books (due to the thaumaturgic and apotropaic powers of such knowledge), the amount of fifty thousand pieces of silver for the value of the books is still a huge figure and probably indicates the extent to which magic was entrenched in the city.

In Paul's letter to the Ephesians, the apostle subtly alludes to magical practices in Ephesus in a couple of passages. In 1:19 Paul prays that the Ephesians' eyes might be enlightened so that they might know the surpassing greatness of God's "power" which is manifest in "the working of the strength of His might." Notice in this verse that Paul used three different, yet synonymous terms for God's power (in Greek: *dynamis*, *kratos* and *ischus*). One of the only places where these three terms "power, strength and might" are found together in all of ancient literature is in a Jewish magical text. The fact that Paul encountered Jewish magicians in Ephesus (Acts 19:13-17) suggests that Paul may be using terms commonly associated with magic to magnify the power of God. Instead of appealing to the powers of magic, Paul seems to be extolling the surpassing power of God.

In 4:14 Paul directed the Ephesians to "no longer be children, tossed here and there by waves and carried about by every wind of doctrine, by the trickery of men, by craftiness in deceitful scheming." The words "no longer" suggest that the Ephesians were already being manipulated by spiritual frauds. The word "trickery" is a rare word in ancient Greek and most commonly refers to playing with dice, such as the magical dice (*astragalos*) mentioned above. Other words in this verse, such as "craftiness and deceitful scheming" also imply that Paul was primarily thinking about the deceptive practices of the magicians.

Finally, Paul probably has magic in mind near the end of this letter in 6:10-18 during his discussion of spiritual warfare. The section metaphorically describes the necessity of putting on the military armor of God in order to fight against the "schemes" of the devil (6:11). The word "scheme" is never used anywhere else in the New Testament or the Septuagint except here and in Eph 4:14 (see the above paragraph). Paul reminds his readers that even though these spiritual frauds or magicians may be complicit dupes in the plot, they are not the mastermind. "For our struggle is not against flesh and blood, but against the rulers, against the powers, against the world forces of this darkness, against the spiritual forces of wickedness in the heavenly places." (6:12)

.

Chapter 3

Paul's Disciples in Ephesus and the Surrounding Area

Epaphras and the Origin of the Church at Colossae

It is commonly assumed that Paul was the founding father of the churches that he addressed in his letters. While that was true in most instances, it was not the case with the churches at Rome and Colossae. Paul acknowledged that he had never been to the cities or churches of Laodicea and Colossae (Col 2:1).

If the church at Colossae was not established by Paul, then how did the church originate? It seems that the origins of the church at Colossae were set in motion when Paul opened the school of Tyrannus at Ephesus (Acts 19:8-10). After Paul was expelled from the synagogue at Ephesus, he withdrew from the synagogue and took his disciples to the school of Tyrannus. Here for a period of two years, Paul trained disciples who would replicate his evangelistic efforts and take the gospel to cities and towns throughout the region. As Luke stated: "this took place for two years, so that all who lived in Asia heard the word of the Lord" (19:10).

One of these disciples, Epaphras, journeyed 170 kilometers inland to the east and brought the gospel to Colossae (1:7). Paul described him as a "beloved fellow bond-servant" and "a fellow servant of Christ on our behalf." When Paul added the words "on our behalf" it can be assumed that Epaphras was sent out by Paul for this task. Epaphras was originally a resident of Colossae according to 4:12 and it makes sense that he would return to his home town to share the gospel message with his kinfolk and friends.

It is not clear how Epaphras met Paul, but he was probably in Ephesus for some kind of business or employment when he heard the Christian message. It is also likely that Epaphras was one of the disciples mentioned in Acts 19:9 that Paul instructed in the school of Tyrannus. Following his ministry in Colossae, Epaphras continued to evangelize the nearby sister cities of Laodicea and Hierapolis (4:13). The three cities of Colossae, Laodicea and Hierapolis were located within twenty kilometers of one another in the Lycus River Valley and the cities shared much in common. Later, Epaphras traveled with Paul and he was with Paul at the time when the letter to the Colossians was written (4:12). Colossians was one of Paul's prison epistles, probably written from a Roman prison, and Epaphras was evidently imprisoned with him from the reference to him as Paul's "fellow prisoner" in Philemon 23.

Paul and the Church at Colossae

Scholars have often noted that Paul's letters to the Colossians and the Ephesians are very similar. Almost half of the verses in Ephesians find parallels in the letter to the Colossians. Moreover, similar topics in the letter to the Colossians are usually found in the letter to the Ephesians in the same order. What are we to make of this?

It seems that the problems at the churches in Colossae and Ephesus were similar and that Paul's concerns in both churches were connected. As Acts 19:10 mentioned, the ministry that emanated from the school of Tyrannus affected the vast bulk of Asia, so that "all who lived in Asia heard the word of the Lord." While the word "all" was an overstatement, nonetheless, the major cities of Asia Minor, as well as many of the smaller towns were exposed to the gospel. Since the churches in these towns had no Scripture or resident pastor it is easy to understand how these churches would drift in various theological directions and would adopt teachings from the philosophies, religions, and current thoughts circulating at the time. Clever and persuasive teachers could easily mislead these new Christians in divergent directions. These teachers may have acted innocently out of ignorance, or they could have acted maliciously for self serving purposes. In either case, many of these churches throughout Asia Minor were straying from the traditions of Paul and Christ. Something had to be done to address the problem.

During the two years while Paul was incarcerated in a Roman prison, the apostle was informed of the situation with the churches of Asia Minor. In response, Paul wrote several letters to address the problems in Asia Minor. One letter was sent to the church at Ephesus, another was sent to the church at Colossae and a third was sent to the nearby church at Laodicea. This letter to the Laodiceans has been lost but it is mentioned in Col 4:16. Paul very well may have written additional letters to churches in Asia Minor, but they have also not survived.

These letters appear to be circular epistles. That is, even though the letters were addressed to specific congregations, Paul intended these letters to be copied and circulated among the other congregations throughout Asia Minor. If problems existed at Ephesus, Colossae and Laodicea, these same problems (or similar ones) probably existed in numerous other churches throughout the area. Rather than writing dozens of letters to individual churches, it seems that Paul wrote a few letters that he wanted to circulate among the churches in the many large cities and smaller towns of Asia Minor.

Some of the earliest and best ancient manuscripts of the letter to the Ephesians omit the words: "in Ephesus" at the beginning of the letter in 1:1. Some scholars have suggested that Paul may have made several copies of this letter to be distributed to various churches and that the name of the church could have been filled in later. At the end of his letter to the Colossians Paul requested that "when this letter is read among you, have it also read in the church of the Laodiceans; and you, for your part read my letter that is coming from Laodicea" (4:16). From this statement, it is clear that the problems and issues addressed in these letters were not localized in just one congregation. Rather, these matters were affecting other congregations as well. Thus, it is clear that Paul's concerns spread far beyond the churches mentioned in these letters and that Paul probably wrote other letters that have perished.

These letters were carried by Tychicus who is mentioned as the carrier in Eph 6:21-22 as well as in Col 4:7-9. Tychicus was described as a beloved brother, faithful servant and fellow-bondslave of the Lord's. In both letters Paul stated that Tychicus would supplement the letters with additional information regarding the apostle's welfare and he would interpret Paul's meaning and intentions for the congregations. It was common for letter carriers from that time to interpret ambiguous portions of a letter and to communicate discreet information that would not be appropriate for the entire congregation. They would usually supply additional information and messages that would be better expressed in person. For that reason, the choice of the messenger was an important decision. To assure the churches that Tychicus was trustworthy, Paul added a few words to indicate that Tychicus was a faithful and trusted fellow servant of God. It was not unusual for messengers, teachers and prophets to carry letters of recommendation with them to show to suspicious audiences. Paul himself sarcastically asked the Corinthians if they needed from him a letter of recommendation as other speakers were prone to do (2 Cor 3:1).

Accompanying Tychicus on the journey from Rome to Asia Minor was Onesimus, who was described in the letter to the Colossians as "one of your number," that is, a resident of Colossae. Onesimus was an escaped slave who fled from his master Philemon and made his way to Rome. There, he met Paul and became a follower of the faith. It was common for escaped slaves to travel to Rome, the largest city in the Mediterranean world and a city where a fifth to a quarter of the population was enslaved. In Rome, one could fairly easily disappear among the anonymous masses. Once he became a Christian, however, Onesimus had to do the right thing. He had to return to his owner. Slaves were considered "living property" during the first century and a slave who escaped from bondage was guilty of theft. Paul advised Onesimus to return to Colossae with Tychicus and to submit to his master Philemon.

Paul wrote a letter to Philemon (one of the shortest letters in the New Testament) that Tychicus carried with him to the city. Not only was Philemon a resident of the city of Colossae, he was also deeply involved in the church there. Philemon was a wealthy man, as was evident by the fact that he owned slaves, and he acted as a patron for the church at Colossae. In fact, the church met in Philemon's home (Philemon 2). There were no dedicated structures for churches in those days and all of the early churches were house churches. In large cities there were probably several house churches. Paul appealed in the letter to Philemon (whom he describes as a "beloved brother and fellow worker"), to Apphia his wife, to Archippus his son (who is also specifically mentioned in Col 4:17) and to the church that met in his house. In this small letter Paul pled with Philemon to release Onesimus in order that he might join Paul in ministry.

From Col 4:10 it appears that Paul had encouraged Mark (Barnabas' cousin) to travel to Colossae in order to address some of their problems. Paul included Mark among the greetings at the end of the letter. However in his reference to Mark, Paul added a rather cryptic parenthetical statement: "Mark (about whom you received instructions: if he comes to you, welcome him)." It is impossible to determine what Paul was talking about regarding the "instructions." However, it is likely that Paul (or someone associated with him) had previously contacted the Colossians regarding the possibility of Mark visiting the city. This may be a reference to yet another of the lost letters of Paul (mentioned above), but the reference is too vague to be certain. Since Paul used a conditional "if" ("if he comes to you") the visit seemed to be tentative and uncertain. Paul's companions who traveled with him were often sent to various locations to address problems in the local churches.

What can we say about the problems at Colossae that elicited a letter from the apostle? The problems here were similar to what was happening in Ephesus, but the situation at Colossae was earmarked in a somewhat distinctive manner. That is why Paul's letter to the Colossians was so similar, yet not identical, to his letter to Ephesus. Paul's approach in both letters was gentle and encouraging, yet instructive, therapeutic and tactful. Paul felt that the problems were not serious enough at that point to merit harsh criticism. Consequently, Paul refrained from using the harsh rhetoric that he employed in his earlier letters to the Galatians and Corinthians.

Still, Paul firmly denounced the syncretistic practices in Colossae that were also occurring in Ephesus (Eph 4:14, 17-18). The tendency to merge certain philosophic concepts with the Christian faith was particularly concerning: "See to it that no one takes you captive through philosophy and empty deception, according to the tradition of men, according to the elementary principles of the world, rather than according to Christ" (2:8). Paul also cautioned his readers about certain teachings that were foisted upon the Colossians regarding the consumption of foods and the observance of festal days (2:16). Ascetic practices, the worship of angels and claims of visions by certain persons in Colossae also concerned the apostle (2:18). Paul concluded that "These are matters which have, to be sure, the appearance of wisdom in self-made religion and self abasement and severe treatment of the body, but are of no value against fleshly indulgence" (2:23). From these clues, the problem appears to be that the Colossians collected a pastiche of thoughts from various philosophies, the mystery religions and Judaism. However, Paul realized that the compilation as a whole was misleading and detracted from the tradition of Christ.

The Ancient History and Archaeology of Colossae (near Honaz)

The Ancient History of Colossae

Little is known of Colossae's past (fig. 44). According to Herodotus the Persian king Xerxes crossed Asia and went through the large city of Colossae during his invasion of Greece in 480 B.C. While discussing the journey of the Ten Thousand Greek mercenary soldiers around 400 B.C., Xenophon also described the city as large and prosperous. This army of mercenaries remained in Colossae for seven days before moving on. During the mid fourth century B.C. the area around Colossae appears to have been ruled by two families: the family of Tithraustes and the family of Ariaios. They were probably noble families who controlled large tracts of land in southwestern Phrygia and they probably functioned as Persian overlords to govern the area. However, when Persian power declined in the area following Alexander's conquests, the land in the area was pillaged and perhaps confiscated by officers of Alexander's armies. In the years following this, the city of Colossae appears to have diminished in size and stature. Strabo writing during the Augustan period, appears to list Colossae among some of the small towns in the area around Laodicea. Nevertheless, he also recognized that the Colossians made good money from the soft black wool that they sold. Over the years it may be that several of Colossae's residents moved to Laodicea, as that city grew in size and importance during the Roman period. Based upon coins minted at Colossae, the dominant gods

Fig. 44 Colossae Ancient City Mound

The site of Colossae has been identified, but the ancient city mound (tel) has never been excavated.

Fig. 45 Colossae Ruins

Exploratory trenches and illegal digs have exposed a small portion of the ancient city of Colossae.

Fig. 46 Colossae Theater

Few architectural pieces remain from the Colossae theater. However, the semicircular bowl (the cavea) is evident along with a few fragments hidden among the weeds.

Fig. 47 Colossae Rock Cut Tomb

On the periphery of the Colossae acropolis and across the stream that flows through the site, rock cut tombs are still visible.

were Zeus and Artemis. Like its neighbor Laodicea, the residents of Colossae were probably affluent. The cities of the Lycus Valley benefited from a vibrant textile industry and they were located on an important trade route leading to Ephesus and the Aegean Sea in the west. Colossae and Laodicea were destroyed by an earthquake in A.D. 17, during the reign of Tiberias and were rebuilt. Then again in A.D. 61 another earthquake destroyed the two cities. Laodicea recovered quickly, but Colossae may have continued its decline.

The Current Remains at Colossae

The site is currently unexcavated and only surface surveys and exploratory trenches have been conducted to investigate the remains at Colossae (fig. 45). Unfortunately not much remains above ground at the site. During the late Byzantine period and thereafter, the site was ravaged by local people who reused the building stones and columns for construction elsewhere. The site is dominated by a small acropolis with a few pieces from a defense wall and a number of shards littering the site. Some half dozen columns can be spotted in the field on the lower level of the acropolis. On the eastern slope of the acropolis, near the modern road, the cavea of an ancient theater can be made out (fig. 46). The theater has a few architectural remains, but has mostly disappeared. Much of the stone has been hauled away and used in secondary construction locally. Southwest of the acropolis there is a stone cut tomb. Further north is the Lycus River and a few remains from an ancient necropolis survive on the north bank (fig. 47). Likewise, a few pieces of some unidentified buildings are left on the north bank of the river. Some Byzantine remains including reused pieces from the earlier city, can be found north of the acropolis (fig. 48).

Fig. 48 Colossae Byzantine Remains

Byzantine ruins that reused pieces from ancient Colossae are located a short distance away.

Paul's Letters to Timothy - Paul's Ministry to Ephesus through His Disciple

The authorship of the Pastoral Epistles (1 & 2 Timothy and Titus) is greatly disputed with many scholars opting to believe that these letters were actually written by Paul's disciples. Even a modest discussion of the issue would take more space than what we can devote to these pages. Whether written by Paul or written by one or more of his disciples in the years following Paul's death, these letters were in all probability written after his letter to the Ephesians and before the letters of John. Thus, in terms of the development of the church at Ephesus, these letters were written sometime in the intermediate years between the mid 60s and the early 90s. For the sake of this discussion, I will assume Pauline authorship, which would place these letters in the mid 60s. For those who see the letters as written by Paul's disciples, a later date perhaps in the 80s would be preferable. In either case, 1 & 2 Timothy testify to a midway transitional stage between the time of Paul's founding of the church and John's later ministry to the Ephesians.

The opening words of the first letter to Timothy place Timothy in Ephesus: "remain on in Ephesus in order that you may instruct certain men not to teach strange doctrines nor to pay attention to myths and endless genealogies" (1:3). Whether the letter was written to a fictitious "Timothy," as some scholars would maintain, or written to the disciple of Paul matters little for our purposes since in either case the letter clearly was written to address problems in the city of Ephesus. It would make no sense to add the words "remain on in Ephesus" if the letter was created to address problems elsewhere.

In the case of 1 & 2 Timothy, the rhetoric employed by Paul was much more harsh and confrontational than what was evident in his earlier letters to the Colossians and Ephesians. The tone of the letters to Timothy suggests that the apostle recognized that the problems mentioned in Colossians and Ephesians had not subsided, but rather had gotten worse. Thus, the apostle utilized an aggressive polemic to deal with the problem.

In the earlier letters Paul employed a redemptive and pastoral approach with his adversaries, hoping that the false teachers would recognize their errors and would adjust their teaching. In the earlier letters Paul refused to name the culprits, realizing that to do so would put them on the defensive, embarrass them and perhaps drive them further away from the apostle's instruction (fig. 49).

In 1 & 2 Timothy, however, the apostle threw away the pleasantries and exposed his opponents for what they really were: frauds and agents of the devil. Here Paul clearly identified the troublemakers: Hymenaeus and Alexander, who "have rejected their

Fig. 49 Ephesus Celsus Library

The Celsus library was destroyed in an earthquake in 262 A.D. and was restored between 1970-1978.

good conscience and have suffered shipwreck in regard to their faith" (1 Tim 1:19-20). Consequently, Paul has "delivered them over to Satan, so that they may be taught not to blaspheme." Those who follow such teachings were paying attention to deceitful spirits and the doctrines of demons (1 Tim 4:1).

The problem was not isolated to Ephesus alone, as 2 Tim 1:15 asserted that "all who are in Asia have turned away from me." Of course, the expression "all who are in Asia" cannot be taken literally. The statement is a rhetorical exaggeration, but the remark does tell us that the false teaching had proliferated throughout the churches in Asia Minor. More specifically, Paul named Phygelus and Hermogenes as individuals who had rejected his teaching and had gone astray (1:15). A few verses later, Paul criticized the "irreligious and foolish talk" of persons such as Hymenaeus and Philetus, whose teachings Paul described as "gangrene" (2 Tim 2:16-17). The same exact expression "irreligious and foolish talk" (in Greek τάς βεβήλους κενοφωνίας) can also be found in 1 Tim 6:20 where Paul described such talk as "the opposing arguments of what is falsely called 'knowledge.'"

Paul's caustic expressions in these letters surpassed the terminology and the approach that he typically took when addressing problems in various churches. One exception is the situation Paul experienced when he wrote 2 Corinthians. At Corinth Paul faced an unresponsive congregation that he had addressed on several occasions and in several letters. When Paul wrote 2 Corinthians the congregation was terribly fractured and was in open rebellion against Paul's teaching. The ringleaders in Corinth were similarly described as "false apostles and deceitful workers" who were servants of Satan (2 Cor 11:13-15). The scenario was similar to what we have found in the Pastoral epistles and consequently, the apostle used a similar approach, reprimanding them with strong language.

Returning to the false teaching at Ephesus, is it possible to clarify how it is that the situation progressed from bad to worse? Also, do we have additional information from 1 & 2 Timothy that would clarify the nature of the false teaching? By placing Paul's correspondence to the Ephesians and Colossians alongside his letters to Timothy, it is possible to see the theological trajectory that was spinning out of control from Paul's perspective. Recognizing that the letters to the Ephesians and Colossians were written around A.D. 60-62 and that the letters to Timothy were written later (three or four years later - if written by Paul, or perhaps twenty years later - if written by his disciples), we can see a development and clarification of the teaching of Paul's opponents.

In Ephesians and Colossians the aberrant teaching is vaguely described. There were probably minor distinctions between the teachings in each of these communities, but in large part the errant concepts shared common notions and beliefs. As we mentioned earlier, this is probably why Paul sent circular epistles that were exchanged and passed along from one congregation to another. Paul wanted the churches to see that they were not alone in this struggle and he wanted the churches to consider the strategies that other churches were using to deal with the problems. The false teaching in these letters is similarly described:

Colossians

2:8 Philosophy
     Empty deception
     Tradition of men
     Elementary principles of the world
2:11 Issue concerning circumcision
2:16 Issues with food and drink
     Issues regarding new moon & Sabbath
2:18 Self-abasement
     Worship of angels
2:23 Appearance of wisdom
     Self-made religion
     Self-abasement

Ephesians

2:2 Course of this world
2:11 Issue concerning circumcision
4:14 Children tossed by waves
     Carried by every wind of doctrine
     Trickery of men
     Craftiness in deceitful scheming
4:17 Futility of their mind
     Darkened in their understanding
     Ignorance that is in them
     Hardness of their heart
5:6 Deception with empty words
6:12 World forces of this darkness

Both of these letters contained a section that referred to the issue of circumcision (Col 2:11-14 & Eph 2:11-19). The letter to the Colossians also contained a section dealing with the permissibility of consuming food and drinks and the observance of the Sabbath and festal days (Col 2:16-17). Since both letters were addressed to congregations that were predominantly Gentile, the introduction of these issues demonstrates that the false teachings somehow promoted the continuance of Jewish customs.

Perhaps more importantly, a common element of the aberrant teaching, variously worded throughout these letters, was a particular wisdom or knowledge which was described by Paul as "philosophy," "empty deception," "the tradition of men," "wind of doctrine," "trickery of men," "craftiness in deceitful scheming," "futility of the mind," a "darkening of understanding," "ignorance," a false "appearance of wisdom," "self-made religion," and "deception with empty words."

The subject matter of this phony "wisdom" cannot be precisely determined from these letters. However, the terminology that Paul used in these letters offers a clue to what was happening in Asia Minor and Ephesus during this time. The region surrounding the Aegean Sea was awash with a wide variety of philosophies that competed with one another for adherents. The leading philosophers of the day were skilled speakers who were trained in rhetoric and prided themselves in their ability to manipulate an audience. Without any

Scripture to guide them and lacking pastors who were trained in the faith, the new Christians became trusting and naïve pawns for hucksters who would easily lead them astray. Thus in these letters, Paul cautioned the churches about philosophies, empty deception, traditions of men, the trickery of men, the appearance of wisdom, deception with empty words and self-made religion. These aberrant thoughts were merged with elements of the Christian faith (a process known as syncretism) to form something foreign to what Paul knew to be true.

We also know that the Aegean region was littered with mystery religions - secret cults with strange and enticing rites. These mystery religions attracted adherents to closely bonded communities and appealed to new initiates with the secrecy and mystique of the cult. Paul's frequent use of the term "mystery" in these letters (and the fact that Paul claims that this mystery is centered upon Christ) suggests that the aberrant teaching in Asia Minor had the trappings of a mystery religion. The word "mystery" was uncommon in the New Testament. However, Paul used the word ten times in these small letters to the Colossians and Ephesians.

For those who were trumpeting this secret "wisdom" or "knowledge" (Greek – γνῶσις), Paul responded by claiming a "higher knowledge" (Greek – ἐπί –γνῶσις). This higher knowledge was given by God and was a fuller understanding of God and his ways through Christ. This is the upshot of Paul's discussion in Col 2:2-4 where the apostle hopes that his readers would attain "the wealth that comes from the full assurance of understanding, resulting in a true knowledge (ἐπίγνωσις) of God's mystery, that is, Christ himself, in whom are hidden all the treasures of wisdom and knowledge (γνῶσις). I say this in order that no one may delude you with persuasive argument." Likewise in his letter to the Ephesians, Paul's discussion of the mystery of Christ reaches a climax with the words: "that you may be able to know the love of Christ which surpasses knowledge, that you may be filled up to all the fullness of God" (3:19).

Now turning to 1 & 2 Timothy, it becomes apparent that the situation has gotten worse. The "strange doctrines" (1 Tim 1:3) have not only crystallized into clearly heterodox beliefs, but these teachings have now become entrenched within the Ephesian community. As a result, Paul's letters reflect a more feisty approach to deal with the problem and to reaffirm the tradition passed on by Paul. As mentioned above, Paul now identified the false teachers by name: Hymenaeus, Alexander, Phygelus, Hermogenes and Philetus. Moreover, the false teaching has acquired a name: "the opposing arguments of what is falsely called 'Knowledge' which some have professed and thus have gone astray from the faith" (1 Tim 6:20-21).

Paul acknowledged that these teachings were known as "gnosis" – "Knowledge," although Paul himself refused to recognize it as such. The name "gnosis" is important since a heretical form of Christianity emerged in the second century which used the same term to identify itself. The movement known as "Gnosticism" was promoted by the great Gnostic teachers Basilides and Valentinus in the early second century and the movement continued alongside orthodox Christianity for more than three centuries. Since the name Gnosis was used in 1 Tim 6:20, many scholars have concluded (for this and other reasons) that the letters to Timothy were not written by Paul, but were instead written by someone in the second century. But, such a conclusion is not necessary.

Many modern scholars are reluctant to recognize that Gnosticism had its origins in the first century. There are no Gnostic documents that can be dated to the first century. However, many of the early church fathers claim that Gnostic teachers were propagating their teachings in the first century and they name several: Simon (Acts 8), Menander, Saturninus, Cerinthus and the Nicolaitans (Rev 2). Moreover, a Gnostic movement that sprang to life so quickly in the second century probably had precursors earlier in the first century. In my mind, it is hard to discount the testimony of the studious church father Irenaeus from the late second century. Irenaeus had access to many oral traditions and written sources that have long since perished and we do not have today. Yet, Irenaeus was convinced that the Gnostics had their beginnings during the time of Paul. Their theological positions were probably no more solidified than many of the churches at that time. Gnostic thought continued to turn and evolve through the first and second centuries up to the time of Valentinus and beyond.

The false teachings against which Paul was arguing in his letters to the Colossians and Ephesians may not have been Gnostic per se, but the syncretistic blending of philosophic wisdom along with the emphasis upon secret knowledge co-opted from the mystery religions provided many of the ingredients to what later came to be Gnosticism. At the time when 1 & 2 Timothy were written, the term "Gnosticism" had become standard terminology to refer to this movement. Rejecting Paul's admonitions, the leaders continued to forge ahead in this amalgamation of thoughts. And as we will soon see, in the years leading up to the end of the first century, this momentum continued.

Unknown Disciples and their Ministries in Asia Minor (Acts 19:10)

The Church at Hierapolis

As far as we know, Paul never wrote a letter to the church at Hierapolis and this church was not addressed in the book of Revelation. However, the congregation at Hierapolis was mentioned in Col 4:13 so we know that a church existed there during the first century. The city of Hierapolis was located only nine kilometers from Laodicea (visible across the Lycus Valley) and twenty kilometers from Colossae. As we have mentioned previously, the church was likely founded by Epaphras (Col 4:12-13), one of Paul's disciples who was trained in the School of Tyrannus (Acts 19:9-10). Since these three cities were closely connected to one another and since the three churches in these cities were probably all established through the ministry of Epaphras, it is logical to assume that they had much in common – including many of the problems that were mentioned in Paul's letter to the Colossians and some of the issues that were brought up in the Apocalypse's letter to the Laodiceans. Paul ordered that the letter to the Colossians was to be circulated in the church at Laodicea and that a lost letter to the Laodiceans should be read in the Colossian congregation (Col 4:16). We can assume that Revelation's letter to the Laodiceans probably had a wider audience as well. Unfortunately however, since we have nothing more concrete to draw upon, we cannot precisely describe how these problems and issues were being handled by the church in Hierapolis. Does the lack of a letter to Hierapolis from Paul and John (in Revelation) indicate that the church at Hierapolis was thriving and was avoiding the problems experienced by their neighbors? Probably not, but not much more can be said about the early history and progress of this church.

The Ancient History and Archaeology of Hierapolis (Pamukkale)

The Ancient History of Hieropolis

An inscription found at the theater of Hierapolis mentioning ancestral family names suggests that the founding of the city goes back to the Seleucids during the late fourth or third century B.C. But, very little is known about this period. After the defeat of the Seleucids at the battle of Magnesia (189 B.C.), the city came under the dominion of the Pergamene kings. An inscription from the site testifies of Pergamene control. This inscription contained a decree of King Eumenes II (197 – 159 B.C.). The Romans inherited the Pergamene Kingdom and in 129 B.C. included Hierapolis in the Roman province of Asia. Like its neighbors Laodicea and Colossae, Hierapolis was famous for quality textile production. Hierapolis however, was also famous for its hot springs and white travertine formations. The white calcium deposits formulating pools with stalactites can still be seen and gives the impression of a frozen waterfall. The hot springs were thought to be therapeutic and drew visitors from across the ancient world. Coins from ancient Hierapolis commonly have images of the healing gods Asklepios or Hygieia. Hierapolis' chief god, however was Apollo (who was also a chief healing god and the father of Asklepios). Apollo was thought to be the founding deity and a temple to Apollo was established in Hierapolis from its earliest days.

In A.D. 17, during the reign of Tiberius, Hierapolis was destroyed by an earthquake. The city was quick to recover from the tremor, but in A.D. 60 the city was devastated by yet another earthquake. Again, its citizens rebuilt the city. Hierapolis continued to flourish and reached it's peak in the second or third century when in A.D. 220 it was named *neokoros*, or 'temple warden' for the imperial cult.

Fig. 50 Hierapolis Tomb of Philip

In 2011 it was announced that the tomb of Philip was discovered near the monumental Philip Martyrium.

Christian Beginnings at Hierapolis

As with Laodicea and Colossae, it seems quite probable that Epaphras, one of Paul's helpers, was the founding father of the church at Hierapolis. When writing to the Colossian Christians (2:1) Paul insinuated that he (Paul) had not yet been in the area of Colossae, Laodicea (and probably Hierapolis). Instead, Epaphras first shared the Gospel with the Colossians (1:7) and his abiding concern for the churches at Laodicea and Hierapolis (4:13) probably stems from the fact that he shared the Gospel in those cities as well. This reference in Colossians is the only place Hierapolis is mentioned in the New Testament. Yet, Hierapolis had a rich heritage of Christian leaders.

Second century traditions connect Philip with Hierapolis. The New Testament refers to two Philips: an apostle and an evangelist who had four daughters who were prophetesses. It is not clear which Philip was associated with the city. The early church historian Eusebius claimed that Philip and his daughters' tombs could still be seen in Hierapolis at the end of the second century. However, a local inscription claimed that a church was built in honor of Philip the apostle. Whatever the case may be, an octagonal early fifth century martyrium was constructed on the hill to the northeast of the city. With more archaeological work over the last few years, the tomb of Philip has been discovered. The tomb was near the martyrium enclosed in a Byzantine church (fig. 50). Another important early Christian was associated with Hierapolis. Papias

Fig. 51 Hierapolis Papias Funerary Stele

Second century tombstone (funerary stele): "Papias Klesos Pastor, highly regarded, Christian: farewell to those who pass by."

(A.D. 60 - 130) was a disciple of John's and an associate of Polycarp (another disciple of John's). Papias collected and wrote five volumes of the oral traditions of Jesus called the 'Expositions of the Sayings of the Lord'. Papias claimed to have contact with the disciples of the Lord, from whom these sayings came. But unfortunately, very little of these writings have survived. Papias served as bishop of Hierapolis until his death around A.D. 130. An interesting funerary inscription dated to the second century at the Hierapolis Museum refers to a person named Papias who was described as a pastor (shepherd) and "Chrestos," a term that may be a misspelling of Christian (fig. 51). The inscription was found at nearby Laodicea. However, considering the date of the funerary inscription, the nearby location of Laodicea and what appears to be Christian titles accompanying "Papias," one wonders if the inscription marked the burial place of Hierapolis' first bishop.

89

Fig. 52 Hierapolis Travertine Formations

The beautiful and massive Travertine formations at Hierapolis have attracted visitors in the past and present. The site has been declared a World Heritage Site by UNESCO.

Fig. 53 Hierapolis Necropolis

The largest ancient necropolis in Turkey was at Hierapolis. The necropolis surrounded Hierapolis on the north, east and south sides of the city.

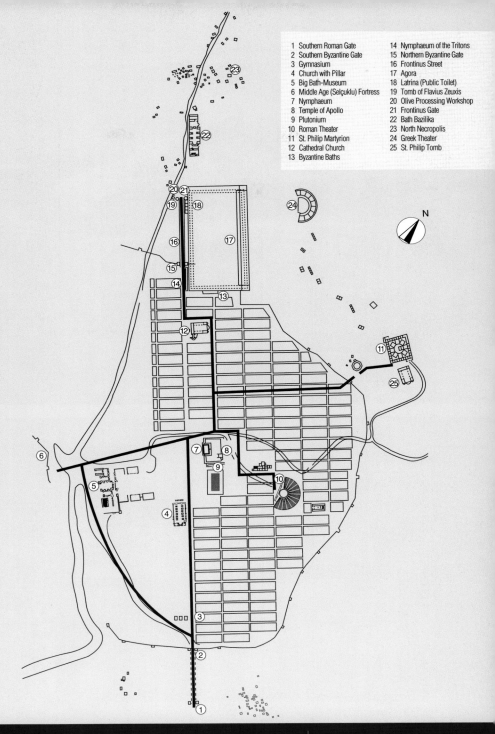

1 Southern Roman Gate	14 Nymphaeum of the Tritons
2 Southern Byzantine Gate	15 Northern Byzantine Gate
3 Gymnasium	16 Frontinus Street
4 Church with Pillar	17 Agora
5 Big Bath-Museum	18 Latrina (Public Toilet)
6 Middle Age (Selçuklu) Fortress	19 Tomb of Flavius Zeuxis
7 Nymphaeum	20 Olive Processing Workshop
8 Temple of Apollo	21 Frontinus Gate
9 Plutonium	22 Bath Bazilika
10 Roman Theater	23 North Necropolis
11 St. Philip Martyrion	24 Greek Theater
12 Cathedral Church	25 St. Philip Tomb
13 Byzantine Baths	

HIERAPOLIS

Design by **TUTKU TOURS**

Fig. 54 Hierapolis Sarcophagus Menorah

Several tombs in the necropolis at Hierapolis have symbols or inscriptions of Jews who lived in the city. This lid has a lion's head and menorah.

Fig. 55 Hierapolis Sarcophagus Menorah

Another Hierapolis sarcophagus with a menorah and palm branch.

The Current Remains at Hierapolis

Most visitors to Hierapolis spend the bulk of their time examining the impressive white travertine deposits and wading into the warm waters of the hot springs. The massive travertine terrace pools and hot springs have been recognized as a World Heritage Site (fig. 52). The waters were thought to be therapeutic and in the past many people came to Hierapolis to be healed. However impressive these calcium formations might be, the ancient remains at Hierapolis are even more impressive. Approaching Hierapolis from the north, one first encounters an incredible necropolis, the largest in Turkey (fig. 53). The necropolis, stretching for two kilometers, is a damning reminder of the supposed healing powers of the city's chief deities: Apollo and Asklepios. Tombs in the necropolis represent a wide variety of burial practices, including sarcophagi, tumulus tombs, mausoleums and house tombs. They include tombs from the Hellenistic period through the early Christian era and on to the Byzantine period. Many tombs have inscriptions identifying their occupants. Twenty-,three tombs bear Jewish inscriptions, including a few with menorahs inscribed on the side (figs. 54 and 55). Further south prior to enter-

ing through the city gates, there are the well preserved Northern Baths. These baths were built in the late second or early third century A.D. and were converted into a Christian basilica in the fifth century.

South of the baths the road enters through the main gate of the ancient city, the Domitian Gate (fig. 56). This triple arched gate was flanked by towers, is in excellent shape and dates to A.D. 83 when Julius Frontinus, the proconsul of Asia dedicated it to the emperor. The gate opened to the main street heading south (known as Frontinus Street) and was lined with colonnaded porticoes on both sides. Behind the porticoes the street was lined with shops and various buildings. The latrines were just inside the gate on the left. East of Frontinus Street there was a huge agora, one of the largest in the ancient world, dating to the second century A.D. The agora measured approximately two hundred meters by three hundred meters and had colonnaded porticoes along the sides. On the eastern side of the agora there were eighteen steps leading up to a long and narrow portico at the front of a basilica running the three hundred meter

Fig. 56 Hierapolis Domitian Gate
Domitian's Gate constructed in 83 A.D. was the main entrance to the city from the north. The colonnaded Frontinus Street was the main street extending south to the hot springs.

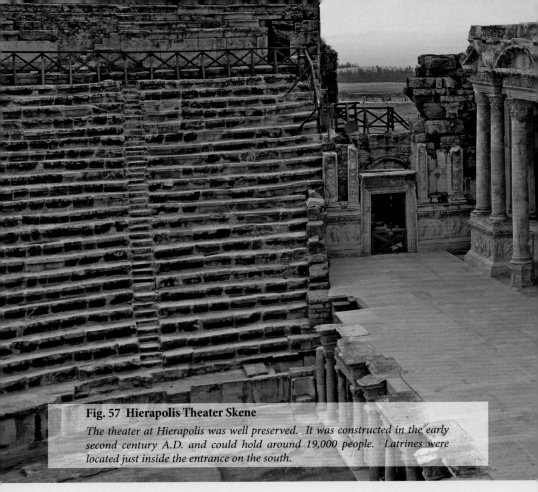

Fig. 57 Hierapolis Theater Skene

The theater at Hierapolis was well preserved. It was constructed in the early second century A.D. and could hold around 19,000 people. Latrines were located just inside the entrance on the south.

length of the agora. A little northeast of the basilica and up the slope of the hill there are the remains of a poorly preserved Hellenistic theater.

A fourth or fifth century Byzantine Gate stood at the south end of Frontinus Street and just inside the gate (to the south) there was the early third century Triton Nymphaeum, a beautifully decorated fountain. Beyond that, a vast stretch of land has only been partially excavated. Here one can view the extensive remains of a fifth or sixth century Christian basilica and follow the course of a few excavated city streets with several intersecting streets that have not been fully excavated. Turning east and traveling up the hillside one will cross a Byzantine city wall and enter into another necropolis. Climbing further, near the top of the hill there are the remains of a square structure with an octagonal domed structure within. This was the early fifth century martyrion of Philip, built to commemorate the saint who purportedly was martyred on this spot. The tomb of Philip was found in a Byzantine church next to the martyrion. Descending the hill and crossing a small ravine to the south an ancient street leads to the Roman theater (fig. 57). This theater is well preserved and was originally built in the second century A.D. The stage building (skene) is in good shape and many of the friezes, statues and columns remain in place. East of the theater there is yet another necropolis.

Descending the hill from the theater and heading west, a fresh dig has exposed a second century A.D. peristyle house with Ionic capitals. Further to the west there are four terraces. The highest terrace contained the foundations of a large Ionic peripteral temple dating to the time of Tiberius. This has been identified as the famous sanctuary of Apollo, the patron deity of the city. Next to this, another temple, built in the third century A.D. and previously identified with Apollo, is now considered part of the Plutonium, a sanctuary dedicated to the god of the underworld, Pluto. At the southwest corner of the temple there is a small arched opening that led to a cave leading to the underworld. The city of Hierapolis was constructed over a volcanic crevasse, which was the source of the hot springs in the city. The area of the Plutonium covered a cave that emitted hazardous vapors. Since the cavity still emits noxious vapors (as it did in the past) the opening has been sealed shut, but further east more of the Plutonium has been excavated and the deadly vapors still kill birds that venture into the precinct (fig. 58). West of the Apollo Temple is a fourth century A.D. nymphaeum and west of the numphaeum is the Sacred Pool. This pool was surrounded by a colonnaded portico during the Roman period, but the only remaining columns are now visible underwater (fig. 59). The south baths were located southwest of the pool. Today these baths are the location of the excellent Hieropolis Museum. Finally, southwest of the Museum are the beautiful calcium deposits from the hot springs.

Fig. 58 Hierapolis Plutonium

The Plutonium was thought to be the entrance to the underworld. Poisonous vapors emanated from the underground chambers. Sacrificial animals were overcome by the noxious gases, but priests (who held their breath) were able to perform their duties without harm.

Fig. 59 Hierapolis Sacred Pool

The hot springs fed the Sacred Pool which was decorated with columns and statues. The pool may have been dedicated to Apollos the patron deity of the city.

Was There a Church at Aphrodisias during the First Century?

The city of Aphrodisias was never mentioned in the New Testament. In addition, the earliest Christian writings do not mention the city. Thus, one cannot say with certainty that a church existed in Aphrodisias during the first century. However, we must bear in mind that some other cities with early Christian congregations were not mentioned in the New Testament. Moreover, we have few Christian sources outside of the NT that date to the first century. Thus, the absence of a reference to a church in Aphrodisias is not entirely surprising.

On the other hand, Acts 19:10 asserts that Paul's two year ministry in Asia Minor was so productive that "all who lived in Asia Minor heard the word of the Lord, both Jews and Greeks." This statement was an exaggeration, but it was also Luke's way of making a declaration of the extent of Paul's work (along with his coworkers) without enumerating all of the individual cities, towns and villages with Christian congregations. Such a list may have been quite extensive.

There were many ancient cities in Asia Minor where churches may have been established during this time. Cities not far from Ephesus such as Magnesia, Tralles, Nysa, Orthosia, Antioch ad Maeandrum, Tripolis, Apollonia, Notion, Colophon, Metropolis, Teos, Klazomenai, Erythrai, Priene, Alinda, Alabanda, Herakleia, Labraunda, Stratonikia and Aphrodisias were all sizeable cities within a fifty mile radius of Ephesus and many of these may have

Fig. 60 Aphrodisias Jew and God Fearer Stele

Aphrodisias had a large Jewish population. This stele lists the names of sixty-eight Jews, three proselytes and fifty-four God Fearers (θεοσεβἰς).

Fig. 61 Aphrodisias Menorah Panel

A wall panel in the Sebasteion at Aphrodisias was inscribed with at least three menorahs along with additional graffiti.

had churches that were founded at this time. While a case may be made for any of these, Aphrodisias is a particularly likely location where a church may have started in the first century.

As we have mentioned previously, Paul's missionary strategy focused upon cities that contained Jewish populations. In such cities Paul and his followers would have an opportunity to share the gospel in the synagogues of these towns. As a Jew, Paul evidently felt an obligation to share the gospel with Jews first and foremost. When he wrote to the Romans, Paul claimed that the gospel was the power of God for salvation to the Jew first and also to the Greek (Rom 1:16). The word in this verse for "first" can be translated "foremost" or "most importantly." Thus, Paul may have claimed that ministry to the Jews was to be done first (in terms of time) or that such ministry to the Jews was of foremost importance. Either way, it is apparent that cities with Jewish populations were probably Paul's primary targets for ministry. As God's covenant community, Jews in these cities were a priority for Paul and his disciples.

Aphrodisias had a large Jewish population. From archaeological evidence alone, Aphrodisias had a larger Jewish population than any other Anatolian city, with the pos-

Fig. 62 Aphrodisias Pavement Menorah

Several more menorahs were etched on the pavement stones of Aphrodisias.

sible exception of Sardis. An inscription found in the city listed the names of 125 Jewish men and God Fearers (fig. 60). The inscription probably only listed those who contributed to a construction project in the city and the inscription only mentioned men. So it is logical to assume that the inscription only mentioned a fraction of the Jewish population in the city. Additionally, a large number of Jewish symbols such as menorahs were inscribed in the city (figs. 61, 62 and 63). Many of these menorahs were found in the Sebasteion, a lavishly decorated structure dedicated to Rome and the

Fig. 63 Aphrodisias Column Menorah

This unusual ten branched menorah on a column in Aphrodisias may have had another menorah (now defaced) above it.

Fig. 64 Aphrodisias Bouleuterion Jewish Inscription

The Aphrodisias bouleuterion had a section marked "place of the blue faction, the Hebrew elders."

imperial family. Another Jewish inscription was found in the bouleuterion (fig. 64). Such Jewish finds in the Sebastion and bouleuterion probably indicates that many Jews in Aphrodisias were politically empowered.

With such a large Jewish presence in Aphrodisias and with its proximity to Ephesus, it is hard to imagine that the city of Aphrodisias was ignored by Paul and his followers. We know that a church existed in the city during the Byzantine period. The church occupied the ruins of the temple to Aphrodite, the city's patron deity and the bishop's residence was adjacent to the former temple. However, a Christian presence during the Byzantine period tells us little of what existed there in the first century.

Christian remains for the first three centuries are very difficult to identify. Christian symbols were not firmly established and widely used until at least the second or third century. Moreover, since the Christian community was viciously persecuted for the first three centuries, Christians were reluctant to identify their locations by placing symbols or inscriptions upon their homes or meeting places. Additionally, the Christian church was essentially an underground movement for the first three centuries. Church buildings as we have them today were not constructed and the congregations met in homes until the time of Constantine when basilicas were first constructed.

Was there a church in Aphrodisias during the first century? We will never know for certain. But the odds favor it.

The Ancient History and Archaeology of Aphrodisias (Geyre)

The Ancient History of Aphrodisias

Findings at the small acropolis at Aphrodisias reveal that the site was occupied from at least the Bronze Age. Around the sixth century B.C. a cult site for a local fertility goddess was established at this site. The place may have been called Ninoe, which some scholars have connected to the Akkadian goddess Ishtar, who was also known as Astarte, Nin or Ninai, the goddess of love and war. If this line of thought is correct, the site changed its name to Aphrodisias during the Hellenistic period as the local goddess was identified with the Greek goddess of love Aphrodite. When the Romans began to exert their influence in Asia Minor in the second century B.C., the city of Aphrodisias quickly gained stature. Aeneas, the legendary founder of Rome was thought to be the son of Venus, the Roman goddess of love who was identified with the Greek Aphrodite. Since the sanctuary at this location was the primary site for the worship of Aphrodite in Caria, the cult site grew into a city and the Romans adopted Aphrodisias as their own. Appian stated that in 82 B.C. the dictator Sulla was advised by the Delphic Oracle to send gifts to the Carian Aphrodite. No doubt, Sulla's gifts were sent here. Theater inscriptions at Aphrodisias indicate that Julius Caesar offered gifts to the sanctuary at Aphrodite and in 39 B.C. the city was granted special privileges, freedom and tax exemption by Roman decree. Several additional honors were bestowed upon Aphrodisias by later Roman emperors. These honors were recorded on the stage building at Aphrodisias. From the beginning of the Roman period Aphrodisias came to be a center and school for the arts, particularly sculpture. Sculpture from Aphrodisias was bought and transported throughout the Mediterranean world. Aphrodisias was damaged by several earthquakes through the years, the most damaging being in the middle of the fourth century A.D.

Fig. 65 Aphrodisias Sebasteion

The Sebasteion of Aphrodisias was erected in the first century in honor of Caesar Augustus. It extended 265 feet and had three story porticoes on both sides of the street.

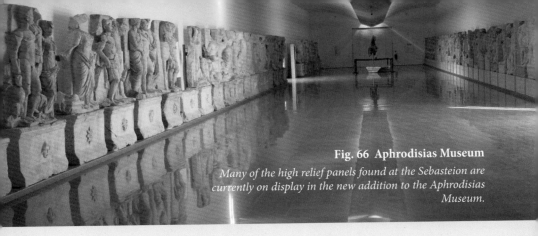

The Current Remains at Aphrodisias

The remains at Aphrodisias are extensive and well preserved. As a center for sculpture, the on-site museum is loaded with statues, sarcophagi and other artifacts. On the east side of the site there was a Sebasteion from the first century A.D. (fig. 65). This consisted of a wide eighty meter street running east-west with colonnaded porticoes on both sides. The porticoes were three stories in height and the niches between the columns on each story were filled with reliefs of gods, mythological figures and the imperial families. On the west end of the street there was a 24 column propylon (a monumental gate) with statues of Aphrodite and the imperial family. On the east end of the street stood a Corinthian temple. Much of the Sebasteion has been reconstructed and dozens of

Fig. 67 Aphrodisias Theater

The theater at Aphrodisias was constructed in the second half of the first century B.C. and was renovated during the early Roman period. It could hold approximately 10,000 people.

Fig. 68 Aphrodisias South Agora

The South Agora at Aphrodisias was dedicated to the emperor Tiberias and had a long 170 meter pool lined with palm trees.

frieze panels from the Sebasteion are on display in the new addition to the museum (fig. 66).

To the south, an excellent first century B.C. theater lies at the southeastern corner of the site, resting on the eastern side of the small acropolis (fig. 67). The theater could hold eight thousand people and was extensively remodeled in the second century. As mentioned earlier, the walls of the stage building are loaded with inscriptions acknowledging the gifts and benefactions received by the city. In front of the theater a commercial agora was constructed in the fourth century A.D. after earthquakes brought permanent flooding to the earlier agora (fig. 68). The new agora, called the Tetrastoon was surrounded on all four sides by a colonnaded portico. Located south of the agora was a second century A.D. bath with a colonnaded hall preceding it.

North of the theater are two agoras, both dating to the first century A.D. The agora furthest to the south was 212 meters by 70 meters and was surrounded by Ionic columns. The northern agora was 205 meters by 120 meters and was surrounded by Doric columns. Recent investigations in the southern agora have shown that a pool or courtyard measuring twenty by twenty-seven meters existed in the agora during the Hellenistic period. Southwest of the agoras was a first century basilica, that was probably used for political and legal purposes. West of the agora were the second century Baths of Hadrian complete with cold, warm, hot water baths, dressing rooms and a palaestra. North of the Agoras was a second century A.D. covered odeon or bouleterion that could hold 1,700 people (fig. 69). West of this, a peristyle complex from the Byzantine period has been identified as the bishop's residence.

Further north there are fourteen columns still standing from the temple of Aphrodite. Although a sanctuary may have stood here dating back to the sixth century, the current remains date to a rebuilt structure from the time of Augustus. In the fifth century the temple was converted into a church. North of the temple about three

Fig. 69 Aphrodisias Bouleuterion

The bouleuterion was constructed in the late second century B.C. and had a seating capacity of 1750 people.

Fig. 70 Aphrodisias Stadium

Aphrodisias' stadium is one of the best preserved ancient stadiums in the world. It was 270 meters in length, had 30 tiers of seats and had a capacity of about 30,000 people.

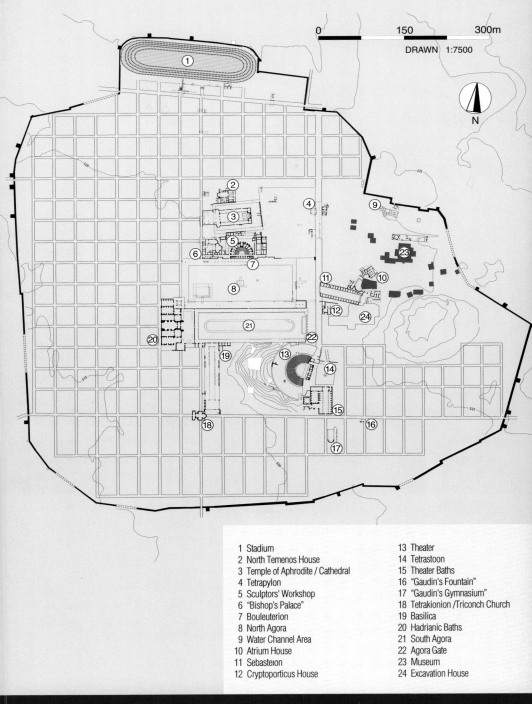

0   150   300m

DRAWN 1:7500

N

1 Stadium	13 Theater
2 North Temenos House	14 Tetrastoon
3 Temple of Aphrodite / Cathedral	15 Theater Baths
4 Tetrapylon	16 "Gaudin's Fountain"
5 Sculptors' Workshop	17 "Gaudin's Gymnasium"
6 "Bishop's Palace"	18 Tetrakionion /Triconch Church
7 Bouleuterion	19 Basilica
8 North Agora	20 Hadrianic Baths
9 Water Channel Area	21 South Agora
10 Atrium House	22 Agora Gate
11 Sebasteion	23 Museum
12 Cryptoporticus House	24 Excavation House

APHRODISIAS

Design by **TUTKU TOURS**

Fig. 71 Aphrodisias Tetrapylon Gate

The Tetrapylon was a monumental gate on the main north south street of Aph-
rodisias. The gate was constructed in the second century A.D.

hundred meters is one of the best preserved stadiums in the Mediterranean world (fig. 70). The stadium from the first century A.D. could hold 30,000 people and was 262 meters long and 59 meters wide. East of the stadium and a little south is a second century A.D. tetrapylon, a huge entrance with four gateways (fig. 71). Each gateway is supported by four spirally fluted Corinthian columns, topped by pediments on the east and west.

How and When Were Churches Established at Troas and Assos?

How far did Paul's Ephesian ministry extend? There is clear evidence of churches at Troas (Alexandrian Troas) and Assos during Paul's lifetime. But, how and when were they established? The first time Troas was mentioned in Acts was following Paul's failed attempt to preach in Asia and Bithynia during his second journey (Acts 16:6-11). It was at Troas that Paul had a vision of a Macedonian man who beckoned Paul to preach in Macedonia. Crossing the Aegean Sea, Paul spent the better part of the next two years in Macedonia and Greece. Nothing was mentioned of Paul preaching or doing ministry in Troas (or Assos) during this time, although it would not have been surprising if he had.

After Paul was forced from Ephesus during the third mission, he returned to the Macedonian churches (Acts 20:1). Since Troas was the chief port for entrance into Macedonia from Asia, it is likely that Paul made his way through Troas on this journey. However, Luke's abbreviated narrative gave no details of the journey.

After spending another three or four months in Macedonia and Greece, Paul returned to Asia Minor through Troas. Paul and his disciples stayed here for seven days before moving on. At this time Luke documented a story of Paul speaking to a crowd at Troas. The discussions extended long into the night. A young man, Eutychus, fell asleep and tumbled out of a third floor window. Although he had apparently died, Paul revived the young man (Acts 20:5-13). This was one of the "we" sections of Luke's narrative. As we have mentioned earlier, the "we" sections ostensibly were times when Luke recorded his own participation in the events that he recorded.

This narrative never mentioned a church at Troas, but it is evident that a church existed there prior to Paul's arrival. Several clues lead us to that conclusion. First, Luke tells us that Paul's traveling companions arrived in Troas five days earlier. It is probable that they arrived early to minister to the Troas congregation. Second, after Paul arrived, the company of travelers remained in Troas for another seven days (v.6). Since Paul was in a hurry to get to Jerusalem before Pentecost (20:16), the most likely reason he spent an additional week at Troas would be to minister to a church at Troas. Third, Luke mentioned that Paul celebrated the Lord's Supper ("broke bread" – v.7) on the first day of the week with the group that was hosting them. Finally, the fact that Paul extended his message through the night and into the morning implies that Paul had urgent matters that he needed to deal with before departing from the congregation.

Fig. 72 Chryse Roman Road

The roman road that Paul took from Alexandria Troas to Assos ran through Chryse. Chryse was the site of the Apollo Smintheon Temple mentioned in Homer's Iliad.

Troas was mentioned in two other places in the New Testament. In 2 Cor 2:12-13 Paul commented on his earlier visit to Troas during the second mission. Here Paul stated that he "came to Troas for the gospel of Christ" and that "a door was opened for me." In this passage, Paul did not mention the vision of the Macedonian man, as Luke did in Acts. However, Paul continued, saying that "I had no rest for my spirit" (perhaps a vague reference to the vision) and he went on to Macedonia (2:13). This brief reference to what happened in Acts 16:8-10 does not tell us enough to conclude that Paul established a church at Troas during this visit, but the statement that he "came to Troas for the gospel of Christ" is a purpose statement that may be interpreted that way.

The last place where Troas is mentioned is in 2 Tim 4:13, the concluding remarks of the final letter to Timothy where Paul asked Timothy to come to him and to bring the cloak and books that Paul left at Troas with Carpus. Nothing is known of Carpus, but he must have been a Christian resident at Troas who provided Paul with housing.

Evidence for the church at Assos is more unclear than for the church at Troas. Assos is only mentioned twice in the New Testament, both in Acts 20:13-14. After

Fig. 73 Roman Road from Alexandria Troas to Assos

Several roman roads still survive in the Troad. This one a short distance from Assos presents the traveler with a fork in the road.

spending seven days in Troas and still intent upon making it to Jerusalem by Pentecost, Paul made the unusual decision to walk from Troas to Assos instead of taking the ship with his disciples. The distance of 34 kilometers was a rather short two or three day trip on foot, but for someone who was in a hurry to get to Jerusalem, the trip would have been covered in one day by ship and the port at Assos could have been skipped if the captain had no business in Assos.

Why did Paul choose to walk to Assos? The best explanation for Paul passing up the ship on the journey was because he wanted to do ministry as he walked on the way. It is probable that members of the Troas church accompanied Paul to Assos. But, it is also likely that Christians from Assos were in Troas during the seven days that Paul ministered there. They would have returned to Assos with Paul. Acts 20:4-6 explains that many of Paul's disciples who had been traveling with him throughout Greece and Macedonia arrived in Troas five days earlier than Paul. Their arrival prior to Paul's arrival at Troas was to gather together Christian leaders from the Troad (the region around Troas, so named for the nearby ancient city of Troy). Five days would have been enough time to gather church leaders from Assos.

Fig. 74 Alexandria Troas Structures near the Augustan Temple

Excavations surrounding the Augustan Temple have exposed city streets, monuments and civic structures.

Paul left Troas earlier than he wished. People usually do not deliver messages throughout the night unless they are pressed for time. Then, the choice to walk to Assos would be pointless unless there was a church at Assos. Paul could have boarded the ship at Chryse (modern Gülpinar) where the temple of Apollo Smintheus existed. Chryse was half the distance to Assos and the road would have taken Paul right past the site. Yet, Paul pressed on to Assos in order to spend more time with leaders of the church at Assos. On his journeys, Paul used the time frugally by teaching and training his followers. Both Acts and Paul's own writings frequently mention many of his disciples who travel with him on these long journeys. In this case, Acts 20:13 indicates that Paul's disciples got on the ship. It is unimaginable to think that Paul took the journey from Troas to Assos alone (fig. 73).

We still have not directly addressed the question of how and when churches were established at Troas and Assos. Let me throw out two suggestions. First, following Paul's failed attempt to preach in Asia during the second mission (Acts 16:6), Paul wandered through Phrygia and Galatia before arriving in Mysia. Luke's narrative does

110

not offer specific details of the cities that Paul visited during that time, but Alexandrian Troas and Assos were included in the region of Mysia. From Mysia Paul attempted to penetrate Bithynia (16:7), but his efforts were thwarted. Returning to Mysia, Paul came to the port city Troas (16:8). During his ventures in Mysia, it is possible that Paul first established churches in Assos and Troas.

Second, as we have mentioned previously, Luke claimed that all of Asia was evangelized during the two years that Paul trained disciples at the school of Tyrannos (Acts 19:10). Any of those disciples who wandered north along the Asian coast would probably put into port at Assos and Troas. Troas was the major port in the north. Travel north by ship to Assos or Troas would have been just as easy as traveling inland to any of the many cities on a fifty mile radius of Ephesus.

Alexandria Troas (near Dalyan, 16 km. south of Troy)

The Ancient History of Alexandria Troas

The first settlement at this site according to Strabo was a Greek colony called Sigeia. But, the settlement seems to have been small and insignificant. In 310 B.C. Antigonus I Monophthalmus, one of Alexander's generals established a larger city and moved nearby residents from the city of Neandria to the site. The city was named Antigonia. In 301 B.C. Antigonus was defeated and killed by Lysimachus who renamed the city Alexandria. There were fifteen cities named after Alexander the Great, so this one came to be known as Alexandria in the region of the Troad, or Alexandria Troas. During the Hellenistic period the city grew and, due to its location at the junction of Europe and Asia with access to the Black Sea, Alexandria Troas soon became the wealthiest and most populous city in the region. Julius Caesar considered moving the Roman capital to Alexandria Troas and conferred upon it the privileges of a colony. Augustus established a Roman colony in the city and Alexandria flourished during the early imperial period. The city declined during the Byzantine period as Istanbul increased in power and significance. Adding to this, around the sixth century the harbor seems to have silted up contributing to the decline of Alexandria Troas.

Christian Beginnings at Alexandria Troas

Paul visited Alexandria Troas at least three times and probably more. During the course of his second mission Paul came to Troas after passing through Phrygia, Galatia and Mysia (Acts 16:7-8). There Paul had his vision of the Macedonian man who bid him to enter Europe. Since this is the beginning of the "we" sections of Acts, it seems probable that Luke joined him at Troas. It is possible that Paul traveled through Troas on his return journey and perhaps again on his third mission heading into Macedonia, although Acts is silent on the travel itinerary. On Paul's return journey of the third mission, it is stated that Paul stayed seven days at Troas (Acts 20:6). A final reference to Troas occurs in 2 Tim 4:13, where Timothy is requested to pick up a cloak and books that were left at Troas (fig. 75).

Additional information about the church at Troas comes

Fig. 75 Alexandria Troas Market Building

A newly excavated building near the Augustan temple appears to be a market building (macellum). The entrance on the left is still largely buried. Above, the slots for timbers indicate that the building had a second floor.

from the beginning of the second century (A.D. 110) when Ignatius, bishop of Antioch traveled to Troas on the way to his execution in Rome. While awaiting his ship, Ignatius wrote three of his last letters from Troas. From Polycarp's writings we may imply that two other prisoners joined Ignatius at Troas.

The Current Remains at Alexandria Troas

Although the ancient city purportedly covered more than one thousand acres, little of the ancient city has been excavated today. The ancient city walls which were eight kilometers in length survive in part. Other visible remains include the huge baths constructed by Herodes Atticus early in the second century A.D. (fig. 76). Herodes Atticus was a personal friend of Hadrian and was appointed to an administrative post in Alexandria. A short distance to the south of the baths, there was a nymphaeum, dating to the second century A.D. At the newest excavation, a short distance to the west, archaeologists have found the foundations of an Agora Temple constructed near the end of the first century B.C. and perhaps dedicated to Dionysus. A large vaulted platform supported the temple precincts. The temple was bordered by a street with a colonnaded portico and a nymphaeum. The vaulted substructure on the west side of the agora may have been used as a cryptoporticus (a subterranean gallery) with shops lining a recently exposed lower street. This paved street ran along the west side of the temple precincts heading south. Along the southern side of the temple precinct there is the footing of a podium. Further to the east is a small bouleuterion (Odeon). Three hundred meters to the south there is a large theater that is unexcavated. The harbor which has silted up, contains damaged columns from the city that were intended to be hauled away for secondary construction elsewhere (fig. 77).

Fig. 76 Alexandria Troas Baths

The large baths at Alexandria Troas were constructed by Herodes Atticus in the 2nd century B.C. and were originally 123 meters by 84 meters.

Fig. 77 Alexandria Troas Harbor

Alexandria Troas was the major harbor controlling sea traffic through the Dardanelles and on to the Black Sea. Paul traveled to Macedonia through this port.

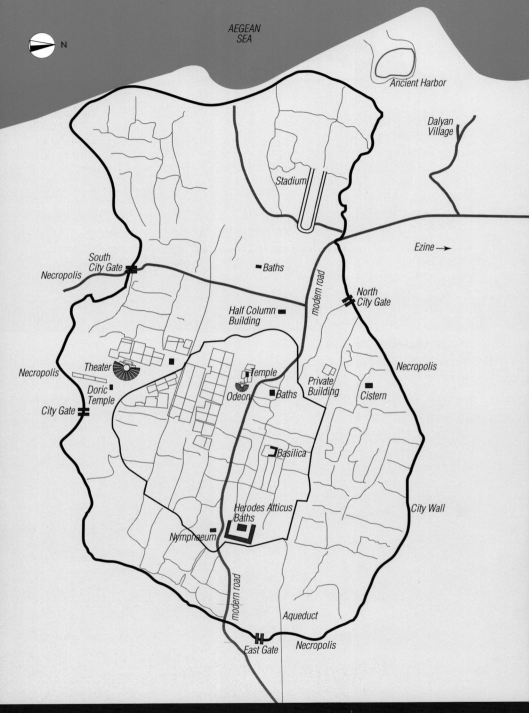

N

AEGEAN SEA

Ancient Harbor

Dalyan Village

Stadium

Ezine →

South City Gate

Necropolis

Baths

modern road

North City Gate

Half Column Building

Necropolis

Theater

Temple

Necropolis

Private Building

Cistern

Doric Temple

Odeon

Baths

City Gate

Basilica

City Wall

Herodes Atticus Baths

Nymphaeum

modern road

Aqueduct

East Gate

Necropolis

ALEXANDER TROAS

Design by **TUTKU TOURS**

Assos (Behramkale)

The Ancient History of Assos

According to Strabo, Assos was founded in the seventh century B.C. by Greeks who crossed the eleven kilometers between the island of Lesbos and the mainland at Assos. Early in the sixth century B.C. King Croesus of Sardis captured Assos and added it to his expanding Lydian Kingdom. But in 546 B.C. the Persians swept into western Asia Minor, crushing the Lydians and taking over Assos. In the fifth century Assos joined together with western Asia Minor cities and threw out their Persian overlords and then joined the Delian League, led by Athens. Later Hermias, a student of Plato's (along with Aristotle) was appointed leader of Assos. He invited Aristotle to Assos and the noted philosopher lived in Assos from 348-345 B.C. In 345 B.C. the Persians recaptured Assos and put Hermias to death. Alexander the Great did away with Persian control of the area in 334 B.C., and after his death Assos fell into the hands of the Seleucids. Around that same time the Stoic philosopher Cleanthes was born in Assos, later traveling to Athens and succeeding Zeno as the head of the Stoic school. The expanding Pergamene Kingdom absorbed Assos in 241 B.C. and a little more than a hundred years later the Romans received Assos along with the rest of the Pergamene Kingdom. In the second half of the first century, the apostle Paul traveled from Troas to Assos near the end of his third mission (Acts 20:13-14). At Assos Paul caught a ship heading to the south and east.

Fig. 78 Assos Athena Temple

The Athena Temple at Assos was built around 530 B.C. and is the oldest Doric temple in Anatolia. Portions of the frieze from the temple (unusual for a Doric temple) are in the Louvre and Istanbul Archaeological Museum.

Fig. 79 Assos City Walls

The 4th century B.C. city walls and towers at Assos still stand at a height of 14 meters and are some of the most impressive Hellenistic walls in the world.

Fig. 80 Assos Theater

The 3rd century B.C. theater at Assos could hold around 5,000 spectators.

Fig. 81 Assos City Gate

The roman road led past the necropolis at Assos and entered into the city through the 4th century B.C. city gates.

The Current Remains at Assos

The remains at Assos are truly impressive and the ancient city, which was built upon the slopes of a steep acropolis occupied a picturesque location overlooking the sea. The views at the top of the acropolis at Assos are spectacular, looking over the Aegean Sea to the island of Lesbos and to the ancient city below. The acropolis is crowned with the Temple of Athena, built in 530 B.C. The Doric peripteral temple had six columns on the ends and thirteen along the sides (fig. 78). The walls surrounding the acropolis are Byzantine. South of the acropolis in the lower city there was a Hellenistic agora with a 125 meter two story stoa on the north side and a 70 meter three story stoa on the south side. At the east end of the agora there was a bouleterion twenty meters square with a bema (speaker's podium) in front. At the west end of the agora there was a temple that was later converted into a church. All of the buildings in the agora date to the third or second century B.C.

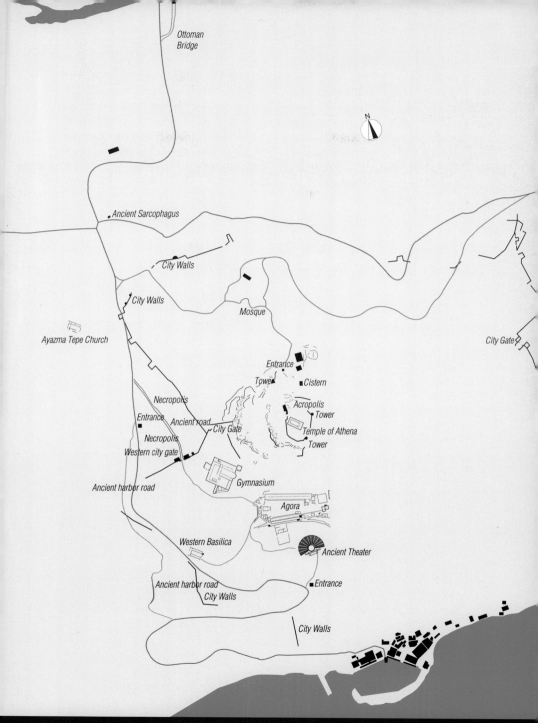

Ottoman
Bridge

N

Ancient Sarcophagus

City Walls

City Walls

Mosque

City Gate

Ayazma Tepe Church

Entrance

Tower   Cistern

Necropolis

Acropolis
Tower

Entrance   Ancient road

Temple of Athena

Necropolis   City Gate
                                              Tower

Western city gate

Ancient harbor road   Gymnasium

Agora

Western Basilica

Ancient Theater

Ancient harbor road   Entrance

City Walls

City Walls

ASSOS

South of the agora there was a third century B.C. theater that was modified during the Roman period. Further south is the ancient harbor, nothing of which remains from the ancient period. A second century B.C. gymnasium was west of the agora. The courtyard (palaestra) of the gymnasium measured 32 by 40 meters and was surrounded by Doric columns. West of the gymnasium are the remains of the Hellenistic city walls and a gate with two towers dating to the fourth century B.C. The walls were originally three kilometers in length and sections are in excellent shape, at times rising to fourteen meters in height. These are some of the most impressive and well preserved city walls and gates in all of Anatolia. Several sections of the road from Alexandria Troas and Chryse remain in excellent shape north and west of Assos. Upon approaching Assos the ancient paved road passed through the necropolis before entering into the city through the massive well preserved western city gate (fig. 81).

Chapter 4

1 Peter – Peter's Ministry to Churches in Pontus, Galatia, Cappadocia, Asia and Bithynia

The authorship of 1 Peter is disputed. However, if it is granted that Peter wrote the letter, then the epistle should be dated around A.D. 65. The letter was written from Rome (5:13) to Christians in Pontus, Galatia, Cappadocia, Asia and Bithynia. The sequence of the provinces as they were listed in 1 Peter 1:1 suggests that the person who carried the letter traveled a circuit, landing at a port in Pontus (perhaps the major Black

Fig. 82 Zelve Valley, Cappadocia
Hundreds of Cave churches, such as this one in the Zelve Valley, were created in Cappadocia and Phrygia as the church went underground in order to retreat from the world and to escape persecutions.

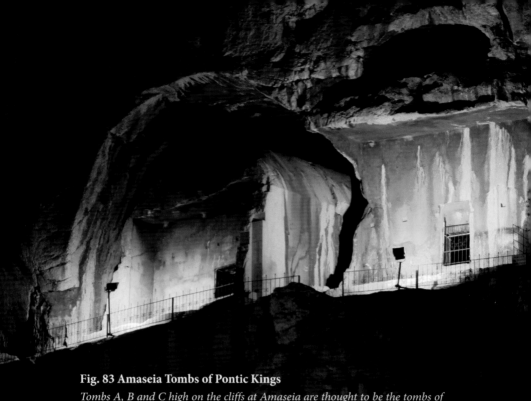

Fig. 83 Amaseia Tombs of Pontic Kings

Tombs A, B and C high on the cliffs at Amaseia are thought to be the tombs of the Pontic kings Mithridates I, Mithridates II and Ariobarzanes. The tombs were probably built in the late 3rd century B.C.

Sea port at Sinope), traveling south to Galatia and Cappadocia and then traveling west to Asia and north to Bithynia (perhaps departing from the port at Nicomedia). The New Testament mentioned nothing about Peter's travels in this area. However, Eusebius, relying on Origen's commentaries, claimed that Peter preached the gospel to Jews in these regions (*Eccl. Hist.* 3.1.2, 3.4.2) and Epiphanius of Salamis claimed that Peter frequently visited Pontus and Bithynia (*Panarion* 27.6.6).

The problems addressed in 1 Peter have nothing to do with false teaching or false prophets. That is not to say that such problems did not exist in these churches. Paul's letters and John's letters indicate that there were significant doctrinal concerns in the churches of Asia Minor. However, Peter either was not aware of what was being taught in these churches or he considered the threats to the church to be a more significant issue and focused his remarks on them. It is also possible that false teaching was not a problem in all of these provinces. In a letter addressed to multiple churches in such a broad area (practically all of middle and northern Anatolia), statements addressing

heterodox teaching would not be relevant for all congregations. So, it is not surprising that 1 Peter fails to mention problems with false teachings.

On the other hand, 1 Peter attests to serious problems that the churches in Pontus, Galatia, Cappadocia, Asia and Bithynia were facing dealing with harassment and persecutions. As a community that was "slandered" by others (2:12 & 3:16), "intimidated" (3:14) and "rejected by men" (2:4) Peter referred to these Christians as "aliens" and "temporary residents" (1:1 & 2:11). In the letter, Peter talked about "unjust suffering" (2:19; 3:17), yet he exhorted his readers to keep their behavior excellent, to obey governing officials and to honor all people (2:12-19) and to not give others a pretext for persecuting them (2:20; 3:16-17). Throughout the five chapters of the letter, there are numerous references to "sufferings" (2:19, 20; 3:14, 17; 4:1, 13, 15, 16, 19; 5:9), "the fiery ordeal" (1:7; 4:12), "various trials" (1:6) and the letter implies that Christians were being dragged before the courts where they were intimidated and slandered (3:14-16). Peter inspired these churches by referring to Christ's unjust suffering as an exam-

Fig. 84 Ephesus St. John Basilica

The walls surrounding the Basilica of St. John have twenty towers and four gates. The walls were constructed with secondary use stone (spolia) from the Artemision and the city of Ephesus, particularly the stadium.

ple to follow (2:21; 4:1) and he prepared them by suggesting that such suffering was unavoidable (2:21; 4:1, 12).

One of the noteworthy features of this letter is that it is the earliest testimony of widespread and systematic persecution against Christians in Anatolia. No other document offers testimony of such tribulations in Asia Minor this early in the first century. The lack of corroborating evidence is one of the reasons why some scholars question whether 1 Peter was written during Peter's lifetime. Yet the lack of supporting testimony should not be surprising. Other historical sources were not interested in documenting the troubles of this new religion.

The harassment and persecution of the Christian community was not an imperial policy at this time and the local governing officials probably had no consistent approach to deal with these Christians. Christians withdrew from the civic cults and refused to worship the local patron deities. Moreover, although they submitted to Roman authorities and obeyed the law, the Christians refused to venerate the imperial family and to offer sacrifices to the imperial cult. The withdrawal of a sizeable group of Christians from the important social gatherings at the temples and community festivals was bound to raise suspicions and to create tensions within the cities. The slander, harassment and intimidation mentioned in 1 Peter would be a natural outcome of these tensions. In time, the hostilities would increase as the local officials either ignored the harassment or they implicitly encouraged it. During this time, there was no official policy for dealing with the Christians and consequently, no records would be kept. Nevertheless, a broad and persistent pattern of persecution against the Christian community was developing throughout Asia Minor. These actions were probably not consistent from one city to another or from one region to another. Yet, these actions had an inertia that carried through to the time of Domitian. When Domitian came to power, the pattern became even more widespread and consistent throughout these regions. Domitian demanded that he be acknowledged as a living god and his firm insistence upon absolute obedience empowered local officials throughout Anatolia to compel Christians to renounce their faith. This was the situation in Asia Minor at the time when the apocalypse (Revelation) was written. In the book of Revelation, John wrote seven letters to seven churches in Asia Minor that were confronted with the imperial demands of Domitian and the pressures exerted upon them by hostile civic officials and individuals from the local population. Not every church or believer responded to these pressures in the same way. Some buckled under the pressure and apostatized, while others stiffly resisted the opposition. Still others found a middle ground and compromised their faith in ways that disturbed John.

John's Ministry in Ephesus and the Surrounding Areas

Early church testimony is solid in its witness that the apostle John spent his later years in Ephesus, although the details of how and when John arrived are not clear. Eusebius, an early church historian, claimed that John fled Jerusalem along with the other apostles and they were scattered to separate regions of the Mediterranean world. According to Eusebius, John went to Asia and after an extended ministry in Ephesus, he died and was buried there. During this time, John trained disciples, just as Paul had done earlier in Ephesus. In time, these disciples ministered to churches throughout Asia Minor. Eusebius and Irenaeus (an earlier Christian writer) passed on traditions related to John from two of his closest disciples: Papias and Polycarp. Papias later became the leader (bishop) of the church at Hierapolis and Polycarp was appointed bishop of the church at Smyrna. According to Eusebius and Irenaeus, Polycarp relayed a story of John fleeing a bath house at Ephesus when he discovered Cerinthus (a Gnostic teacher) within.

Fig. 85 Christ Pantocrator

The eleventh century Pammakaristos Church in Istanbul contains some of the most beautiful Byzantine mosaics in the world. Here depicted is Christ Pantocrator ("Christ Almighty"), an expression used in the book of Revelation nine times.

Eusebius also handed down a few quotations from Papias. Papias authored a five volume collection of Jesus' sayings (many more than what are recorded in the canonical gospels) called the Expositions of the Sayings of the Lord. Unfortunately, these volumes are lost and the few quotations of these volumes from Eusebius are all that remain. In one section Papias referred to John twice. This led Eusebius and others to conclude that there were two persons named John in the early church: John the apostle and John the elder.

The fourth gospel, the letters of 1, 2 and 3 John and the apocalypse (Revelation) were all attributed to John by the early church fathers. But, if there were two people named John, which one wrote these books? Later church fathers seem to dissolve this distinction and assert that both of the titles refer to one and the same person: John the Apostle (who also called himself an elder). Some of these early church fathers believed that the apostle was the author of the gospel, epistles and apocalypse. Others however, suggest that the apostle wrote the gospel and epistles, while another John wrote the apocalypse. Regardless of how this issue is answered, it is clear that the fourth gospel, the epistles and apocalypse were all written in or around Ephesus. Likewise, scholars are agreed that these writings were some of the last writings in the New Testament, written in the late 80s to the mid 90's. Thus, these writings give us clues as to what was happening near the end of the first century in Ephesus and Asia Minor.

The Muratorian Canon and Clement of Alexandria both pass on an account of how John wrote his gospel after the other gospel accounts had been written. John, aware of the other gospels and uninterested in writing his own account, was coaxed to write his own gospel from his perspective. Since the chief focus of John's gospel narrative was upon Jesus and his ministry in Palestine, practically nothing can be learned about the church at Ephesus based upon this gospel. Some scholars have looked at passages like John 9:22 and 16:2 and have suggested that the references to being cast out of the synagogue were added by John to reflect the experiences of his fellow Christians in Ephesus. But this is a bit of a reach, and even if it is true, it tells us little more than what was happening when Paul himself was dismissed from the synagogue and began his work in the school of Tyrannus (Acts 19:8-9).

When John came to reside in Ephesus he quickly became the patriarch of churches throughout Asia Minor. His first letter was probably written to the churches in Ephesus and the surrounding area, while the second and third letters were likely written to congregations and persons elsewhere in the region. With the passing of Paul, John because the chief apostolic authority in Asia Minor. With numerous churches in this populous region, John realized the importance of raising up disciples and training them for ministry to churches without stable and knowledgeable leaders. This was a daunting task,

Fig. 86 Chora Church - Istanbul

One of the earliest churches still standing in Istanbul, the Chora Church was built in the early fifth century and contains beautiful frescoes and mosaics of the life of Christ.

since the problems encountered by Paul two decades earlier were still plaguing the churches during John's days.

In the middle of the last decade of the first century, John was banished to the island of Patmos by the emperor Domitian. There, John received a vision of the risen Lord and he was commanded to write letters to seven churches in western Asia Minor. The seven churches were located in some of the largest and most prominent cities in the area. The letters were placed in the book of Revelation in an order that suggests a circuit that the apostle or his disciples would have taken as they traveled to these churches and ministered to their congregations. On a map, the route began at Ephesus and then continued north to Smyrna, roughly 65 kilometers. Then the route extended another 110 kilometers to the north to Pergamon. From there, the route turned inland and southeast for about 70 kilometers to Thyatira and then ran south for another 65 kilometers to Sardis. Philadelphia was located another 45 kilometers to the southeast of Sardis and the final church Laodicea was located another 70 kilometers southeast of Philadelphia. From there, the traveler on the itinerary could head due west for 160 kilometers on a road that led directly to Ephesus, where the journey began. Because of these long distances separating the seven churches, the evangelists stopped at a number of cities and villages in between. Churches probably existed in most of these unknown towns.

John's Ministry in Ephesus - 1 John

As we mentioned above, Polycarp passed on a story of John fleeing from the bath house in Ephesus at the sight of the false teacher Cerinthus. The story was repeated by Irenaeus and Eusebius. Irenaeus, an early church father, believed that John's gospel was written in part to refute the teachings of Cerinthus and some scholars believe that 1 John likewise may have been written to address Cerinthian or Gnostic tendencies in Asia Minor. Whether Cerinthus, or some other heretical teacher, it is clear that all three letters of John were written to counter a false teaching that had emerged in Ephesus and Asia Minor.

In the first letter John asserted that many "false prophets" and "antichrists" had emerged in the area (1 Jn 2:18, 4:1). John stated that these antichrists were initially a part of the congregation, but they dissociated themselves from the Christian community and they alienated their followers from the church: "just as you heard that antichrist is coming, even now many antichrists have arisen . . . . They went out from us, but they were not really of us; for if they had been of us, they would have remained with us; but they went out, in order that it might be shown that they all are not of us" (2:18-19).

The use of the word "antichrist" to describe John's opponents tells a great deal about John's perception of these people. The term was harsh and portrayed John's rivals as individuals who were not only opposed to John's teaching but also persons who were opposed to Christ himself. John's letter indicates that his readers had already heard about the coming antichrist – an apocalyptic individual who embodied evil and who opposed the cause of Christ. However, John does not indicate where this information came from. Paul, in his second letter to the Thessalonians, referred to an eschatological "man of lawlessness" who was similar to this antichrist, but Paul never used the term antichrist. John himself may have explained this person in his earlier contact with the church. He used the term again in 2 John 7 (which may have been written before 1 John) and the concept was prevalent in the book of Revelation, although the term was never used in the apocalypse. Here in 1 John however, the term was broadened to include several people who split from the church.

A further description of these antichrists can be found a few verses later in 1 Jn 2:22 "who is the liar but the one who denies that Jesus is the Christ? This is the antichrist, the one who denies the father and the son." And still more clarification is found in 4:1-3

Fig. 87 Hagia Sophia - Istanbul

At the entrance to the Hagia Sophia in Istanbul an ancient mosaic welcomes guests with an enthroned Christ holding the scriptures, saying "Peace be to you. I am the light of the world." The first church built at the site was constructed by Constantine the Great early in the fourth century. Most of the present church dates to the time of Justinian, early in the sixth century, who rebuilt the church after it was destroyed by fire.

"Beloved, do not believe every spirit, but test the spirits to see whether they are from God, because many false prophets have gone out into the world. By this you know the Spirit of God: every spirit that confesses that Jesus Christ has come in the flesh is from God; and every spirit that does not confess Jesus is not from God; this is the spirit of the antichrist, of which you have heard that it is coming, and now it is already in the world."

The crucial test for John was the belief that Jesus Christ had come in the flesh. Denial of the physical existence of Christ was a heresy that came to be known as Docetism. Docetism was one of several tenets that eventually became a component of Gnostic theology. Banking on Platonic thought, Docetic and Gnostic thought proposed a dualism between the spiritual realm and the physical realm. Accordingly, the spiritual realm was wholly good and pure, but the physical realm was irredeemably evil. The spiritual realm was the realm of pure light and of pure knowledge and the physical realm was a realm of darkness and utter ignorance. The Docetic theology asserted that the Gnostic redeemer (Christ) descended from the highest heaven (known as the pleroma) to earth. The purpose of the redeemer was to impart knowledge (gnosis) to the inhabitants of the lower earth, whereby they could ascend successively to the higher realms and eventually reach the pleroma. Several realms existed between the highest spiritual realm (the pleroma) and this world. Each successive lower realm was more physical, more enshrouded in darkness and more ignorant, and thus more evil. The problem was that if the redeemer (Christ) descended into the lower realms, he too would acquire a physical form and would become evil like everyone else. Moreover, it was thought that the light and knowledge of the redeemer would be extinguished as he descended through the realms of darkness and the redeemer would be incapable of leading himself and others to the pleroma.

The Gnostics resolved this dilemma by positing the belief that the redeemer (Christ) masqueraded as an incarnate being, but that in reality Jesus was only a disembodied spirit. As such Christ communicated the knowledge (gnosis) to his disciples and then departed for the pleroma. The Docetics and Gnostics denied the physical death and resurrection of Jesus and denied that the cross was the means by which salvation was achieved. Instead, it was believed that individuals achieved salvation through the acquisition of knowledge.

The teachings described above were still in the developmental stages at the time when John ministered in Ephesus and the surrounding region. It is not known how far these teachings had progressed at the end of the first century. We do know that these thoughts were systematized early in the second century by Basilides and Valentinus, the two best known Gnostics. It is probably also true that various teachers at the end of the first century had assorted Gnostic-like theologies. Marcion, a heretic around this time, has sometimes been described as a Gnostic, but his teachings, although Gnostic like, also differed from standard Gnostic thought, if such a thing existed at this time. Other than the clearly described Docetic teachings described in 1 Jn 4:1-3, it is not known what else might have been disputed by John.

The frequent contrast between the "truth" and "deceit" found in all three of John's letters (1 Jn 1:6-8; 2:4, 8, 21, 26-27; 3:7, 18-19; 4:6; 5:6, 20; 2 Jn 1-4, 7; 3 Jn 1-4, 8, 12) as well as the frequent contrast between "light" and "darkness" (1 Jn 1:5-7, 2:8-11) may in fact be John's attempt to sway the theological argument toward the truth and light manifest in the person of Jesus Christ. John may have been using terminology utilized by the false teachers. However instead of supporting the teachings of the schismatic frauds, John realigned these concepts of truth / deceit and light / darkness with a more accurate understanding of the faith of Christ.

Fig. 88 Crown of Life

John's words to the church at Smyrna: "Be faithful even to the point of death and I will give you the crown of life" Rev. 2:10. Second century Hellenistic Royal Crown – Ephesus Archaeological Museum.

John responded to these false teachings with a scathing attack on the propagators of such doctrines. In addition to referring to these opponents as antichrists, John also branded them as "liars." "If we say that we have fellowship with Him and yet walk in the darkness, we lie and do not practice the truth" (1 Jn 1:6). "The one who says 'I have come to know Him', and does not keep His commandments, is a liar" (1 Jn 2:4). "Who is the liar but the one who denies that Jesus is the Christ? This is the antichrist" (1 Jn 2:22). "If someone says, 'I love God', and hates his brother, he is a liar" (1 Jn 4:20). The repeated contrast between the truth and the lie (or false teaching) found in all three of these letters emphasizes the issue at stake for John. False teachers (also known as Antichrists or liars) have infiltrated the Christian communities in Ephesus and Asia Minor and have spread doctrines contrary to the traditions of Christ.

John's Ministry in Asia Minor - 2 John

The order of John's three letters is not certain and some scholars believe that Second and Third John may have been written before First John. The current placement of the letters in the New Testament is not according to chronology. The arrangement of the twenty-one epistles in the New Testament follows an order of declining size with letters grouped among authors.

First John was an open letter to a church, or it could have been a circular letter to several churches, similar to Paul's letters to the Ephesians, Colossians and to the Laodiceans (see above). These letters were intended to be circulated among a number of churches in Asia Minor. Second and Third John however, were more specific. Second John was directed to a particular church and Third John was addressed to a particular individual (Gaius).

The letter of 2 John was sent to "the chosen lady and her children" (2 Jn 1). The term "lady" was a metaphor to describe the church. In the New Testament, the church was depicted as the bride of Christ. The most common title used to refer to Jesus – "Lord" – is a translation of the Greek word "Kurios." The corresponding term for a woman in Greek was "Kurie," the term used here in 2 John 1 and translated as "Lady." The "Lady" was also described as "chosen." This word could also be translated as "elect" and this was a term that was commonly applied to Israel as the chosen or elect covenant people of God. In 2 Jn 1, the chosen Lady refers to the church in its covenant relationship with God.

It is interesting to note that John also indicated that he had encountered some of the church's "children" who were "walking in the truth" (Jn 4). These children were members of this church that John had met somewhere. It is not likely that John just bumped into these people during his travels. Rather, these children appear to have sought out John to inform him of the troubles at their church. We should suppose that these Christians traveled to Ephesus where they met with John and described to him what was happening back at their home church. John used similar terminology at the end of this short letter when he closed the note with "the children of your chosen sister greet you" (2 Jn 13). Naturally, the children and chosen sister mentioned here were members of the church where John was located – probably at Ephesus.

The messengers who found John brought news to him that false teachers (here described as "deceivers") had infiltrated the church and were misleading the people in the congregation. John described these deceivers as persons "who do not acknowledge Jesus Christ as coming in the flesh" (2 Jn 7). The description here in 2 John is practically identical to John's description of the "false prophets" in the first letter: "Every spirit that confesses that Jesus Christ has come in the flesh is from God and every spirit that does not confess Jesus is not from God. This is the spirit of the antichrist" (1 Jn 4:1-3). The key words here are the words "Jesus Christ coming in the flesh." As mentioned above, this was the false teaching known as Docetism, a doctrine advocated by the Gnostics of the second century. We can safely assume that the false prophets, deceivers, or antichrists mentioned in both epistles were promoting the same false teachings.

About twenty years after John wrote these letters, Ignatius the leader of the church at Syrian Antioch, was arrested and taken to Rome where he was martyred. As he passed through Asia Minor he wrote letters to several churches including a letter to the church at Smyrna, a short distance north of Ephesus. In his letter to the church at Smyrna, Ignatius used similar terminology to describe the false teaching (Docetism) that was still circulating in the area in A.D. 109. Ignatius stated that some unbelievers still maintained that Jesus was a spirit and only appeared in the flesh. Ignatius however, insisted "I know and believe that he (Jesus) was in the flesh even after the resurrection" (*Smyrnaeans* 3).

It is possible that John was targeting the same culprits in both 1 and 2 John, but such a conclusion is not necessary since both letters claim that "many" such false prophets or deceivers "have gone out into the world" (1 Jn 4:1 & 2 Jn 7). The number of deceivers had multiplied to such an extent that John was clearly alarmed: "Watch yourselves, that you do not lose what we have accomplished, but that you may receive a full reward" (2 Jn 8).

John was also concerned that such deceivers not be given an opportunity to address the congregation. These teachers were persuasive and many disciples had already fallen victim to their doctrines. When John ordered the church not to allow the deceivers "into your house" and not to give them a "greeting" (2 Jn 10), this was not an issue of being rude or inhospitable. All churches at that time were "house churches" that met in the homes of Christians. John was instructing the church not to allow these people an opportunity to enter "your house," that is, the church. Along the same lines, John was commanding these churches not to offer the deceivers a "greeting." The greeting in this instance was an opportunity to greet (or to speak to) those worshipping in the church. Such a "greeting" was usually offered to traveling Christians, or to those who claimed to be Christians, as these deceivers declared themselves to be.

It is not known where this church was located, but John was not close by. He concluded the letter with the hope that he would be able to visit them shortly (2 Jn 12) in order to deal with these issues. John also stated that there were other concerns that he felt were better addressed in person: "Though I have many things to write to you, I do not want to do so with paper and ink. But I hope to come to you and speak face to face" (2 Jn 12). Sensitive information, particularly if it deals with specific individuals, may not be tactfully or strategically addressed with a written copy, which could fall into the wrong hands. Also with a letter written to a congregation, it may be appropriate to omit names so that the transgressors (either the deceivers or their followers) might be more easily brought back into the congregation. Perhaps John was hoping that the Spirit's conviction would bring about repentance among the apostates and that they would be restored to the church.

John's Ministry in Asia Minor - 3 John

Of the three letters, 3 John was the most specific. Here John was not addressing several congregations (as may be the case with 1 John), and he was not addressing a specific church (as was the case with 2 John). Rather, 3 John was addressed to a specific individual named Gaius. Gaius was described in positive terms. John affirmed that Gaius was "beloved" and that his "soul prospers" (3 Jn 1-2). It was claimed that Gaius was "walking in the truth") and by referring to Gaius as one of "my children," it can be implied that Gaius was one of John's converts (3 Jn 4). We can conclude from the contents of this letter that Gaius was a leader of a church in the area. It is quite possible, perhaps even probable, that this church was the same congregation that was addressed in 2 John. Without getting into the details of it all, in the discussion that follows, I will assume that Gaius' church is the same as that in 2 John.

Like what we found in 2 John, we can see that people (described here as "brethren") had come from Gaius to John to explain what was happening at Gaius' church (3 Jn 3). In the time since John sent the earlier letter, the situation had gotten worse. These brethren were mentioned again in 3 Jn 5-8, where it is clear that these brethren were messengers originally sent out by John to attend to the problems at Gaius' church. Gaius was evidently providing hospitality for these messengers and John commended Gaius for doing so, even when they were unknown "strangers" to Gaius (3 Jn 5). These messengers were sent by John on an itinerary that included Gaius' church. When they had finished their task, they continued their journey to other churches before returning to John and giving an account of what happened. Thus, John encouraged Gaius with the words: "You will do well to send them on their way in a manner worthy of God" (3 Jn 6). It was necessary to supply these Christian workers with food and water for their next stop on the itinerary (3 Jn 6-8).

These "fellow workers" carried letters from John to the various churches on the itinerary. It is likely that many of these churches were dealing with problems similar to what we read about in the three letters of John. However, there were no doubt, some distinctions between the churches, so these letters probably differed from one another in some small details. We probably have a situation similar to what we read about in the book of Revelation, where John was instructed to write seven letters to seven churches surrounding Ephesus. The letters in the apocalypse were probably sent to churches on an itinerary similar to what we see in 3 John. We will discuss the book of Revelation shortly.

When these messengers returned to John, they reported that Gaius was a trustworthy partner with John and they testified of Gaius' love and support (3 Jn 5-6). They

135

also reported that an individual named Diotrephes was opposed to John's teaching and that Diotrephes refused hospitality to John's messengers and refused to allow such messengers to speak to the church (3 Jn 9-10). Moreover, Diotrephes harassed other Christians in the congregation who wished to welcome John's messengers by excommunicating them from the church (3 Jn 10). Perhaps Gaius was one of those who was excommunicated from Diotrephes' church.

It is not known how Diotrephes secured a position of authority within the church, but it does not appear to have been with John's consent. John declared that Diotrephes "loves to be first among them" (3 Jn 9) and we may assume from this that Diotrephes was an assertive individual who muscled his way into the position. Perhaps Diotrephes was persuasive and perhaps Diotrephes was one of the ringleaders of the false teaching that was sweeping the countryside. Diotrephes may have been one of the "deceivers" mentioned in 2 Jn 7.

Gaius, on the other hand, may have been a meek person who simply ceded power to Diotrephes without realizing the later outcome. Now in this letter however, John was asking Gaius to step forward and do what was necessary: that is, to challenge the authority and teaching of Diotrephes. Whether Gaius was still inside of the church or whether he was excommunicated from the church, he still had the respect of the Christian community in the city. From either perspective, the task would be exceedingly difficult, particularly if Gaius did not possess the charisma and speaking abilities of Diotrephes.

One other person was cited in the text of this short letter. Demetrius was mentioned in 3 Jn 12, where John claimed that Demetrius had received good testimony from "everyone." He also received good testimony from "the truth itself" and he was given an outstanding recommendation from John. Demetrius was one of John's disciples who carried this letter to Gaius. Traveling speakers (philosophers, potential politicians or public servants) often brought letters of recommendation with them to usher support for their appearance. Paul himself mentioned reference letters like this (1 Cor 16:3, 2 Cor 3:1-2). When it was stated that Demetrius had received good testimony from "everyone," we can take it for granted that Demetrius was an experienced itinerate speaker who faithfully communicated the gospel and John's messages to congregations throughout the region. Demetrius not only communicated well, it appears that John had complete confidence in his ability to faithfully convey his messsage. John added his personal recommendation to that of the others. Interestingly, John claimed that Demetrius had received good testimony from "the truth itself." One can only conclude from this that John was aware of some mystic spiritual or perhaps miraculous confirmation of Demetrius in his ministry. One can only guess what this might have been.

John's strong recommendation of Demetrius may be taken as an indication that he wanted Demetrius to oppose Diotrephes, rather than to have Gaius to take on the assignment. Gaius would need to support Demetrius on this mission and to organize support for John and his many messengers. The reference to a previous letter in 3 Jn 9 may be a reference to 2 John, but it may equally refer to another letter now lost. It is hard to tell how many letters and how many messengers John sent to the congregation. Diotrephes' attacks did not stop with criticism of John's teachings, Diotrephes also directed his hostility to John personally, "unjustly accusing us with wicked words" (3 Jn 10).

In the time between the writing of 2 John and 3 John, there was a progression in John's approach to dealing with the problem. Similar to how Paul dealt with the issue earlier (see above), John also initially refrained from mentioning names in 2 John. However in this last letter, John clearly drew the lines of demarcation and specifically named individuals. Gaius, the brethren and Demetrius were approved by John and they were opposed by the deceivers, Diotrephes and his followers. As with the earlier letter (2 John), John indicated that he did not want to issue a written copy of everything that needed to be dealt with. Instead, John indicated that he would come to Gaius' church to deal with the issue personally (3 Jn 13-14). Aside from Diotrephes, John's hope was that many of Diotrephes' followers would repent and return to Gaius's leadership. If these errant followers of Diotrephes were mentioned by name, it might complicate John's efforts to repatriate them to the church. John could be discreet by not mentioning names and those who turned back would not have the stigma associated with apostasy.

Fig. 89 Alinda Watchtower

Alinda, an ancient Carian city, was an important commercial city located only 50 kilometers from Ephesus. The city was visited by Alexander the Great and continued to be an influential city throughout the Roman imperial period. Was there a church in Alinda during the first century?

Chapter 5

Asia Minor in Turmoil – Revelation and the Letters to the Seven Churches

The identity of the author of the apocalypse (the book of Revelation) is no less debated than the author of the fourth gospel and the letters of John. The earliest Christian sources concur that the author was John the apostle, but many scholars believe this book was written by a different person named John. The vocabulary and syntax of the book of Revelation is so different than what can be found in the gospel and epistles that many scholars do not believe that the same person authored all of them. Thus, three different persons named John have been proposed as authors of these books: John the Apostle, John the Elder and another John who authored the apocalypse. Some scholars believe that the apostle wrote all of these works, but many others believe that these books were authored by any combination of the three Johns.

The earliest Christian sources (Justin Martyr, Irenaeus, Clement of Alexandria, Origin, Tertullian and Hippolytus) indicate that the apocalypse was written during the latter years of Domitian's reign. Domitian ruled the Roman Empire from A.D. 81-96, so Revelation should be dated somewhere in the middle 90s. Roman historians, such as Tacitus, Pliny the Younger, Dio Chrysostom, Suetonius, and Dio Cassius provide us with ample testimony that Domitian's rule was marked by evil, corrupt, tyrannical and despotic actions. The emperor demanded that others address him as "our Lord and our God" and his autocratic rule incurred the animosity of both the general public and the senate.

Fig. 90 Ephesus Domitian Temple

The two story façade of Domitian's temple was capped with male and female figures representing the conquered barbarian tribes. After Domitian's murder and the senate's decree of damnatio memoriae the temple was dedicated to Vespasian, Domitian's father. Domitian's name was also removed from a number of inscriptions and replaced with Vespasian.

During Domitian's reign a new imperial temple was built in Ephesus for the worship of the emperor and pressures were exerted upon all citizens to participate in the imperial festivals and to pay homage to Domitian as a living god (fig. 90). Emperor worship had been the practice of the imperial family since Caesar Augustus, but deification had been conferred upon the emperors after their death. Prior to the time of Domitian, worship at the imperial temples was not demanded of all citizens. Things changed with Domitian. Domitian was not content with a posthumous deification and he demanded to be recognized as a living god. Domitian was feared and hated and in the years following Domitian's death, the Senate decreed "damnatio memoriae." The decree ordered that Domitian's image and name be removed from all inscriptions, monuments and statues. The decree was a condemnation of Domitian's memory.

The emperor was the preeminent patron and benefactor in the empire and the patron with the deepest pockets. A portion of the taxation that was collected from the provinces was redistributed to the cities and provinces that showered the emperor with adulation. These funds could be used for the construction of aqueducts, public baths, fountains, temples, roads, libraries, stadiums, theaters, or other public buildings to improve the quality of life in the cities and provinces. Additionally, a great deal of civic pride was associated with the honor of imperial benefactions. Participation in the imperial temples and at the imperial festivals was the primary way of demonstrating loyalty and devotion to the emperor. Communities across the Mediterranean world were vying for the emperor's patronage and the competition necessitated the participation of everyone in the empire. If large segments of the population refused to participate, the fortunes of the cities might suffer. With large Christian communities in the cities of western Asia Minor who refused to acknowledge the divinity of the emperor and who refused to participate in the imperial festivals, concerned citizens and leaders of these cities exerted pressure upon the Christians in these regions. In many instances, the Christians were harassed, intimidated and persecuted by others in the community. Most of this opposition was generated locally, by the residents and civic officials of the cities and provinces, rather than by imperial orders.

The harassment and persecution took on various forms. The Christians experienced verbal abuse involving mocking, derision and slander, physical mistreatment, ranging from simple assaults to whippings and even death, and economic harassment involving the seizure of property, the boycotting of Christian shops and businesses and the refusal to sell food and goods to members of the church. Martyrdoms figure prominently in Revelation, such as in Rev 6:9-11 where the martyrs were found under the altar crying out for vengeance. Likewise instances of economic abuse can be found throughout the book. Most explicitly, Revelation reports that those who refused the mark of the beast (Rev 13:16-17) could neither buy nor sell. Also, the economic hardships mentioned in

Fig. 91 Patmos Acropolis Ruins

Hellenistic and Roman ruins remain at the top of the hill adjacent to the Monastery. Revelation 1 notes that John was banished to Patmos at the time when the apocalypse was revealed to him.

Rev 6:5-6 and 18:11-17 probably reflect the pressures to succumb to imperial veneration. These problems were most poignantly reflected in the letters that John wrote to the seven churches of Asia Minor during the reign of Domitian.

John was banished to the island of Patmos, a small volcanic island off the western coast of Asia Minor, "because of the testimony of Jesus" (1:9) (fig. 91). John described himself as a "fellow participant in the tribulation" and at Patmos he was visited by the Lord where he received the visions of the apocalypse. John was told to write letters to seven churches at Ephesus, Smyrna, Pergamon, Thyatira, Sardis, Philadelphia and Laodicea.

Although the book of Revelation has commonly been interpreted futuristically, John was explicitly told to "write the things which you have seen, and the things which are, and the things which will take place after these things" (1:19). Thus, a study of the book of Revelation must come to grips with the past developments in Asia Minor. John was told to respond to the distressing, hopeless and unbearable circumstances that had befallen the Christian communities at the end of the first century. In the rush to speculate on the future, this aspect of the apocalypse has been largely ignored by interpreters of the book. However, an understanding of the last decades of the first century in Asia Minor is vital to understanding the book of Revelation.

Revelation: The Letter to Ephesus (Rev 2:1-7)

The continued struggle with false teachers in Ephesus is evident in the first letter of Revelation (2:1-7). Here however, compared with John's letters which were written a few years earlier, it seems that the Ephesian church was making some progress in combating the false teachers and kicking them out of the congregation. The church was commended for not tolerating "evil men" (2:2). They had "tested" people who called themselves apostles and had found them to be "false" (2:2). The wording here is similar to the cautions that John issued in 1 Jn 4:1-3: "test the spirits to see whether they are from God, because many false prophets have gone out into the world." An early Christian writing known as the Didache, probably written in the first century, refers to traveling itinerate prophets and instructs Christians to "test" these speakers to see whether they are true or false (12:1). In Revelation, Ephesians' struggle to uproot these teachers was apparent in the words that John used to describe this conflict with the heretics: "work," "toil" and "perseverance" (used twice). Yet as John stated, "you have not grown weary" (2:3).

The Ephesians were also commended because they detested "the deeds of the Nicolaitans" (2:6). The Nicolaitans are distinct from the evil men and false apostles mentioned in 2:2. These Nicolaitans were mentioned again in the letter to the church at Pergamon (2:15), but otherwise they are not cited in the New Testament. Irenaeus, a late second century church father, described the Nicolaitans as early Gnostics. They were also mentioned by Clement of Alexandria, Hippolytus, Epiphanius and Eusebius who assert that they came from Nicolas of Antioch (Acts 6:5). Some of the church fathers attributed these doctrines to the aberrant teachings that Nicolas adopted later in life. However, Clement of Alexandria asserted that the followers of Nicolas distorted his teachings. The text in 2:15 seems to equate the teachings of the Nicolaitans with the teachings of Balaam (Num 22-24). In spite of the fact that Numbers never associates Balaam with the libertine practices of eating food sacrificed to idols and sexual immorality, Rev 2:14 suggests that these practices were supported by the Nicolaitans.

Although the church at Ephesus was successfully warding off the false teachers, not all was well at Ephesus. John issued a stern warning against those who "had left their first love" (2:4). The meaning of expression is not entirely clear. The verb here can be interpreted to mean "you have divorced your first love." As we have mentioned previously, the church is often portrayed as the bride of Christ (see 2 Jn 1 above) and the meaning "divorce" would suggest that members of the Ephesian church had apostasized to such an extent that they no longer had a relationship with Christ. On the other hand, John's earlier commendations of the Ephesians seem to indicate that they had

Fig. 92 Ephesus Celsus Library

The Celsus Library and the southern agora gate (Mazaeus and Mithridates Gate)

largely overcome the false teachers (2:2-3, 6). Another way to interpret this statement is to read the statement as "you have neglected your first love." This would suggest that the passion and zeal with which the members had previously served the Lord had waned. There are problems with this interpretation as well, since (v. 3) stated that the church had persevered and had not grown weary.

Ephesus was the largest city in Asia Minor and there were several churches in the city. These churches probably responded to the false teaching and persecutions in various ways. We cannot assume that all Christians in Ephesus were united in their response to the problems. John's choice of words here presumably reflected various aspects of life in different churches at Ephesus. Most of them responded well to the problems. They tested the false teachers and rejected their doctrines. Likewise, they spurned the Nicolaitans. However, there were others who seemed to have pandered these teachers or have simply grown apathetic and thus they compromised their faith. In a big city with a large Christian population we cannot assume that the entire Christian population was handling the harassment and persecution well. Thus, John cautioned those who had left their first love.

The construction of Domitian's temple at Ephesus was a significant honor bestowed upon the city and it came with additional benefits for the residents of the city. Perhaps some Christians in the community, looking at the bigger picture and the benefactions, offered token support for the imperial cult. The perspective advanced by the author of the apocalypse was an intolerant, no concession approach toward the imperial cult. Some Christians at Ephesus appeared to have adopted a less harsh attitude and may have cooperated with the cult. For John these people had left their first love. One could not be married to both God and Domitian.

Revelation: The Letter to Smyrna (Rev 2:8-11)

From what we gather in Revelation's letter to the church at Smyrna, the situation for Christians in the large port city was more bleak. The letter began with the words "I know your tribulation and your poverty, but you are rich" (2:9). As in most of these cities in Asia Minor severe persecutions were levied against Christians who refused to participate in the imperial cult and the pagan festivals. No doubt, the intensity and manner of persecution varied from city to city, but from what we understand of these seven letters that were written to the largest cities of western Asia Minor, the persecution was powerful enough to cause many within these Christian communities to buckle under the pressure. When John wrote these letters, he generally offered support and encouragement to the church along with negative criticism for the ways that some people within the congregation had compromised their faith.

In the case of the letter to Smyrna, John's letter offered encouragement, but no negative criticism. Although Smyrna was smaller than Ephesus, it was still a large city. Thus, we can assume that there were several Christian congregations throughout the city, just as there were in Ephesus. The lack of negative criticism to the church however, suggests that these congregations were more united in their opposition to false teachers and the imperial cult than the churches in Ephesus. The church at Smyrna as a whole remained faithful in the face of these troubles. This letter is one of only two letters in Revelation that does not offer negative criticism. Instead, the church was encouraged to persist in the faith even if it should lead to death. Those who persevered were told they would be given the crown of life (2:10) and were assured that they would not experience the second death (2:11).

John's epistles referred to a docetic teaching that was circulating throughout Asia Minor at this time. Docetic teachers insisted that Jesus was not a fleshly human, but that he only "appeared" to have a body. Ignatius' letter to the church at Smyrna strongly condemned this teaching while contending that Jesus was in fact "in the flesh." The fact that Ignatius' short letter dwelt upon this issue so much tells us that this heresy was a significant threat near the end of the first century and continued to be a problem at the beginning of the second century. Revelation's letter to the church at Smyrna, however, does not suggest that docetism had made any inroads into the church at Smyrna. The church was commended without reservations.

The statement "I know your tribulation and your poverty, but you are rich" is a perceptive declaration. As mentioned above, much of the persecution against the Christian community was economic pressure and harassment. Since the reference to persecution was bundled together with poverty in 2:9, it is probable that the poverty of the Christians in Smyrna was brought about by the detrimental economic measures imposed upon the Christians. Christians may have lost their jobs, or their businesses may have been boycotted. If Rev 13:16-17 pertains to the seven churches (as it seems likely) the Christian community was not allowed to buy or sell, simply because they did not take the "mark of the beast" (that is, worship Domitian). John's words of encouragement "but you are rich" may contain the faint echo of Jesus' words not to store up treasure on earth, but rather to store treasures in heaven (Mt 6:19-20). The Smyrnan church was divested of wealth on earth, but was rich in righteousness.

Some of John's sharpest rhetoric was reserved for the Jewish community in Smyrna. From the beginning of the imperial period, the Jews had been exempted from emperor worship and thus they were not subject to the daily harassment experienced by the Christians in the city. Earlier in the first century the Christians were included in this exemption since Christianity was looked upon as a sect within Judaism. Jesus was Jewish along with all of his early followers. However as time progressed, more non-Jewish Gentiles joined the faith, particularly outside of Palestine. As we enter into the latter years of the first century, the split between the synagogue and the church became concrete. At that time, the exemption from emperor worship was slowly taken away from Christians and Christians were obliged to participate in the imperial cult like everyone else. Ancestrally, most of the Christians in Asia Minor were non-Jewish. Thus, the expectations for them were the same as for other people in the empire.

The harsh criticism of the Jews in Smyrna was unusual. The description of the Jewish community as a "synagogue of Satan" indicates that the synagogue was instrumental in the opposition to the Christian community. It is not possible to precisely identify the "blasphemy" of the Jews in 2:9, since blasphemy can be variously construed. Blasphemy can refer to words or actions that were deemed contrary to the cause of Christ, but here it appears to refer to verbal abuse of the Christians in Smyrna. The blasphemy could simply refer to the Jewish community's rejection of the gospel or its denunciation of the church in Smyrna. However, other Jewish communities that also rejected Christianity were not described in these terms. Thus, these harsh words probably refer to words or actions beyond the simple rejection of Christian claims. John's remark "those who say they are Jews and are not" implies that the synagogue at Smyrna had forfeited its claim to be the covenant people of God. John, himself a Jew, insinuated that those who supported the cause of Christ were the true covenant community. That community consisted of Jews and Gentiles alike.

Remarkably, John spoke in the future tense of an impending tribulation lasting for ten days. The ten days may be figurative and simply mean a short period of time. This tribulation was described by John as a "test" – the same term used in 2:2. In 2:2 the test was to determine the authenticity of false apostles, while in this case (2:10) the test was for Christians in Smyrna to prove their faith in Christ. In the same sentence with the "test," it was revealed that some Christians would be imprisoned. Prisons in the first century were not used for punitive purposes and were not designed to hold prisoners for long periods of time. Instead, prisons were used to temporarily restrain defendants accused of serious crimes until their trials and they were used to hold the condemned until their execution. Since the next sentence encouraged the people of Smyrna to "be faithful until death," we can safely assume that the Christians at Smyrna were facing condemnation and death.

The Ancient History and Archaeology of Smyrna (Izmir)

The Ancient History of Smyrna

The earliest settlement at Smyrna was located at Bayrakli, a suburb of modern Izmir located about four kilometers northeast of the city center. The earliest occupation of that site dates back to the third millennium B.C. At that time the settlement was on a small peninsula and the bay extended inland as far as Bornova. Strabo, citing earlier traditions, asserted that the site was founded by the Amazons. However, when Aeolian colonists arrived they found the Lelegian people occupying the site. Pottery indicates that the Aeolians migrated from Greece to Smyrna in the tenth century B.C. and Smyrna was numbered among the cities of the Aeolian League. Aelius Aristides, a long time resident of Smyrna, claimed that Homer was born in Smyrna and that a heroon (honorific tomb) to Homer existed in the city. Herodotus recounted that in the last half of the eighth century B.C. Smyrna welcomed Ionian refugees from Colophon, who repaid their hospitality by expelling the Aeolians from the city. Thereafter, Smyrna became part of the Ionian League. In 600 B.C. Smyrna was sacked and destroyed by King Alyattes of Lydia. The city was rebuilt, but the site at Bayrakli never fully recovered its former glory. In 546 B.C. Smyrna came under the dominion of the Persians and Smyrna dwindled in size and influence for the next two centuries.

According to Pausanias, Smyrna was regenerated by Alexander the Great who purportedly received a message from the Nemeses (goddesses of vengeance) indicating that he should build a new city on Mt. Pagus and move the old inhabitants from Bayrakli to the new site. The

Fig. 93 Smyrna Aqueducts
Two Roman aqueducts crossing the Meles River in southeast Smyrna.

Fig. 94 Smyrna Theater
The recently exposed Roman theater in ancient Smyrna may have held 16,000 spectators. Few seats remain, but the stage (pictured) remains intact.

Fig. 95 Smyrna Agora

The agora at Smyrna was very large. Recent excavations on the western perimeter of the agora have revealed the bouleuterion (where the town council met) and a large basilica, the use of which is not yet known.

Fig. 96 Smyrna Agora Cryptoporticus

Underneath the agora, the vaulted substructures created a cryptoporticus for storage and shops. Some of these shops were open on the north where the surface level declined.

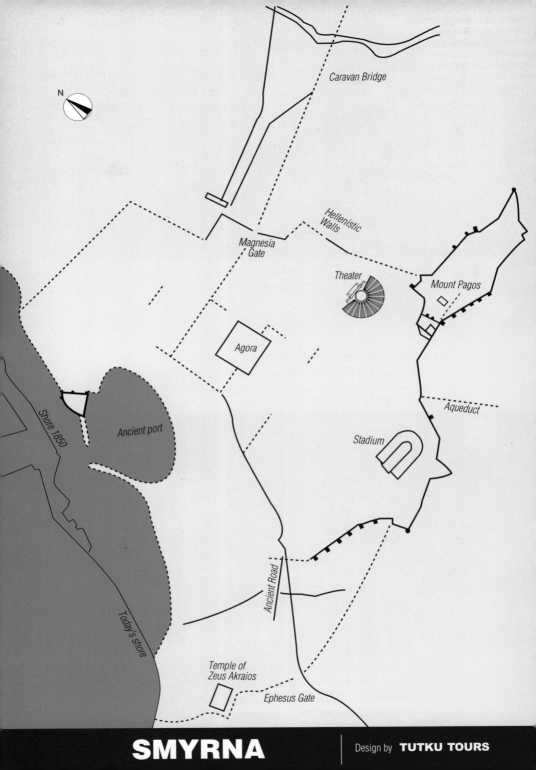

N

Caravan Bridge

Hellenistic Walls

Magnesia Gate

Theater

Mount Pagos

Agora

Aqueduct

Shore 1850

Ancient port

Stadium

Today's shore

Ancient Road

Temple of Zeus Akraios

Ephesus Gate

SMYRNA

Design by **TUTKU TOURS**

Fig. 97 Smyrna Agora Graffiti

An earthquake in 178 A.D. flattened the city and buried the agora shops until recent excavations have begun the process of digging them out. Vast amounts of graffiti covered the walls of these shops. Scholars believe some of the graffiti may be the earliest examples of Christian graffiti.

new city was built around 300 B.C. and in 288 B.C., the city was welcomed into the Panionic League. Like many of the other Aegean cities of Asia Minor, Smyrna fell to the Pergamene Kingdom and then was given to the Romans, whereupon it was incorporated into the Roman province of Asia Minor in 129 B.C. Under the Romans, Smyrna grew and prospered. The city may have had as many as 200,000 people during the first century A.D. The city was thrice named neokoros (guardian of the imperial temple). This great honor was given to the preeminent cities of the Roman provinces. Smyrna received this privilege once under Tiberius, again under Hadrian and finally again during the reign of Caracalla. Smyrna possessed a temple dedicated to Asclepius the chief healing god and the city was known for its work in science and medicine. In A.D. 178 a devastating earthquake destroyed most of the city, but Smyrna was rebuilt within three years with the assistance of the emperor Marcus Aurelius.

Christian Beginnings at Smyrna

The only reference to Smyrna in the Bible occurs in the book of Revelation (2:8-11) where one of the seven epistles is addressed to a church there. The origin of the church is unknown, but one might speculate that the church began with extensions from the work that Paul began in Ephesus, about 65 kilometers to the south. Paul spent more than two years at Ephesus during his third mission and he and his associates moved around Asia Minor during that time. The apocryphal *Acts of Paul* 8 suggests that Paul visited Smyrna before coming to Ephesus.

151

Fig. 98 Smyrna Agora Graffiti

This wall exhibits a gladiator and proclaimed Smyrna as the "Foremost city of Asia." Someone later added the small letters "Ephesus" between the larger letters. Both Ephesus and Smyrna vied for the honor of preeminence in Asia.

However, the letter of *Polycarp to the Philippians* (11:3) implies that the church was founded some time after Paul's ministry. *The Acts of John* 37, 45 & 55 tells of a visit by the apostle John and his disciples, but the date is uncertain. John's Apocalypse referred to tribulation that the church was experiencing and coupled this with a reference to their poverty and the blasphemy of the Jews in the city. The cause of the church's poverty was not identified, but the context of the passage leads scholars to believe that the Christians were being discriminated as a consequence of their faith. The reference to the Jews contained a disclaimer. Although they claimed to be Jews, John stated that they constituted a synagogue of Satan. This vitriolic statement was followed by a prognostication that some of the Smyrnean believers would be cast into prison by the Devil. This seems to indicate that Jews were thought to be using the legal system to harass the Christian community.

Early in the second century Ignatius stopped in Smyrna and met with church leaders during his journey to martyrdom in Rome (A.D. 107). While there, Ignatius wrote four letters to churches encouraging them to maintain the faith. Later on the journey Ignatius sent another letter to Polycarp, the bishop of Smyrna. Polycarp was a disciple of John the apostle and served the church at Smyrna for fifty years. In A.D. 156 Polycarp himself was martyred in the city's stadium as he was burned at the stake. During the reign of Decius in A.D. 250 Pionius was likewise martyred after the emperor decreed the execution of Christians who refused to offer sacrifice.

The Current Remains at Smyrna

A rather large excavation exists at Bayrakli with mud brick city walls that date back to the ninth century B.C. These walls were largely destroyed by King Alyattes in 600 B.C. A stone wall from the mid-seventh century reinforced this wall. The stone wall was significantly damaged by Alyattes, but was refurbished at the beginning of the sixth century B.C. and is still intact for a length of 180 meters on the east side and 75 meters on the south. A temple to Athena was constructed as early as 725 B.C. This too was destroyed by Alyattes, but was reconstructed in the sixth century, only to be destroyed again by the Persians. Houses from the site date from the ninth to the seventh centuries B.C. Another unknown temple and two megarons (meeting houses) from the seventh and sixth centuries B.C. have been uncovered in recent excavations.

On Mt. Pagus an excellent citadel exists. This dates to the medieval period, but rests upon Hellenistic foundations. Inside the fortress, there are the barrel arches of a massive underground cistern that dates to the Roman period. These cisterns were fed by an aqueduct. The best surviving sections of the aqueduct (and some of the best in Turkey) are east of the city center in Buca where the aqueducts retain their full height with huge arches two and three tiers on top of one another (fig. 93). Down the eastern slope of Mt. Pagus there are few remains of a theater and the stadium where Polycarp was martyred.

Several buildings on the slope have been demolished and portions of the theater and the stage have now been exposed (fig. 94).

Further toward the coast, the state agora is Izmir's most interesting ruin. The agora was part of Marcus Aurelius' rebuilding project after the A.D. 178 earthquake. The excavated portion of the agora currently measures 120 meters by 80 meters (fig. 95). The western and eastern sides had colonnaded porticoes 17.5 meters in width with two rows of columns dividing the porticoes into three sections. These porticoes were two storied. On the north there was a two storied basilica 28 meters in width with a nave and two aisles running the 120 me-

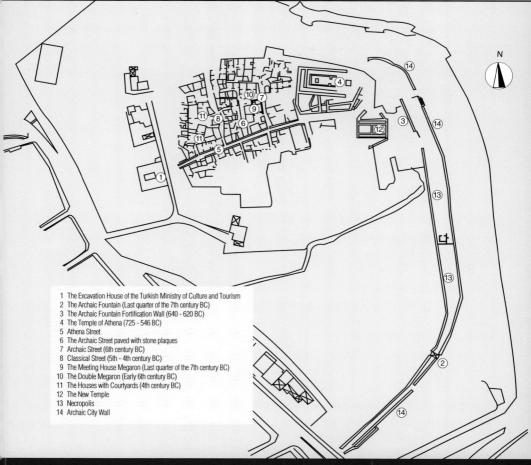

1 The Excavation House of the Turkish Ministry of Culture and Tourism
2 The Archaic Fountain (Last quarter of the 7th century BC)
3 The Archaic Fountain Fortification Wall (640 - 620 BC)
4 The Temple of Athena (725 - 546 BC)
5 Athena Street
6 The Archaic Street paved with stone plaques
7 Archaic Street (6th century BC)
8 Classical Street (5th - 4th century BC)
9 The Meeting House Megaron (Last quarter of the 7th century BC)
10 The Double Megaron (Early 6th century BC)
11 The Houses with Courtyards (4th century BC)
12 The New Temple
13 Necropolis
14 Archaic City Wall

OLD SMYRNA (BAYRAKLI)   Design by TUTKU TOURS

ter length. Underneath this basilica ran a cryptoporticus which may have opened to the street on the northern side (fig. 96). Sections of the cryptoporticus have a large amount of ancient graffiti written on the plaster. Of most interest are several graffiti that have recently been identified as the earliest Christian graffiti ever discovered (fig. 97). Dating to the late first century or early second century are the Greek words: *logos onoma* (the logos is a name), *kurios* (Lord), *pistis* (faith) and *ho dedokos to pneuma* (the one who has given the spirit). Another interesting graffiti proclaimed Smyrna "The foremost city of Asia." Within the letters, a later writer in small letters wrote "Ephesus" (fig. 98). The cities of Ephesus and Smyrna engaged in a rigorous rivalry for highest honors in Asia Minor. The later graffitist cleverly changed the original piece, so as to transfer the honor to Ephesus. Recently the graffiti has been covered while authorities decide how to best preserve the writings. The northwest corner of the agora contained an exedra (a semicircular recess) where legal proceedings were undertaken. In the same area a fountain still churns out water from an underground spring. A cryptoporticus also existed under the western side of the agora. Izmir has two excellent archaeological museums where finds from ancient Smyrna and the surrounding region are displayed (fig. 99).

Revelation: The Letter to Pergamon (Rev 2:12-17)

The letter to the church at Pergamon began with a reference to Pergamon as "Satan's throne" and the place "where Satan dwells" (Rev 2:13). Of the seven churches mentioned in Revelation, the opposition against the church was the most intense at Pergamon. Persecution in the city resulted in the martyrdom of Antipas, who was described as "My witness" and "My faithful one." The term "witness" (in Greek, μάρτυς) was a word that later came to be used for Christians who were dragged into the courts and accused of treason (failure to participate in the imperial cult). Those who maintained their faith and refused to worship the images of the emperors were executed. The Greek term μάρτυς (witness) came to be a technical term to refer to martyrs – those who kept their testimony and died for it. The fact that the Christians of Pergamon were being dragged into the courts is also suggested by the phrase "you hold fast my name and did not deny my faith." It was asserted that Antipas "was killed before you," implying that Antipas had a public trial during which he upheld his faith in Christ and that he was publicly executed in front of other Christians. Perhaps Antipas was singled out as an example in order to deter others from following his example of defiance.

It has been popular to point to the altar of Zeus found on the acropolis at Pergamon as "Satan's throne" and there is some merit to this suggestion. The huge "U" shaped altar was prominently displayed at the top of the acropolis in broad view of those in the city. Also, it is logical that John would portray Zeus as Satan.

However, Satan's throne more likely referred to the Asklepion (fig. 101). The Asklepion was a healing facility (an ancient hospital of sorts) that was dedicated to the god Asklepius, the son of Apollo. Asklepius was the chief healing god in the Greco-Roman world and the cult site at Pergamon was the largest and most famous in all of Anatolia. Asklepius was always represented with a staff and a snake wound around it. This symbol (staff and snake) is used today by the American Medical Association as its emblem. Snakes were also brought into the facility and were placed in the beds of

Fig. 100 Pergamon Temple of Trajan

Dominating the acropolis at Pergamon is the temple of Trajan, the Roman emperor from A.D. 98 to 117. Trajan ruled shortly after Domitian who ruled from A.D. 81 to 96, the time when Revelation was written. Domitian was the first living emperor to demand the honor of emperor worship. These demands and Christian refusals to acknowledge them brought about the crisis in the churches of Asia Minor mentioned in Revelation chapters 1-3.

Fig. 101 Pergamon Altar of Asclepius

The Sacred Way led to the monumental entrance of the Asclepion (known as the propylon). An inscription over the propylon read: "Death may not enter here." Inside, a round marble altar to Asclepius was decorated with reliefs of serpents drinking from a libation dish (patera). Sculpture of Asclepius has the god holding a staff with a serpent wound around it.

Fig. 102 Pergamon Asclepion Patient Quarters

The sanctuary of Asclepius (known as the Asclepion) was a healing center where patients came to be healed of various infirmities. Patients brought gifts to the god and slept on the grounds while under the care of the priests and physicians. The famous physician Galen (A.D. 129-217) was born and educated in Pergamon and worked at this Asclepion. The grounds were infested with snakes which were thought to be guardians of health and welfare. The god Asclepius was almost always depicted with a snake.

patients, believing that the presence of the snakes would bring about healing (fig. 102). Pergamon was exceedingly proud of this facility and the snake became the symbol of the city. Almost all coins minted at Pergamon had snakes represented on them.

However in both Jewish and Christian minds, the snake was associated with Satan. As the chief center for the worship of Asklepius and the abundant presence of snakes in the city, it would not be surprising for John to refer to Pergamon as Satan's throne. Additionally, the temple at the site was dedicated to Asklepios Soter (Asklepius Savior). The term savior was a title that the Christians applied to Jesus, not to Asklepius. Numerous inscriptions have been found at the Asklepion that were dedicated to "Asklepius the Savior" thanking him for healing (fig. 103). Jesus' healing ministry (amply attested in the gospels) can be understood as a challenge to the prevalent belief in the healing powers of Asklepius and the other healing cults. The question was: who really is the "savior"?

Although the Pergamon church had been through the trauma of Antipas' execution and they were probably still enduring persecution at the time this letter was sent, John recorded some misgivings: "I have a few things against you" (2:14). Some within the church had compromised their faith, crossed the line and were tacitly (or perhaps more explicitly) supporting the imperial cult. They were accused of following the teachings of Balaam (an infamous prophet) and had consumed things sacrificed to idols and had committed acts of immorality. "Balaam" was a substitute term for the false teachers at Pergamon. These charges could refer to Christians who lent support to the imperial cult by attending the festivals and by purchasing and consuming meat that previously had been sacrificed to the emperor. More seriously, these charges could refer to Christians who participated in the sacred meals at the temple for the imperial cult. In either case, these Christians were singled out as apostates who needed to repent.

The Nicolaitans, mentioned earlier in the letter to the church at Ephesus (Rev 2:6) were brought up again in Rev 2:15. It is not clear if the people who followed the Nicolaitans were connected to those who followed the teachings of "Balaam"(2:14), or if they were an entirely separate group. Irenaeus identified the Nicolaitans as Gnostics and as we have mentioned previously, early Gnostic ideas were clearly circulating in Asia Minor at this time and earlier. Whereas the Ephesians were commended for repulsing the Nicolaitans, the Christians at Pergamon were reprimanded because some of them were attracted to the Nicolaitan teachings.

The word "you" is emphatic in the text: "Thus, you even have some who hold the teaching of the Nicolaitans." John was astonished that the community was so divided. It seems that there was a dichotomy within the church at Pergamon. Some were

Fig. 103 Pergamon Asclepion Inscription

Numerous honorific and dedicatory inscriptions still litter the grounds of the Asclepion. These inscriptions commonly refer to the god as "the Savior Asclepius" (ΤΟΥ ΣΩΤΗΡΟΣ ΑΣΚΛΗΠΙΟΥ in line 7). Some scholars believe that the presence of the Asclepion at Pergamon is what is referred to in Revelation 2:13. Satan was commonly depicted as a serpent in Jewish and Christian art and literature. Moreover, the numerous references to Asclepius as "Savior" and as a healer were challenges to similar roles attributed to Christ.

staunchly upholding the faith and refusing to accommodate the imperial cult in any way, while others were succumbing to the pressures and were offering support for the emperor.

The Ancient History and Archaeology of Pergamon (Bergama)

The Ancient History of Pergamon

The origins of Pergamon are enshrouded in myth. The founder of the city, Telephus, was the grandson of the Peloponnesian King Aleus of Tegea. Upon visiting the Delphic Oracle Aleus was told that his daughter's son would harm his family. Telephus, the son of Hercules and Aleus' daughter, slew Aleus' sons as prophesied and then traveled to Asia Minor where he became King of Mysia and founded the city of Pergamon. This story is the underlying tradition for the migration of people to Pergamon. Thus, the earliest rulers of Pergamon, the Attalids, claimed descent from Telephus, Hercules and Zeus. The earliest settlements on the acropolis at Pergamon date to the eighth century B.C.

The earliest reference to Pergamon comes from Xeno-phon who indicates that Greek soldiers passed through Pergamon in 399 B.C. At that time Pergamon was controlled by the Persians. However, in 334 B.C. Alexander the Great defeated the Persians and Pergamon was free. Following Alexander's death, the Pergamon rulers (the Attalids) were able to maintain their independence by strategically forming alliances with the kingdoms that were jockeying for power in the region. Alliances with the Macedonians, Seleucids, Ptolemies and Romans allowed Pergamon to grow in power and influence. When the Romans, assisted by the Attalid King Eumenes II, finally defeated the Seleucids at the battle of Magnesia ad Sipylum in 189 B.C., the Romans ceded all of Asia Minor up to the Taurus Mountains to the Pergamene Kingdom. The city of Pergamon went through fifty years of great

Fig. 104 Pergamon Roman Bridge

There are four Roman bridges visible today crossing the ancient Selinus River in Pergamon. Most of them are still used, a tribute to Roman bridge construction. The Roman arch could support incredibly heavy loads and was used not only for bridges, but also for the construction of theaters, stadiums and numerous other structures. One of Pergamon's bridges is 643 feet wide and functions as the substructure supporting the Red Basilica above. This was the widest bridge in the Roman world. The bridge pictured here is located a short distance south of the larger bridge and is used today for foot traffic.

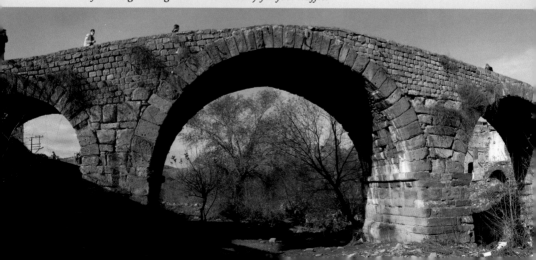

Fig. 105 Pergamon Amphitheater

Amphitheaters, such as this one in Pergamon, are rare in the eastern Roman empire, though they are more common in the western Mediterranean. In A.D. 157 the renowned Galen was appointed as physician to the gladiators and significantly reduced the rate of death among the competitors in the Pergamon arena. Amphitheaters were used primarily for the "spectacles," shows which included such entertainments as animal hunts (venationes), gladiator contests and public executions, where the condemned were tortured, burned, torn apart by beasts (damnatio ad bestias), dragged, crucified or killed in theatrical productions (fatal charades). It is not known how Antipas was killed (Rev. 2:13), nor whether he was executed in the amphitheater, but it is clear that he was martyred for his faith in Christ. The Greek word used to describe Antipas as "my witness" is the same word that was later used to describe martyrs. Later in the second century, three Christians, Papylus, Carpus and Agathonike, met their deaths as martyrs in this arena.

prosperity and most of the temples and important public buildings were constructed at this time. Attalos III had little interest in maintaining the dynasty and kingdom and upon his death in 133 B.C. the Pergamene Kingdom was bequeathed to Rome.

In 129 B.C. Rome established the new province of Asia Minor in the western portions of the former Pergamene Kingdom. Pergamon probably functioned as the capital of the province for a few years until Ephesus assumed that position. In 88 B.C. Pergamon joined together with

160

Fig. 106 Pergamon Temple of Trajan

The temple of Trajan was begun during the latter years of Trajan and was completed under Hadrian. It was used as an imperial temple honoring both Trajan (A.D. 98-117) and Hadrian (A.D. 117-138), his successor. Trajan continued the policies of mistreatment for the Christians in Asia Minor that were instituted by his predecessor Domitian. In an exchange of letters between Pliny the Younger, the governor of nearby Bithynia, and Trajan, both writers acknowledge that the trials Christians who had committed no offenses were commonplace. Executions for those who persisted in confessing Christ were normal and such practices received Trajan's support.

Mithridates VI, King of Pontus along with several other cities in a revolt against the Romans. When the revolt was put down, the Romans punished Pergamon. Fifty years later, Pergamon regained its stature. In 29 B.C. Augustus granted Pergamon the right to build an imperial temple, an honor that was highly sought among ancient cities. During this time the population of Pergamon was probably 150,000 – 200,000 people. New building activity was initiated during the reigns of Trajan and Hadrian in the early second century A.D. when another imperial temple was constructed. Then, with the dedication of a temple to Caracalla in the early third century, the city was named Neokoros (guardian of the imperial temple) for the third time.

Christian Beginnings at Pergamon

Pergamon is another one of the seven churches of Revelation whose origins are a mystery. It is possible that Paul could have visited the city during the course of his second or third missions since Pergamon was along the route that he travelled. It is known from Cicero that a large Jewish population existed in Pergamon and it is also known that Paul frequented synagogues in large cities during his travels. The Apocalypse (Rev 2:12-17) indicates that at the end of the first century the city had a vibrant and diverse congregation. The church was commended because they did not deny their faith in the face of persecutions. An individual, Antipas, was cited as a martyr who was slain during these troubles. On the other hand, the church at Pergamon was rebuked because there

161

Fig. 107 Pergamon Acropolis Theater

The acropolis theater at Pergamon could seat as many of 10,000 people. Due to the slope of the acropolis hill upon which it was built, this is the steepest theater in Asia Minor and provided attendees with an amazing view of the lower city. The theater was built in the third century B.C. and was later modified by the Romans. The stage and background (known as the skene) were constructed of wood and was removable. The fittings for the wooden posts are still visible.

were some within the congregation who were holding to the teachings of Balaam and others who were following the teachings of the Nicolaitans. The former group may have compromised their faith by participating in imperial festivals and emperor worship. The Nicolaitans may have been a primitive Christian-Gnostic group.

Galen, the most famous ancient physician was born in Pergamon in A.D. 129. He was trained at the sanctuary of Asklepius in Pergamon and traveled to medical schools throughout the Mediterranean world. After returning to Pergamon, Galen became the physician of the gladiators who were injured in the amphitheater at Pergamon. He learned a great deal of anatomy, physiology and medicine by operating upon the wounded gladiators and examining the remains of those who died in the spectacles. The amphitheater was used for not only the gladiator contests, but also for public executions. Galen mentioned the Christians in his writings and no doubt some of his exposure to the Christians came from those who had been thrown to the beasts or slaughtered by gladiators in the amphitheater. The third century church historian Eusebius reported the martyrdoms of Carpus, Papylus and Agathonike in Pergamon during the reign of Marcus Aurelius around A.D. 170.

Fig. 108 Pergamon Dionysus Temple

The patron deity of theatrical productions was Dionysus. Many theaters throughout the ancient Greek world had sanctuaries or altars of Dionysus nearby or even within the theater (such as at Priene, to the south). This temple to Dionysus was located on the periphery of the theater. The temple contained an entry of twenty five steps and was first erected in the second century B.C. This was later rebuilt during the reign of Caracalla in the third century A.D.

The Current Remains at Pergamon

Pergamon has some of the best ancient remains in Turkey. Most of the remains are located at two sites: on the acropolis and about a kilometer away at the Asklepion. The bulk of the Roman city sat between the acropolis and the Asklepion, straddling the ancient Selinus river. Three ancient Roman bridges still span the river. They are all in excellent shape and are used by the residents of Bergama, the modern city. Elsewhere in the city one can see the Red Basilica (originally a second century A.D. temple to Serapis and later converted to a fifth century Christian basilica), and three more poorly preserved Roman struc-

tures: a theater, a stadium and an amphitheater. The remains of the amphitheater are impressive and important. There are only three known amphitheaters in all of Anatolia. Such structures were rare in the eastern empire. The excellent Bergama Museum also lies between the acropolis and the Asklepion (figs. 104 and 105).

The acropolis is loaded with ancient structures that have been well excavated and are in good shape. There are three tiers of the Acropolis. The ruins on the upper acropolis mostly date from the Hellenistic period. At the south

Fig. 109 Pergamon Roman Road

A second century B.C. road snakes it's way up to the acropolis from the lower city. Roman roads were durable stone paved thoroughfares constructed upon a gravel base designed to divert water away from the road. Many of these roads survive today throughout Turkey. The smooth grades of these roads facilitated travel and trade throughout the Roman empire and contributed to a great increase in the interchange of goods and ideas as people and cultures became more mobile during this time.

Fig. 110 Pergamon Altar of Zeus

Some of the best preserved remains of the acropolis at Pergamon are currently housed in the Pergamon Museum in Berlin. The Germans were ome of the early excavators at Pergamon and the remains of the great altar of Zeus were brought to Berlin and wonderfully reconstructed. What currently remains on the acropolis are the five steps of the crepidoma, the base of the structure. The altar was constructed in the middle of the second century B.C. and was built in the shape of a squared U. A large frieze encircled the altar depicting the battle between the gods and the giants. Many scholars believe that the reference to "Satan's throne" in Revelation 2:13 alludes to this altar. Others believe Satan's throne refers to the Asklepion

near the entrance gate is an early Hellenistic heroon, where the Attalids were honored. Northwest of this was the third century B.C. Temple of Athena and further north, the famous 200,000 volume Pergamon Library, the second largest in the ancient world. On the east side of the acropolis there are several peristyle residences from the early Hellenistic period. These are assumed to be the Palaces of the Attalid kings. Dominating the upper acropolis is the Temple of Trajan (early second century A.D.) (fig. 106). The temple was supported by large barrel vaults that are still present and it had colonnaded porticoes on three sides. The temple itself had six Corinthian columns on the ends and ten columns on the sides. Both Trajan and Hadrian were worshipped here. The 10,000 seat Pergamon acropolis theater was on the western slope of the acropolis (fig. 107). This structure was built in the third century B.C. and was modified by the Romans. The theater had eighty rows of seats and had a removable stage

Fig. 111 Pergamon Acropolis Building Z

This building, designated as Building Z, was first constructed at the beginning of the second century B.C. The structure was enlarged in the following years and by the time of the Roman period the building had become a peristyle dwelling with an atrium, mosaic floors and frescoes. The building may have been used for cult purposes and may have been associated with the nearby sanctuary of Demeter, which was constructed at about the same time.

(skene) of wood. The fittings for the wooden posts are still present. Not surprisingly a Temple of Dionysus was at the bottom of the theater and a bit to the north (fig. 108). The twenty-five stepped temple was originally built in the second century B.C. and was rebuilt and dedicated to Caracalla in the early third century A.D. South of the theater and west of the heroon was the Altar of Zeus (fig. 109). All that remains of the altar are the five steps of the base. The rest of the altar was removed and has been reconstructed in the Pergamon Museum in Berlin. The mid-second century B.C. altar was dedicated to Athena and Zeus and had colonnaded porticoes shaped in a 'U'.

The large frieze that encircled the altar contained scenes of the battle between the gods and the giants.

A second century B.C. street led from the upper acropolis to the middle acropolis (fig. 110). After a short walk down this street, one passes Roman baths on the right and then a Heroon complex on the left dedicated to Diadoros Pasparos built around A.D. 100. The heroon complex included a public latrine, baths, an Odeon and a cult hall. Further down the street there was a large cult hall for Dionysus from the second century A.D. Still further down the hill on the right a Sanctuary of Hera was built

Fig. 112 Pergamon Acropolis Gymnasium

This gymnasium, located on the lower terraces of the acropolis, was originally constructed during the Hellenistic period and was supplemented during the Roman period. The gymnasium was constructed on three terraces with exercise areas on each terrace and included a narrow running track, an odeon for music and poetry and baths on both the eastern and western ends. The upper terrace, the largest, had a large open air palaestra surrounded by colonnaded porticoes. The middle terrace had a small temple and altar dedicated to Hercules and Hermes, the patron deities of athletic competition.

in the second century B.C. and to the west of this there was a peristyle building that has been recently opened for public viewing. The second century B.C. Hellenistic building has been enclosed to protect the mosaics and portions of painted frescoes that were unearthed (fig. 111). The building probably served as a cult building for Demeter. Next to the villa are the interesting remains of the Sanctuary of Demeter. The sanctuary from the second century B.C. had a small propylon leading to the temple precincts that contained five altars. The largest altar has been reconstructed and is situated seven meters in front of the temple. On the south side of the temple precinct, overlooking the city, stood a long colonnaded portico. On the western side, ten rows of seats provided space for worshippers during the ceremonies. A huge three tiered Gymnasium complex occupied the remaining space on the middle acropolis. The Gymnasium complex was built during the Hellenistic period and was altered during the Roman period. The top tier was the largest and had a large palaestra surrounded by colonnaded porticoes (fig. 112). At the northwest corner of the complex there was a small one thousand seat Odeon and at the eastern end there was a large bath complex. The lower tiers of the Gymnasium complex were for younger children and were

167

Fig. 113 Pergamon Sacred Way

A Roman road, known as the Sacred Way, leads from Pergamon's acropolis and the lower city to the city's chief claim to fame, the medical facility, dedicated to the chief healing god of the Greco-roman world, Asclepius. Although Asclepius' most important sanctuary was at Epidaurus about 25 miles southeast of Corinth, the facility at Pergamon ran a close second. Desperate people seeking medical treatment came from all corners of Asia Minor to be healed. Their hopes were pinned upon primitive medical practices coupled with gifts to the god and bribes paid to the priests.

smaller in size. The largest structure of the lower acropolis was the Lower Agora with two storied colonnaded porticoes on all sides. Shops were located behind the stoas.

The Asklepion was a healing center named after the chief god of healing Asklepios, the son of Apollo. Although there were numerous asklepions throughout the ancient world, the Asklepion at Pergamon was one of the three most prominent. Galen, a court physician to three Roman emperors was born here and practiced medicine here before moving to Rome. Pergamon's Asklepion was preceded by an eight hundred meter colonnaded Sacred Way that led from the ancient city at the foot of the acropolis to the Asklepion (fig. 113). The Sacred Way terminated at a square courtyard with three colonnaded porticoes. In the middle of the courtyard stood an altar to Asklepios with reliefs of serpents (the symbol of Asklepios and the city of Pergamon). The uncolonnaded side (the west) had a second century A.D. propylon with four

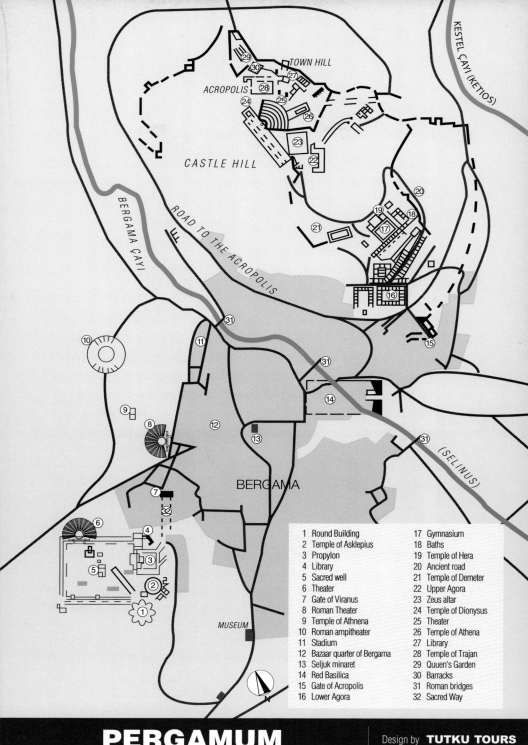

KESTEL ÇAYI (KETIOS)

TOWN HILL

ACROPOLIS

CASTLE HILL

BERGAMA ÇAYI

ROAD TO THE ACROPOLIS

(SELINUS)

BERGAMA

MUSEUM

N

1	Round Building	17	Gymnasium
2	Temple of Asklepius	18	Baths
3	Propylon	19	Temple of Hera
4	Library	20	Ancient road
5	Sacred well	21	Temple of Demeter
6	Theater	22	Upper Agora
7	Gate of Viranus	23	Zeus altar
8	Roman Theater	24	Temple of Dionysus
9	Temple of Athnena	25	Theater
10	Roman ampitheater	26	Temple of Athena
11	Stadium	27	Library
12	Bazaar quarter of Bergama	28	Temple of Trajan
13	Seljuk minaret	29	Quuen's Garden
14	Red Basilica	30	Barracks
15	Gate of Acropolis	31	Roman bridges
16	Lower Agora	32	Sacred Way

PERGAMUM

Design by **TUTKU TOURS**

Corinthian columns that functioned as the main entrance to the Asklepion. The temple of Asklepios was a round domed structure twenty-six meters in diameter located south of the propylon. The temple was constructed in A.D. 150. To the west of the propylon and temple was a large square with columns lining the north, west and south. In the northwest corner of the square there was a 3,500 seat Roman theater with a three storied stage building, although little of the stage has survived. Three healing pools were found in the square along with three small Hellenistic temples dedicated to Asklepios, Apollo (his father) and Hyieia (his daughter), the three primary gods of healing. A Doric portico branched off to the west from the middle of the western portico and a gymnasium was located south of this portico. Both the portico and the gymnasium date to the Hellenistic period. In the middle of the large square, steps led underground to an 85 meter walkway (or cryptoporticus) that ran in a southeastern direction to a large two storied round building that scholars guess was a treatment center. The building was built in the second century A.D.

Revelation: The Letter to Thyatira (Rev 2:18-29)

The letter to the church at Thyatira was similar to the letter sent to Ephesus (Rev 2:1-7). Both began with an acknowledgment that the Lord "knows your deeds (or works)." For the Ephesians these deeds consisted of toil and perseverance and for the Thyatirians these deeds involved "love, faith, service and perseverance." The letter gives evidence that John had previous contact with this church, since he added "your deeds of late are greater than at first" (2:19). While the Ephesian church was chastised because they left their first love, the church at Thyatira was trending upwards. It may be that John had visited the church at Thyatira earlier or that one of his messengers had been there previously. Whatever the case, the church at Thyatira was demonstrating their faith and commitment better than before.

As with most of the letters in Revelation, however, there were problems at Thyatira. The church was tolerating a woman prophet, whom John labeled "Jezebel." In the Old Testament Jezebel was the Phoenician wife of Ahab, a king over the kingdom of Israel. She induced her husband and the northern tribes to follow the Canaanite god Baal, thus committing apostasy. Although the name Jezebel was used metaphorically, just as Balaam was used metaphorically in 2:14, the reference was clearly to a woman who was spreading false teaching at Thyatira.

The description of the teachings of the woman prophet "Jezebel" was identical to the teachings of the "Balaam," who was misleading the church at Pergamon. Both were enticing Christians "to engage in acts of immorality and to eat things sacrificed to idols" (2:14 & 20). If this Balaam was connected to the Nicolaitans, (as 2:15 may imply), then we should assume that this Jezebel was also a leader within the Nicolaitan movement. The accusations of immorality and eating food sacrificed to idols were stock criticisms levied against opponents and these statements may simply describe Jezebel's practice of participating in the paganism of the imperial cults.

John or his messengers had confronted the woman prophet earlier, but these efforts did little to correct her teachings: "I gave her time to repent and she does not want to repent of her immorality" (2:21). As a result, John prophesied of doom – sickness, trouble and death - for the prophet and "her children" (those who followed her teachings).

The teachings of Jezebel were designated "the deep things of Satan" (2:24). It is hard to imagine that a quasi-christian sect would describe its teachings as the deep things of Satan, but John states that the term was a self designation. Some scholars think that John parodied the cult's expression "deep things of God" (a common expression within Gnostic thought) and changed it to "the deep things of Satan." Others think that the followers of Jezebel were involved in black magic in order to manipulate the demonic world. The followers of Jezebel claimed a special knowledge, as all of these Gnostic groups did. The Nicolaitans were a sect that arose within the emerging, developing and expanding world of Gnostic thought. Knowledge of the deep things of Satan would enable the Nicolaitans to avoid the harassment and lures of Satan.

The church at Thyatira, like all of the seven churches of Revelation, was composed of Christians who had no Bible as we have it today. These Christians, sincere as they may have been, were heavily dependent upon the traveling disciples, teachers and prophets who came their way to share the gospel. These churches had no resident pastors who were trained in the traditions of Christ. Thus, they were easily influenced by persuasive speakers who tapped into the rapidly growing Christian movement and used their influence for their own selfish purposes. The words of Paul, written to churches in this area years earlier, were still pertinent: "See to it that no one takes you captive through philosophy and empty deception, according to the tradition of men, according to the elementary principles of the world, rather than according to Christ" (Col 4:8). Not all those in Thyatira were influenced by the teachings of Jezebel. John referenced some who did not follow her teachings (2:19 & 24). For those who have remained faithful, John offered encouraging words to "hold fast" until the Lord's return.

The Ancient History and Archaeology of Thyatira (Akhisar)

The Ancient History of Thyatira

Excavations at the site of Thyatira show an early occupation dating back to 3000 B.C. Pliny the Younger suggested that an early city at this site named Pelopia may have originally been founded by the Lydians. In the early third century B.C. Seleucus I Nicator refounded the city and named it Thyatira. With the emergence of the Attalid rulers and the Pergamene kingdom, Thyatira was incorporated into the kingdom in 189 B.C. and remained a part of it until the kingdom was ceded to the Romans in 133 B.C. Shortly thereafter, in 129 B.C. the Romans created the province of Asia Minor and Thyatira was subsumed in this province.

Due to its advantageous location at the crossroads of vital trade routes, Thyatira grew into an important and wealthy commercial center. From Thyatira one could travel the roads to Pergamon in the Northwest, to Sardis in the South and to Smyrna in the Southwest. Inscriptions indicate that numerous trade guilds existed at Thyatira, including trade associations for tanners, leatherworkers, dyers, wool workers, linen workers, potters, bakers, slave traders and coppersmiths. Textile workers were strongly represented in Thyatira and Acts 16:14 refers to a woman named Lydia who was a merchant in purple fabrics from the city of Thyatira. Purple textiles were sold to wealthy Roman citizens as a sign of their status. Inscriptions also claim that the city possessed temples to Apollo Tyrimnaeus, Artemis Boreitene, Helius and Hadrian. Additionally the city boasted of three gymnasiums with numerous statues, many stoas and shops. The Roman emperor Caracalla made the city a judicial center and was proclaimed the city's founder and savior in the third century A.D.

Fig. 114 Thyatira Ruins
A city block in Akhisar contains remains from the ancient city of Thyatira.

Fig. 115 Thyatira Ruins

Columns, capitals, the arches of a gateway and various architectural pieces litter the ground at ancient Thyatira.

Christian Beginnings at Thyatira

As mentioned above, Thyatira was first mentioned in the Bible in Acts 16:14. When Paul visited the Macedonian city of Philippi, he evangelized some women outside of the gate near a river. One woman named Lydia, a seller of purple fabrics, was from Thyatira. She responded to Paul's message and was baptized. The fact that Lydia sold purple fabrics and that she provided quarters to Paul and his companions is a strong indication that she was a woman of some means. Thyatira is next mentioned in the book of Revelation as one of the seven churches to which the apocalypse was written. Revelation assumes the existence of a church at Thyatira, but there is no clue as to how the church was founded. It is logical to assume that the church was established as a secondary outgrowth of Paul's ministry in Asia Minor. During Paul's extensive stay in Ephesus during his third mission, the apostle established the School of Tyrannus (Acts 19:9-10). Here Paul trained disciples who took the gospel message throughout Asia Minor, "so that all who lived in Asia heard the word of the Lord." Alternately, it could be that the church was established by John the apostle or elder. Early church traditions indicate that John relocated to Ephesus and began ministry there. The church at Thyatira could be an extension of his ministry in Asia Minor. The epistles 2 John and 3 John indicate that the elder had an extended ministry to churches in various locations and Thyatira may very well have been one of those churches. Revelation 2:18-29 indicates that the church in Thyatira was beset with a woman whom John dubs "Jezebel." This woman claimed to be a prophetess and was promoting immorality and the eating of things sacrificed to idols. These teachings were known as the 'deep things of Satan'. Nevertheless, John recognized that their recent deeds were better than at first and that not everyone in the church followed the prophetess' teachings. Later, in A.D. 325 a bishop from Thyatira attended the Council of Nicea.

Little archaeological work has been done at ancient Thyatira. The modern city sets squarely upon the ancient site and covers much of what could be found. A hill in the center of the town is assumed to be the ancient acropolis of the city. A sacrophagus and an inscription can be seen in the garden of the hospital currently occupying the site. It is thought that the Great Mosque (Ulu Cami) was originally a Roman temple that was later converted into a Byzantine church and later transformed into a mosque.

More ruins can be found in the downtown section of Akhisar. A city block has been fenced in where two unidentified buildings probably dating to the fifth or sixth century A.D. can be found. The remains of a colonnaded street and a monumental entrance, dating to the second or third centuries A.D. can be seen here along with some inscriptions, statue bases, an altar and various Byzantine artifacts (figs. 114 and 115).

Revelation: The Letter to Sardis (Rev 3:1-6)

When writing to the church at Smyrna, John described a church with two contrasting fortunes: "I know your tribulation and your poverty, but you are rich" (2:9). The letter emphasized the afflictions and hardships imposed upon the church at Smyrna and the resultant poverty that was crippling the believers. But the letter also revealed the spiritual treasure that the church possessed. The Christian community was experiencing poverty in an earthly sense, but wealth spiritually.

When writing to the church at Sardis, John offered a different metaphor: "I know your deeds that you have a reputation that you are alive, but you are dead" (3:1). Sardis had an illustrious reputation extending back to the days of the wealthy King Croesus who made his capitol in Sardis. The city, and evidently the church as well, continued to thrive at the time when John wrote, but the author warned the congregation that spiritually speaking, the church was dead. To thrive socially and economically in the major cities of Asia Minor during the reign of Domitian meant that one needed to support the imperial cult. The church at Smyrna refused to do this, but the church at Sardis chose to follow the demands of their fellow citizens and to participate in the imperial festivities. Thus, in the letters to these two churches John used the antithetical metaphors of poverty / wealth and life / death in different ways to illustrate the opposite directions that these two congregations were headed.

Not everyone in the church at Sardis was spiritually dead. Rev 3:4 claimed that there were "a few people in Sardis" who had not compromised their faith. The term "few" however, indicates that the faithful were a distinct minority within the congregation. They were described as those who had not "soiled their garments" and those who would be given "white garments" upon the Lord's arrival. The reference to garments was a common metaphor indicating a person's moral righteousness. Isaiah described sin as a soiled garment (Is 64:6) and Zechariah described the high priest Joshua wearing filthy garments (symbolizing iniquity) as he stood before the angel of God (Zech 3:1-5). In contrast to the soiled garments, the white garments were often represented in the apocalypse as the acquisition of righteousness. Thus, in 6:11 the martyrs were given white robes. Likewise, in 7:9 & 13 the multitude of people who came out of the great tribulation were found standing before God's throne clothed in white robes. The wealthy church at Laodicea was advised to buy white garments from Christ in order to cover the shame of their nakedness (3:18, see the comments below).

A third group in the Sardis church was described as those who were about to die (3:2). The verse can be translated either "strengthen the things that remain, which are about to die" or "strengthen the people who remain, who are about to die." The latter seems preferable. Thus, John seems to be exhorting the few devout disciples in the church to wake up and strengthen other Christians who seem to have been straddling the fence. These people were depicted by John as persons who were about to die, as the bulk of the congregation already had.

John challenged them to recollect "what you have received and heard" (3:3). The teachings of Christ were previously shared with the congregation and John warned them to "wake up," and "remember" what they had heard, "keep" these teachings and to "repent." These words were followed by an appeal to Jesus' parable of the thief who came at an unexpected hour in the night (Mt 24:42-44): I will come like a thief and you will not know at what hour I will come upon you (3:3). This parable was also known and repeated by Paul (1 Th 5:1-4), who may have passed it on to the church at Sardis.

John concluded the letter with the words that those who overcame would not only be clothed in white garments, but also that their name would not be erased from the book of life and that Jesus would confess their name before the father in heaven (3:5). It is strangely ironic that Jesus' true followers were promised that their names would not be erased from the book of life, while Domitian's name was erased from all public monuments and inscriptions following his death. Domitian was so greatly hated that the Roman Senate tried to abolish the name and memory of Domitian when they posthumously issued a *damnatio memoriae*, a decree that forbade anyone from speaking or writing about the emperor. Domitian was neither the first nor the last to receive the *damnatio memoriae*, but he was the first Roman emperor to be so condemned.

The phrase "I will confess his name before my father" (3:5) recalls the words of Jesus: "everyone who confesses me before people, I will also confess him before my father who is in heaven" (Mt 10:32). It also evokes thoughts of a judicial proceeding. The word "confess" is not common, but it occurs nine times in the fourth gospel and the epistles of John. Most of these occur in the context of confessing Jesus under an examination by opponents or the confession of right doctrine as opposed to false teaching. In Rev 3:5 Jesus promised to confess his devout followers before the father. This was the reward of a Christian confession before the civic law courts or hostile crowds at Sardis.

The Ancient History and Archaeology of Sardis (Sart Mustafa)

The Ancient History of Sardis

Along with the decline of the Phrygian Kingdom in central Anatolia came the emergence of the Lydian Kingdom in western Anatolia with Sardis as its capital. The Lydians had carved out a small enclave around Sardis early in the first millennium B.C., but it was not until King Gyges (680 - 652 B.C.) and the later Mermnad rulers that the Lydian Kingdom really emerged. Herodotus, the fifth century B.C. historian claimed that the earliest Lydian rulers were part of the Heraclid dynasty that ruled for 505 years prior to Gyges. Gyges murdered the last Heraclid ruler, Candaules, married his wife and established himself as king. In 652 the Cimmerians invaded Sardis, destroyed the city and killed Gyges. The Cimmerian presence in Sardis and Lydia was brief and around 630 they were beaten back and the Lydian Kingdom reemerged.

A later Lydian ruler, Croesus (561 – 547 B.C.) was believed to be the wealthiest person in the world. The source of Croesus' wealth was gold. According to legends, the Phrygian King Midas washed in the Pactolus River in order to get rid of his 'golden touch'. This turned the river deposits to gold. The Pactolus River, which flows to Sardis, in fact still contains small amounts of gold. Excavations next to the river indicate that gold dust panned from the river was refined at Sardis from the late seventh century or the early sixth century B.C. Croesus, after consulting with the Delphic Oracle attacked the expanding Persian Kingdom. However the Persians were not to be deterred and in 547 Croesus and his forces were crushed and the Lydian empire came to an end.

Now under Persian control, Sardis became the capital of the Persian province in Asia Minor. The Athenians, fearing Persian expansion, bonded together with Ionian cities on the coast and attacked Sardis. The city was burned in 499 B.C. and the temple to Cybele was destroyed, but later the Persians regained Sardis and repressed the Ionian revolt. The Persians ruled Asia Minor until Alexander the Great took over western Asia Minor in 334 B.C. After Alexander's death Sardis was incorporated into the Seleucid Kingdom. In 189 B.C. at the battle of Magnesia ad Sipylum (only 50 kilometers to the west), the Romans crushed the Seleucid forces and most of Asia Minor was given to the Pergamene kings as a reward for assisting the Romans. When the Pergamene Kingdom dissolved in 133 B.C. the Romans controlled Asia Minor and Sardis was included in this Roman province. Under the Romans, Sardis prospered due in large part to the Royal Road constructed by the Persians, through which a great deal of trade passed. The population of the city during the first and second centuries A.D. grew to about 100,000 and Sardis became an administrative center. The A.D. 17 earthquake that destroyed Philadelphia also flattened Sardis. Tiberius provided funds to rebuild the city and Sardis continued to flourish. In the third century A.D. Diocletian made Sardis the capital of the province of Lydia.

Christian Beginnings at Sardis

The earliest reference to a Christian community at Sardis comes from John's Apocalypse (Rev 3:1-6), written around A.D. 90-95. There the church was cautioned to wake up and rekindle the faith that was about to die. Evidently the church was struggling, but the short epistle also commended a few people who had not "soiled their garments," who would "walk with Me in white."

It is not possible to determine how the church at Sardis was founded. However, it is known that there had been a strong Jewish presence in Sardis for centuries before Christianity arrived. Jews probably settled in the area shortly after the Babylonian exile. Obadiah 20 mentioned the exiles of Jerusalem who were in "Sepharad" — another name for Sardis. Josephus (a first century A.D. Jewish historian) claimed that the Seleucid king Antiochus III relocated 2,000 Jewish families from Mesopotamia to Lydia and Phrygia at the end of the third century B.C. Josephus also referred to two decrees during the time of Julius Caesar and Augustus that granted Jews in Sardis the right to congregate and to send temple taxes to Jerusalem. Moreover, a large synagogue dating somewhere between the fourth to the sixth century A.D. has been uncovered in the ancient city center (fig. 116). Since most of the Christian missions in the Greco-Roman world focused upon the synagogues, it is not unreasonable to suggest that the church sprang from mission work among this Jewish population and the gentiles associated with the Sardis synagogue.

Fig. 116 Sardis Synagogue

Work at Sardis has revealed the largest ancient synagogue ever discovered. The date of the synagogue is disputed with some opting for the 4th century and others choosing the 6th century. The west end of the Sardis Synagogue contains an eagle table and lion statues. This synagogue was located next to the gymnasium and was a prominent structure in the city.

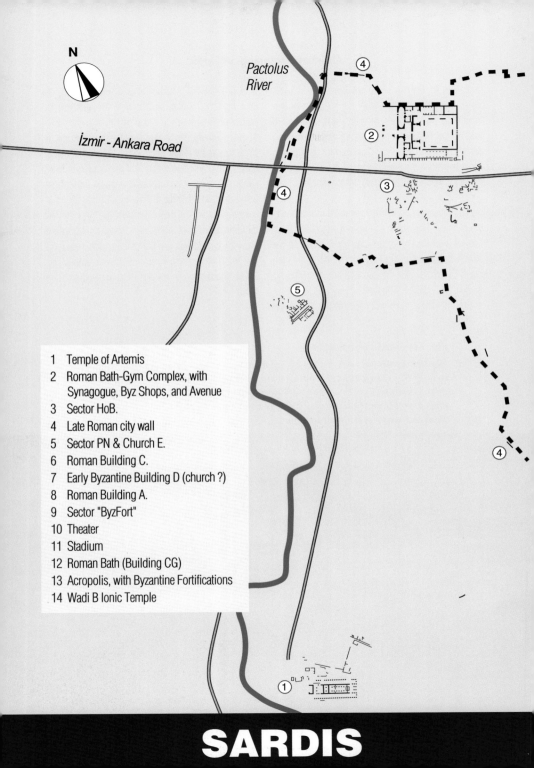

N

Pactolus
River

İzmir - Ankara Road

④
②
④
③
⑤

1 Temple of Artemis
2 Roman Bath-Gym Complex, with
   Synagogue, Byz Shops, and Avenue
3 Sector HoB.
4 Late Roman city wall
5 Sector PN & Church E.
6 Roman Building C.
7 Early Byzantine Building D (church ?)
8 Roman Building A.
9 Sector "ByzFort"
10 Theater
11 Stadium
12 Roman Bath (Building CG)
13 Acropolis, with Byzantine Fortifications
14 Wadi B Ionic Temple

④

①

SARDIS

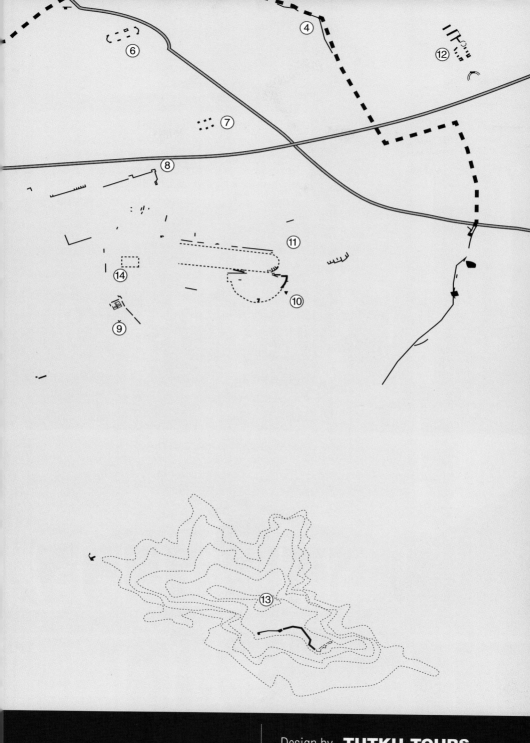

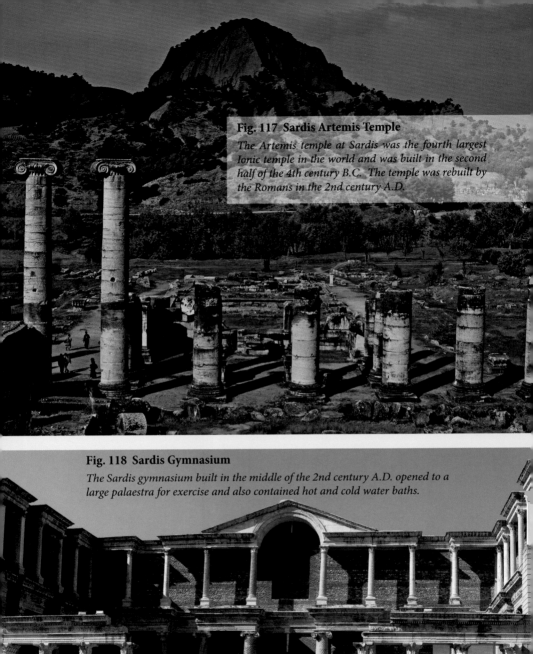

Fig. 117 Sardis Artemis Temple

The Artemis temple at Sardis was the fourth largest Ionic temple in the world and was built in the second half of the 4th century B.C. The temple was rebuilt by the Romans in the 2nd century A.D.

Fig. 118 Sardis Gymnasium

The Sardis gymnasium built in the middle of the 2nd century A.D. opened to a large palaestra for exercise and also contained hot and cold water baths.

Fig. 119 Sardis Synagogue Menorah

The courtyard of the synagogue contains an inscribed menorah. Over eighty Jewish inscriptions have been found in and around the Sardis synagogue.

Fig. 120 Sardis Shop Menorah

Several shops of Jewish residents have been found in Sardis. This shop had two menorot etched on the walls.

During the second century Melito was appointed bishop of the church at Sardis. Among his many writings (few of which survive) Melito gives accounts of Christians who were persecuted in the middle of the second century. The church continued to thrive in the city and maintained a presence and bishopric throughout the Byzantine period.

The Current Remains at Sardis

The remains at Sardis are spread over an area more than two square kilometers. At the top of the hills to the southeast was the ancient acropolis. The acropolis is still accessible, but the final ascent to the top is very steep. The view of the ancient site from the top is spectacular, but the remains at the top are minimal. Erosion has obliterated most of the acropolis, but small portions of the Lydian defense wall (sixth century B.C.) and larger portions of the Byzantine wall can be seen.

Down below the acropolis to the west is the massive temple of Artemis (fig. 117). The original shrine dating to the fifth century B.C. was built a little to the west of the present structure. The temple that now stands was constructed in three phases extending from the third cen-

tury B.C. to the early second century A.D. The peripteral temple with a roofed cella (inner chamber) had eight columns in the front and back and twenty columns along the sides. The temple was one of the seven largest Greek temples in the world. At the southeast corner of the temple a fourth century Christian basilica was built. The sixth or fifth century B.C. altar to the west was probably part of the earlier temple. Further to the west surrounding the Pactolus River is a necropolis. The tombs here date back as far as the sixth century B.C. and include Tumulus tombs, mausoleum tombs and rock cut tombs in the hillside. A large pyramid tomb, perhaps dating to the sixth century B.C. can be found north of the Artemis Temple.

North of all this on the east bank of the Pactolus River,

181

an excavated area contains the sixth century B.C. gold refinery mentioned above. Here also, a square structure housed an altar of Cybele, likewise dating to the sixth century. Other structures located here include a small Roman bath and two churches - a fourth century Chris-

bulk of the construction was finished by the middle of the second century A.D., although the Marble Court (the Imperial Hall at the center of the gymnasium) was finished in A.D. 211. This court has been wonderfully reconstructed. South of this complex, on the eastern end, a fourth

Fig. 121 Sardis Synagogue God Fearer

A mosaic floor at the Sardis synagogue reads: "Aurelius Eulogios, a God Fearer, fulfills his vow."

tian basilica and another late Byzantine church. East of the Pactolus River roughly 300 meters, the ancient city agora is being unearthed. Further east and still south of the modern highway in the foothills of the acropolis there are the scant remains of a theater and stadium dating to the Roman period.

North of the modern highway a great deal of excavation and reconstruction has recreated a portion of the Sardis city center. This section of the city was built after the earthquake of A.D. 17. The main feature of this area is the Palaestra, Gymnasium and bath complex (fig. 118). The

or sixth century synagogue has been found (fig. 116). This synagogue is the largest ancient synagogue found anywhere. The large size and prominent location of this synagogue is an indication of the large Jewish presence in Sardis at that time. A number of menorahs can be found in the synagogue and nearby shops (figs. 119 and 120). Two God Fearer inscriptions can be seen in the atrium forecourt (fig. 121). South of the synagogue there was a colonnaded east-west street paved with marble. This was probably the Persian Royal Road. Two-storied shops from the fourth century A.D. lined the street. On the south side of the street there were upper class villas.

Revelation: The Letter to Philadelphia (Rev 3:7-13)

The church at Philadelphia was one of only two churches in the book of Revelation that was positively commended without any negative corrections. Like the church at Smyrna, the church at Philadelphia was faithfully persevering in the midst of harassment and adversity. As we will shortly note, there were several similarities between the church at Smyrna and the church at Philadelphia.

The letter to the church at Philadelphia described the risen Lord as "the one having the key of David: the one who opens and nobody shuts and the one who shuts and nobody opens" (3:7). Following the statement "I know your deeds" (3:8), John added "I have put before you an open door which no one can shut, because you have little power, and have kept my word and have not denied my name." The emphasis on an open door was not a random comment, but a comment that had a particular point of reference in the life of the church at Philadelphia. The reference to the "key of David" in verse seven was a clear reference to Is 22:22, "I will set the key of the house of David upon his shoulder. When he opens no one will shut. When he shuts no one will open." Isaiah's statement referred to the authority of Eliakim, the son of Hilkiah to exercise power in the kingdom of David. We can imagine that the Christians in Philadelphia were shut out of the rights and benefits given to others in the city. The door was closed to anyone who had not taken the mark of the beast (Rev 13:16-17). The Christians had "little power" (3:8) and it was impossible for them to buy or sell anything in the city. But for the faithful Philadelphians, the Lord, who holds the key of David, promised "an open door which no one could shut." The key may not open doors in Philadelphia, but it would open the door to God's kingdom.

Part of the problem for the Christians in Philadelphia seemed to be opposition by the leaders of the local synagogue. The Jewish community in Philadelphia was described in terms almost identical to the Jewish community in Smyrna. In both cities the Jewish assembly was described as a "synagogue of Satan," an expression loaded with vitriolic displeasure for what appears to be mistreatment of the Christians in Philadelphia by the Jewish community. Also, in both of the letters to Smyrna and Philadelphia, the text conveys the belief that these Jews "say they are Jews, but they are not" (2:9, 3:9). The assertion is a matter of semantics: hereditarily, these people were Jews, but the author believes their actions belie their faith.

Thus, the Lord "will make them come and bow down before your feet, and will make them know that I have loved you" (3:9). This statement recollects the words of

Isaiah, and turns the tables on the concept of the chosen people. Isaiah 60:14 reads "The sons of those who afflicted you will come bowing to you, and all those who despised you will bow themselves at the soles of your feet. And they will call you the city of the Lord, the Zion of the Holy One of Israel" (also see Is 45:14 & 49:23). The passages in Isaiah refer to the tribulation and mistreatment that Israel received at the hands of the Gentiles. God's assurance was that he would vindicate Israel and their opponents would come to bow before their feet. In Rev 3:9 the situation is reversed. The Jews in Philadelphia are judged to be the ones mistreating the church, composed mostly of Gentile believers. By their actions, the Jews of Philadelphia have forfeited their right to be God's people. Using Isaiah's prophecy, John explained that the Christians in Philadephia would be vindicated. John prophesied that the Jews would be forced to bow before the church's feet, acknowledging God's love for the Gentile church at Philadelphia.

Like the churches at Ephesus and Thyatira, the church at Philadelphia was commended for its perseverance. These churches, as well as John himself (1:9) steadfastly endured the verbal, social and physical abuse by their fellow citizens and had maintained their faith in Christ in the face of unabated hostility. The virtue of perseverance was particularly significant in the apocalypse - seven of the twenty-two uses of the noun "perseverance" (the Greek *hypomone*) in the N.T. occur in Revelation (1:9; 2:2, 3, 19; 3:10; 13:10; 14:12). The daily pressure of living in intolerable circumstances had caused many Christians within the churches of these communities to succumb to the demands of the broader society and to participate in the imperial cult. Alternately, others had fallen prey to persuasive teachers who distorted the faith. John praised the many devout Christians who remained steadfast and true – those who sacrificed the honors bestowed upon others by secular authorities in Asia Minor in favor of an unseen honor given by Christ to those who "overcome."

Another similarity to the letter sent to the church at Smyrna was John's reference to the "hour of testing" (3:10). In the letter to the Smyrnans this "test" was described as a period of tribulation lasting ten days (2:10). The word for "test" can be translated as "test" or "temptation" and in this instance the temptation to submit to the persecutors became the test to determine the core of one's faith for Christians in Philadelphia and Smyrna. As with many of the temporal designations in Revelation, there probably was not any difference between the "hour" of testing in Philadelphia and the ten days of testing in Smyrna. Both signify a short period of intense persecution.

Those who persevered in Smyrna and Philadelphia would be given a wreath. The word used here, (in Greek *stephanos*) referred to a victor's wreath, not a royal crown.

The Greek word for a royal crown, *diadema*, can also be translated "diadem." The crown or diadem was used in Rev 12:3, 13:1 and 19:12 where it pertained to kings or royal pretenders. But, the term used in 2:10 and 3:11 is *stephanos*. The Greek victor's wreath was composed of laurel leaves woven together to mimic a royal crown. These crowns were given to victors in athletic contests and to victorious military leaders returning from battle. In fact, many Greek royal crowns consisted of a headdress made of gold that was fashioned into laurel leaves (fig. 88). Kings and royal figures wanted to emit the image of strength and victory and thus these crowns borrowed the imagery of laurel leaves. In Smyrna those who endured the persecution and were faithful until death were given the wreath of life (2:10). In Philadelphia the faithful were encouraged to persist in the faith through the hour of testing in order that they not lose their crown (3:11).

The crown in these instances was a victor's crown received for triumph over the evil forces allied against the church. In all seven of the churches the letters concluded with the words "to him who overcomes" (Rev 2:7, 11, 17, 26; 3:5, 12, 21). The word used in these clauses is *nikao*, a verb used for athletic champions and for victors in battle. The imagery of battle against Satanic forces is found throughout Revelation and the meaning here is a reference to those who have waged war against spiritual forces and have won eternal rewards. The concepts here are not unlike Paul's words to the Ephesians: "Our struggle is not against flesh and blood, but against the rulers, against the powers, against the world forces of this darkness, against the spiritual forces of wickedness in the heavenly places" (Eph 6:12).

The Ancient History and Archaeology of Philadelphia (Alaşehir)

The Ancient History of Philadelphia

An ancient city known as Calletebus existed at Alaşehir before Philadelphia. This city, dating to the first half of the first millennium B.C. was a Phrygian settlement. The city was refounded in the first half of the second century B.C. by either Eumenes II, King of Pergamon or his brother and successor Attalus II Philadelphia, from whom the city received its new name. When the Pergamon kingdom was dissolved and assumed by the Romans, Philadelphia came under Roman dominion. The city was known for grape and wine production and not surprisingly, took Dionysus as its patron deity. Being in an earthquake prone area, Philadelphia suffered from devastating earthquakes in A.D. 17 and again in 23. The emperor Tiberius returned the city's tribute to Rome for five years to assist in the rebuilding of the city. The city in turn, built a temple to honor Tiberius and was briefly known as Neocaesarea. Philadelphia continued to enjoy a close relationship with Rome and dedicated other sanctuaries to Caligula and Vespasian. Caracalla honored Philadelphia with the Neokorus (guardian of the imperial temple) during his reign.

Fig. 122 Philadelphia Byzantine Basilica
Little of the ancient city of Philadelphia can be seen today since the modern city of Alaşehir covers the site. A small plot in the city contains the scant remains of a 6th century Byzantine church along with a few inscriptions, sarcophagi and artifacts.

Fig. 123 Philadelphia Theater

The base of the acropolis at Philadelphia holds a few remains of the ancient city's theater.

Christian Beginnings at Philadelphia

Christianity came to Philadelphia sometime in the first century. The city received one of the seven letters that John addressed to cities of Asia Minor in the Apocalypse (Rev 3:7-13), written around A.D. 90-95. It is not known how the church was established at Philadelphia, but it is probable that it was founded sometime after the cluster of churches at Hieropolis, Laodicea and Colossae. Paul never mentioned a church at the city, so it may have been established sometime later than the churches in those nearby cities. Philadelphia was located on a major road heading north from those cities and its founding may be attributed to an anonymous evangelist from one of those cities. The church at Philadelphia was evidently strong and faithful, since it was one of only two churches among John's churches that received only commendations and no criticisms. At the beginning of the second century Ignatius, the bishop of Syrian Antioch, visited the church in route to his martyrdom in Rome (A.D. 107) and he wrote to the church at Philadelphia later on his journey. Philadelphia was also mentioned in relation to the martyrdom of Polycarp around A.D. 155. According to the *Martyrdom of Polycarp* 19:1 eleven Christians from Philadelphia were martyred with Polycarp.

Earthquakes have destroyed much of ancient Philadelphia. Also, much of what could be seen at Philadelphia is covered with the modern city of Alaşehir. Consequently, there is not much to see at the site today. Most people who make the journey to Philadelphia are dropped off at the Byzantine basilica where four piers for the arches of an ancient church are visible along with a couple of faded eleventh century frescoes, a number of Byzantine inscriptions, a few columns and sarcophagi (fig. 122). The ancient acropolis was located on the hill in the center of town and it is possible to see a few pieces of a Roman theater and portions of a temple on top (fig. 123). The hollowed area of a stadium is evident just off the acropolis to the north. In the north part of town there are portions of a Byzantine city wall with parts of a gate and an inscription.

Revelation: The letter to Laodicea (Rev 3:14-22)

The church at Laodicea was established in the middle of the first century during Paul's ministry in Asia Minor. The church was mentioned five times in Paul's letter to the Colossians. The letter to the Colossians also mentioned a church at Hierapolis. The cities of Laodicea, Colossae and Hierapolis had close relations with one another and were located within 20 kilometers of one another. Although Paul wrote to the Colossians and made references to the churches at Hierapolis and Laodicea, Paul did not establish these churches. In his letter to the Colossians, Paul stated that the Christians at Colossae and Laodicea had never seen him. Thus, it is safe to conclude that Paul was not the evangelist who established the churches in this area. Instead as Col 1:7 indicates, the church at Colossae was founded by Epaphras. Epaphras was one of Paul's students at the school of Tyrannos (Acts 19:9-10) who returned to his home town of Colossae and shared the gospel with his friends and kinsmen. By extension, we assume that Epaphras shared the gospel with the nearby cities of Laodicea and Hierapolis and founded churches in those locations.

In Revelation, the church at Laodicea was described as "neither cold nor hot" (3:15-16), a metaphor to characterize the dispassionate nature of the believers in the city. Mediocrity might be acceptable in some aspects of life, but for the risen Lord bland faith was unpalatable. As a result John wrote "I will spit you out of my mouth."

Perhaps it would be unfair to think of the Laodicean church as apathetic, detached, indifferent or unconcerned about their faith. But, something had changed between the middle of the first century and the end of the first century when Revelation was written. When Paul wrote to the Colossians around A.D. 60 his tone was apprehensive, but he had a positive attitude toward the church and he spoke optimistically of its future.

Remember, the letter to the Colossians was a circular letter that was intended to be passed on to the congregation at Laodicea (4:16). So, the letter to the Colossians reflected the situation at Colossae as well as the situation at Laodicea. Paul was thankful for the faith and love exhibited within the church at Colossae (Col 1:3-4). Paul spoke of the hope laid up in heaven for the Colossians (1:5) and he recounted how the gospel was increasing and constantly bearing fruit from the time of its inception in the church (1:6). Speaking to both the Colossians and the Laodiceans (2:2), Paul claimed that he was "rejoicing to see your good discipline and the stability of your faith in Christ" (2:5). Still, Paul had concerns with false teaching that was circulating in the area: "See to it that no one takes you captive through philosophy and empty deception, according to the tradition of men" (2:8).

This upbeat tone is absent in the letter to the Laodiceans written by John some thirty years later. The church was lukewarm – neither hot nor cold. However this expression is understood, the church had lost its zeal and the faith of the Laodiceans was somehow tarnished.

Most scholars believe that the terminology of hot, cold and lukewarm was chosen by John to echo the physical surroundings of Laodicea, Hierapolis and Colossae. Hierapolis to the north was built upon massive hot springs which continue to flow today. The white travertine deposits can be seen for miles around Hierapolis and the formations are clearly visible from across the Lycus Valley at Laodicea. Not far to the east, the city of Colossae was known for its pure cold water. However, between Hierapolis and Colossae the people of Laodicea had lousy tepid water – not hot enough to be valuable and not cold enough to be refreshing. A water distribution tower found at Laodicea illustrates the water problems in the city. The tower contained dozens of pipes that were continually replaced because of the calcification of the pipes due to the considerable presence of minerals in the water (fig. 124). The metaphor of lousy water – neither hot nor cold and of poor quality – was an apt description of the church in Laodicea.

Laodicea was a very wealthy city and many members of the Laodicean congregation were among the rich. The city was a financial center, located along an important trade route leading to Ephesus and was known for its fine textiles. The ancient city is currently being excavated by archaeologists at a rapid pace and the discoveries are revealing a city of great prosperity (fig. 125). A large number of the streets were colonnaded and the mid-sized city was well outfitted for entertainment, having two theaters, an odeon, a large stadium and at least four bath houses (fig. 126). Many larger cities did not have the architectural perks possessed by Laodicea.

Fig. 124 Laodicea Water Tower

The water supply at Laodicea was a problem. An aqueduct transported water north from present day Denizli to Laodicea where it was distributed throughout the city via this water tower. The water contained so many minerals that the deposits clogged the terracotta pipes and had to be replaced frequently. The tower was greatly enlarged with the accumulation of the water deposits and additional pipes.

Fig. 125 Laodicea Resurrected

*Laodicea was a wealthy mid-sized city. The city is being rapidly excavated
and rebuilt by archaeologists and scholars from nearby Pamukkale University*

Fig. 126 Laodicea Colonnaded Street
The newly restored colonnaded streets of Laodicea display the city's wealth.

The city was frequently damaged by earthquakes. In A.D. 17 during the reign of Tiberias, the city was destroyed by the same earthquake that destroyed Philadelphia. The emperor Tiberias assisted the city to rebuild. Another earthquake in A.D. 60 was similarly destructive. However, the residents of the proud and wealthy city refused Nero's imperial assistance and rebuilt the city with its own resources. Perhaps this is what the letter to the Laodiceans was referring to in 3:17: "you say, 'I am rich, and have become wealthy, and have need of nothing.'" The Laodiceans were affluent and felt that they did not need anyone's assistance – either financially or spiritually. Maybe the wealth of the Laodicean Christians contributed to the transformation of the congregation from the church that Paul commended for its faith, love and stability to the church that John rebuked for its spiritual attrition. Since all of the churches in the book of Revelation were being intimidated and pressured to engage in the imperial cult, the rich Christians in Laodicea figured they had a lot to lose. With wealth comes power and members of the church at Laodicea stood to lose property, possessions, power and positions. It is not entirely surprising that members of the congregation compromised their faith, participated in the imperial cult and became lukewarm. Jesus himself warned how hard it is for a rich man to enter the kingdom of heaven.

While the Laodiceans felt that they were self sufficient and had need of nothing, John continued to write "you do not know that you are wretched and miserable and poor and blind and naked" (3:17). Prosperity sometimes blinds us to our faults. It is doubtful that the Laodiceans felt wretched and miserable, yet the risen Lord assessed them as such. The last three descriptors (poor, blind and naked) were metaphors that were addressed by the advice offered in the next verse. Though spiritually poor, they were advised to "buy from me gold refined by fire, that you may become rich." The metaphor is transparent: the wealthy Laodiceans were advised to figuratively buy gold refined by fire (the fires of tribulation) so that they might become spiritually rich.

The church was also advised to buy white garments so that they might cover the shame of their nakedness. The white garments (a common feature in Revelation) represented righteousness that was acquired by maintaining faith and suffering through the tribulations of that time. The white garments were mentioned earlier in the letter to the church at Sardis (3:4-5, see above). Clothing in all societies past and present communicated a great deal about wealth and social status. The most powerful and important citizens (those of the Senatorial or Equestrian class) proudly wore a red stripe upon their garments to call attention to their status. Here, the church was instructed to wear a plain white garment representing righteousness and purity.

Finally, the Laodiceans were advised to address the problem of their blindness by purchasing eyesalve. This reference probably has a direct link to the ancient city. The ancient geographer Strabo claimed that Laodicea had a medical school where the ophthalmologist Demosthenes Philalethes practiced. Demosthenes Philalethes was the author of the most famous ophthalmalogical textbook in antiquity. Laodicea, a Phrygian city, also had access to "Phrygian powder" which was used in solutions for eye problems.

The Ancient History and Archaeology of Laodicea (Eskihisar)

The Ancient History of Laodicea

Laodicea was established near the Lycus River by Antiochus II who ruled the Seleucid empire from 261 – 246 B.C. Antiochus named the city after his wife Laodice, whom he divorced several years later. Since there were several other cities known as Laodicea, this one came to be known as Laodicea ad Lycum. Pliny the Elder claims that Laodicea was actually built upon an earlier city first called Diospolis, but later known as Rhoas. After the Seleucids were driven out of Asia in 189 B.C. the city was handed over to the Pergamene kings. Then when the Pergamene Kingdom folded in 133 B.C., the Romans assumed control of Laodicea. The city prospered under Roman control. In the first century B.C. the city was known as a banking, administrative and textile center. Major roads gave the city easy access to other cities in the populous region and made it an important stop along trade routes. In 50 B.C. Cicero, at that time the governor of Cilicia, spent time there. In A.D. 60 the city was destroyed by an earthquake. At that time the residents were so wealthy that they refused imperial assistance in rebuilding the city. The city continued to prosper and grew in importance until the second century A.D. when it was awarded the Neokorus of Asia by Commodus. This established Laodicea as the official site of imperial worship in the area. This honor was repeated early in the third century by Caracalla. In A.D. 494 the city was hit with another devastating earthquake from which it never fully recovered. The site was finally abandoned after the Seljuk Turks conquered the territory in the late 11th century.

127 Laodicea Theaters
Most ancient cities were happy with one theater. The prosperous city of Laodicea had two.

Fig. 128 Laodicea Byzantine Church

A large newly excavated church at Laodicea holds a well preserved cross shaped baptistery and opus sectile mosaic floor.

Christian Beginnings at Laodicea

The beginnings of the Christian church at Laodicea are not certain, but it seems probable that Paul's helpers were responsible for first introducing the Gospel to Laodicea. When Paul wrote to the Colossians he mentioned a coworker named Epaphras from nearby Colossae who had deep concerns for those at Laodicea (Col 4:12-13). Since the two cities were only fifteen kilometers from one another, Epaphras seems to have evangelized both cities. Paul himself had a strong stake in the development of the Laodicean church and in fact wrote a letter to the Laodicean church that has been lost (Col 4:16). Near the end of the first century one of the letters of the Apocalypse was written to the church at Laodicea. The short letter mentioned the Laodicean wealth and the textiles for which the city was known. The letter chastised the church for being complacent (or 'lukewarm'), indolent and satisfied with little more than their wealth and possessions (Rev 3:15-17).

The Current Remains at Laodicea

The ancient city of Laodicea is currently being excavated by the local university at Pammukale at such a rapid pace that it is hard to keep up with the new developments. As the ruins emerge from the ground, the affluence of the city becomes more evident. The wealth of Laodicea is reflected in the fact that the ancient city had two theaters and at least four baths. Both theaters are on the northern slopes of the city and both theaters are in fairly good shape. The northwestern one is smaller and was probably built during the second century A.D. The northeastern theater is a bit larger and was built during the Hellenistic period with renovations during the Roman period (fig. 127). Midway between the two theaters is a large Corinthian temple. Southeast of the larger theater is

195

A column fragment from Syria Street was inscribed with a menorah, *shofar* and palm branch. Sometime later a cross was carved growing out of the top of the menorah.

Fig. 130 Laodicea Syria Street Nymphaeum

On Syria Street a decorative two story fountain (nymphaeum) provided water to the residents of the city.

Fig. 131 Laodicea Temple A

It has been suggested that the recently excavated Temple A was originally built for Apollo during the first century A.D. and was later used for the imperial cult. Others believe the temple was originally constructed during the second century. Ancient sources report that an imperial temple dedicated to Domitian was built in Laodicea during the first century.

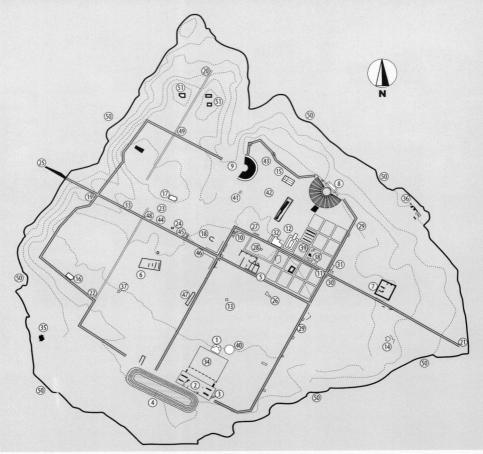

1. Parliament Building (Bouleuterion)
2. Southern Bath Complex
3. First Water Distribution Terminal
4. Stadium
5. Central Baths
6. Western Baths
7. Eastern Baths
8. North Theater
9. West Theater
10. Caracalla Nymphaeum (Fountain)
11. Syrian Road
12. Temple A
13. Rotunda (Circular Roman Structure)
14. Octagonal Roman Building
15. North Church
16. Southwest Church
17. Northwest Church
18. Four armed Byzantine Church
19. Ephesian Gate and Byzantine Gate
20. Hierapolis Gate
21. Syrian Gate

22. Aphrodisias Gate and Southern Byzantine Gate
23. West Agora
24. Macellum on the Ephesian Road
25. Roman Bridge Above Asopos
26. Second Water Distribution Terminal
27. First and Second Memorial Pathways (Propylene)
28. Central Agora
29. Early Roman Walls
30. Eastern Byzantine Gate and Towers
31. Eastern Byzantine Nymphaeum (Fountain)
32. S. Severus Nymphaeum (Fountain)
33. Ephesian Road
34. South Agora
35. South Roman Village
36. North Workshops
37. Southwestern Temple
38. House A
39. Street Water Distribution Center
40. Praetorian (City Guest House)
41. Building Near Western Theater

42. Temple
43. Temple
44. Temple
45. Memorial Walkway
46. Ephesian Portico
47. South Nymphaeum
48. West Nymphaeum
49. Northwestern Byzantine Gate
50. Necropolis
51. Asopos I-II
52. Laodicean Church
53. Central Church
54. Stadium Road
55. Nymphaeum B, Toilets and Water Depo
56. Temple A on the Eastern Road
57. Roman Peristyle Home
58. Holy Way Portico
59. Stadyum Church
60. Rectangular Building

LAODICEA

Design by **TUTKU TOURS**

Fig. 132 Laodicea Stadium

A huge stadium was built at Laodicea with a large bath complex on the perimeter.

a large Byzantine church that has recently been exposed. The church is very well preserved and contained beautiful mosaic floors and an interesting cross shaped baptistery (fig. 128).

South of the theaters there was the major east-west street (Decumanus Maximus) that has been excavated. This road, called the Syrian Street, dates from the late first century A.D. and was paved and colonnaded. Two hundred and eighty meters of the road have currently been exposed. At the center of the city on the south side of the street was the commercial agora. The agora was surrounded on three sides (east, south and west) with a colonnaded stoa and shops behind the stoa. Among the many columns found in this area, one is particularly important. A damaged column section was nicely inscribed with a seven branched menorah flanked by a palm branch and a shofar (ram's horn). Growing out of the top of the menorah is a large cross which may have been inscribed later (fig. 129). This unique inscription can be interpreted in various ways, but the most likely interpretation would be either that the Laodicean church believed that it owed it origin to the Jewish community in Laodicea or the inscription could simply indicate a close

cooperative relationship between the church and synagogue at Laodicea. It is important to note that if the cross was added later, those who inscribed it did not damage the Jewish symbols beneath it.

The central baths backed up to the agora on the south side. During the fourth century these baths were converted into a church. Across the street on the north side of Syria Street was a decorative two storied nymphaeum with columns, niches and statues dedicated to Septimius Severus (A.D. 193 - 211) (fig. 130) and east of the nymphaeum was a temple for the imperial cult (late second century A.D.). (fig. 131). This temple has recently been reconstructed and was one of the chief attractions at the city. Further east on the street was the eastern bath complex. Another nymphaeum, dedicated to Caracalla (early third century), was located much further to the west. Another bath (possibly) was southwest of Caracalla's nymphaeum. The remains here include several arches, but little more has been uncovered to assist in the identification of the nearby structures. Yet another bath is at the southern extremity of the city, just north of the stadium, where the bath was once a part of a gymnasium complex. According to an inscription on the building, this complex was built in the first half of the second century A.D. in honor of Hadrian. North of the gymnasium baths was the state agora with a bouleterion on the north side of the agora. Five rows of seats are visible in the bouleterion. South of the gymnasium baths there was a stadium dedicated to Vespasian in A.D. 79 (fig. 132). The stadium is terribly overgrown, but is enormous, measuring about 350 meters in length. Further south are the remains of an aqueduct and water pipes that led to a water tower near the eastern end of the stadium that functioned as a decorative nymphaeum and castellum (a structure for the distribution of water throughout the city).

On the west side of the city the triple arched Ephesus Gate led to a Roman bridge straddling the Asopus River, a tributary to the Lycus River. The Syrian Gate lay on the eastern side of town. Stone blocks from this gate contain an inscription noting that it was dedicated to Zeus and Domitian around A.D. 84–85.

Chapter 6

Asia Minor in the Years Following the New Testament

The Life and Letters of Ignatius

Very little is known about the early years of Ignatius. He was appointed bishop of the church at Antioch in Syria around A.D. 68 and it is possible, but not certain, that he was a disciple of John the apostle. Ignatius ministered to the church at Antioch during Domitian's persecutions but was caught up in the later persecutions during the reign of Trajan.

Ignatius was arrested for his faith in Christ at Antioch and he was taken through Anatolia in route to Rome where he was executed. Ignatius described the ten soldiers who were assigned to bring him to Rome as ten leopards that grew worse as they were kindly treated (*Ignatius to the Romans*, 5). As he was passing through western Asia Minor Ignatius was able to meet with Christians from a number of churches who had heard of his arrest and impending execution. A reconstruction of the journey seems to have taken Ignatius through the Lycus Valley, where he probably met with members of the Colossae, Laodicea and Hierapolis churches. From there, he traveled north to Philadephia and then east to Smyrna. At Smyrna Ignatius met with members of the churches at Ephesus, Magnesia on the Maeander and Tralles. In Smyrna he also began writing letters to a few of the churches in Asia Minor. From Smyrna, letters were sent to the churches in Ephesus, Magnesia, Tralles and Rome. Ignatius was then taken from Smyrna north through Pergamon and on to the port at Troas. While at Troas Ignatius wrote another three letters: to the churches at Philadelphia and Smyrna along with a personal letter to the bishop of Smyrna, Polycarp. Crossing into Macedonia, they caught the Via Egnatia which led them to Philippi and on to Rome where Ignatius was martyred. According to the early church historian Eusebius the execution took place in A.D. 108.

Ignatius' letters give us valuable information regarding the situation in Asia Minor shortly after the seven letters of the apocalypse. Written little more than a decade after Revelation, Ignatius' letters expose the state of affairs in the churches during the reign of Trajan. Thus, it is important that we examine other ancient cities in Asia Minor where churches existed. Acts, Paul's letters and the book of Revelation only mention a few of the churches in the larger cities. But Christianity had spread throughout Asia Minor by the end of the first century, infiltrating smaller cities and villages.

Two issues emerged as Ignatius' dominant concerns: the struggle with false teaching and how the church should cope with continued persecutions. Of the seven letters five were written to churches in the area that we have been dealing with: Ephesus, Magnesia, Tralles, Philadelphia and Smyrna. Another was written to the bishop (Polycarp) at Smyrna. Thus, we are able to trace the historical trajectory and theological struggles in the churches of Asia Minor up to the beginning of the second century.

In his letter to the Ephesians, Ignatius briefly alluded to the persecutions taking place in the area: "you are a highway for those who are executed for God" (12:2). The use of the term "highway" probably indicates that a large number of Christians had passed through Ephesus (or were executed in Ephesus) at the time of their martyrdom. In response to their antagonists, Ignatius advised the Ephesians to imitate Christ: in response to their anger – exhibit patience, to their slander – respond with prayer, to their cruelty – manifest gentleness (10:2-3). When writing to the Magnesians, Ignatius assured them that they would accede to God, if they patiently endured the abuse of the ruler of this age (1:3).

These concerns were also mentioned in a somewhat later letter of Polycarp to the church at Philippi. The letter was written to inquire about Ignatius' fate and to pass along copies of Ignatius' Anatolian letters to the Christians at Philippi. The letter was written a short time after Ignatius' martyrdom and it also reveals Polycarp's concern regarding the persecutions and troubles that the churches in Smyrna and Philippi were still dealing with. He exhorted the Philippians to "pray for kings and powers and rulers and for those who persecute and hate you" (12:3). He urged Christians to patiently endure their suffering, using Christ as an example of righteous endurance (8:2–9:1).

Perhaps a bigger problem in Ignatius' mind was the threat of false teaching. This matter occurs in his letters more than the issue of persecutions. Ignatius himself was eager to face his martyrdom and thus for Ignatius, the physical welfare of Christians took a back seat to the spiritual threats facing Christians in Asia Minor.

Ignatius praised the Ephesians for successfully resisting false teachers, but he acknowledged that these people were still lurking in Asia Minor. "I have learned that certain people from there have passed your way with evil doctrine, but you did not allow them to sow it among you" (9:1). Also, "There are some who maliciously and deceitfully are accustomed to carrying about the Name while doing other things unworthy of God. You must avoid them as wild beasts" (7:1). To the Trallians (6:1), Ignatius referred to false teaching as "strange plants" (the same term was also used in the letter to the Philadelphians – 3:1). He likened heresy to poison and claimed that the false teachers deceptively mixed their poison with the sweet wine of the gospel (6:2). These issues were also raised in Ignatius' letter to the Philadelphians. The false teachers were described as wolves who attempted to lure astray the sheep of God's flock (2:1). Ignatius exhorted the Christians at Philadelphia to not be deceived by strange doctrines (3:3) and to shun the beliefs of the "tombstones" who echoed the wicked arts and plottings of the prince of darkness (6:2).

Some false teachers insisted that Christians should maintain Jewish practices (the Ebionite heresy). In his letter to the Magnesians Ignatius asserted that such teachings were absurd (8:1 & 10:3). Writing to the Philadelphians he insinuated that some of these Jewish teachings were being disseminated by Gentile Christians (6:1). These Jewish Christian tendencies were evident earlier in this area of Asia Minor in the first epistle to Timothy (1:6-8).

Docetic teachings similar to what we encountered in the epistles of John are also evident among the heretics mentioned by Ignatius. In the letter to the Trallians Ignatius emphasized that Jesus "truly was born . . . truly was persecuted by Pontius Pilate, was truly crucified and killed . . . and was truly raised from the dead" (9:1-2). He also refuted those who claimed that Jesus suffered in appearance only (10:1). A similar reference to false teachers who assert that Jesus suffered only in appearance is found in Ignatius' letter to the church at Smyrna (2:1). Ignatius further contended "I know and believe that he was in the flesh even after the resurrection" (3:1). As we have noted previously, these docetic doctrines were a stock feature of Gnosticism, which first emerged during the latter years of the first century and flourished during the second century.

The Ancient History and Archaeology of Magnesia Ad Maeandrum (near Tekinköy)

The Ancient History of Magnesia Ad Maeandrum

According to Magnesia's earliest traditions and an ancient inscription, Magnesia was founded by soldiers of Agamemnon's army after their return from the Trojan war. Having been instructed by the Delphic Oracle to migrate to Crete, the Magnesians from Thessaly first moved to the island of Crete. After receiving further instructions from the oracle, the Magnesians went through another move to the Manthios (Maeander) River in Asia Minor. An ancient inscription from Magnesia claims that this was the first city in Asia Minor established by Greeks. Even though the city was located in Ionia, the city was founded by Aeolians and was never a member of the Ionian League. Likewise, it was never a member of the Aeolian League.

Early in the seventh century B.C. Magnesia was sacked by the Lydian king Gyges. A short time later (657 B.C.) the city was destroyed by the Cimmerians. The city was rebuilt with the assistance of the Ephesians. By 530 B.C. the city came under the control of the Persians as they absorbed most of the surrounding territory. Later when Themistokles was exiled by the Athenians, he moved to Magnesia around 467 B.C. and lived there until his death. Thibron of Sparta liberated the city from the Persians in 400 B.C. and relocated the city a short distance away to Mount Thorax where the remains are currently located. Shortly thereafter, the Persians regained control of the city and held it until the time of Alexander in 334 B.C. For the next 150 years, the city was controlled by several of Alexander's successors, until the Pergamene Kingdom was given control of the area around 189 B.C. In 133 B.C. the Romans acquired the Pergamene territories. When Mithradates VI of Pontus rose up against the Roman presence in Asia Minor in 88 B.C., the Magnesians resisted Mithridates, and after the Romans regained Asia Minor they rewarded the Magnesians with independence. The A.D. 17 earthquake in Asia Minor destroyed Magnesia and the city was assisted in their recovery with the help of the emperor Tiberius' benefactions. Magnesia flourished and grew during the Roman period and was one of the cities that Ignatius addressed in his letters from Smyrna at the end of the first century A.D.

Fig. 133 Magnesia ad Maeandrum Temple of Artemis

The magnificent temple of Artemis Leucophryeno (Artemis with white eyebrows) at Magnesia was thought to be the most beautiful temple in Asia Minor. Today the remains lie in a heap.

Fig. 134 Magnesia ad Maeandrum Altar of Artemis

The temple of Artemis Leucophryeno was built in the 2nd century B.C. Forty-three panels of the frieze from this temple depicting battles between the Greeks and Amazons are currently at the Louvre.

Fig. 135 Magnesia ad Maeandrum Agora, Eastern Stoa and Propylon

The large 215 by 125 meter agora was surrounded by stoas and an ornamental gateway (propylon) on the east. The propylon can be dated to the first century A.D.

Fig. 136 Magnesia ad Maeandrum Excedras

The western plaza in front of the Athena Temple included three podiums with two excedras between them. The excedras were used for seating and were "U" shaped to better accomodate discussions.

Christian Beginnings at Magnesia Ad Maeandrum

Magnesia Ad Maeandrum is only 25 kilometers from Ephesus and Paul's ministry at Ephesus likely resulted in an evangelistic ministry that extended to Magnesia. At Ephesus Paul established the School of Tyrannus where he prepared coworkers for evangelistic and ministerial work. Ignatius' Letter to the Magnesians (A.D. 108) was further evidence for a first century church at this site. In his letter, Ignatius wrote to the church commending the leader (bishop) of the congregation Damas, along with two presbyters, Bassus and Apollonius, and a deacon, Zotion. These representatives of the Magnesian church traveled to Smyrna and met with Ignatius as he was being taken to Rome for martyrdom. The letter refers to a church that was struggling (or had struggled) with those who continued to cling to Jewish beliefs and practices. This suggests that the church had a strong Jewish Christian presence.

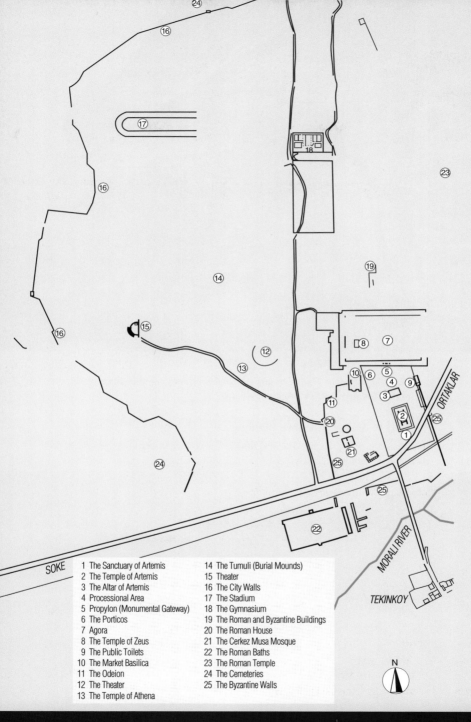

1 The Sanctuary of Artemis
2 The Temple of Artemis
3 The Altar of Artemis
4 Processional Area
5 Propylon (Monumental Gateway)
6 The Porticos
7 Agora
8 The Temple of Zeus
9 The Public Toilets
10 The Market Basilica
11 The Odeion
12 The Theater
13 The Temple of Athena
14 The Tumuli (Burial Mounds)
15 Theater
16 The City Walls
17 The Stadium
18 The Gymnasium
19 The Roman and Byzantine Buildings
20 The Roman House
21 The Cerkez Musa Mosque
22 The Roman Baths
23 The Roman Temple
24 The Cemeteries
25 The Byzantine Walls

SOKE

ORTAKLAR

MORALI RIVER

TEKINKOY

N

MAGNESIA

Design by **TUTKU TOURS**

Fig. 137 Tralles Baths

The three arches of Tralles' second century A.D. bath complex along with portions of the substructure are visible today.

Fig. 138 Tralles Unknown Building

A large building, whose date and function is currently unknown, has been excavated in ancient Tralles.

The Current Remains at Magnesia Ad Maeandrum

Even before the Magnesians relocated to the foot of Mount Thorax, the site was known for its sanctuary of Artemis, which dates to at least the sixth century B.C. The ancient temple that is currently visible at the site was dedicated to Artemis Leukophryene ("the white browed Artemis") and dates to the second or third century B.C. The foundation, portions of the cella and the massive fluted Ionian columns are scattered around the temple (fig. 133). The temple was the fourth largest Hellenistic temple in Asia Minor, measuring 41 by 67 meters, and had a pseudodipteral plan of eight by fifteen columns. It was built by Hermogenes of Priene (the architect of the temple of Dionysus at Teos). Just west of the temple lies the few remaining pieces of the large "U" shaped altar (fig. 134).

Northwest of the temple are the remains of latrines constructed between the third and fourth centuries A.D. and directly west of the temple lies the well preserved agora, surrounded by stoas and fronted with a decorative gateway (propylon) (fig. 135). The agora (with unequal sides roughly 123 by 215 meters) dates to the second or third century B.C., but the propylon was a newer addition dating to the first century A.D. A Byzantine wall constructed around 620 cut off the agora from the temple precincts, but excavators have opened the wall to expose the propylon. Along the eastern side of the agora, facing the temple precincts, are three podiums with inscriptions and two excedras designed for seating, between them

(fig. 136). In 2002, a cryptoporticus was discovered underneath the eastern stoa. A small temple was discovered in the southern part of the agora, dedicated to Zeus Sosipolis, "Zeus savior of the city." This dates to the second or third century B.C.

Outside of the agora, on its southeast side, is the market basilica, constructed in the second century A.D. This remarkable building was a large two-storied indoor market with an apse at its eastern end. Despite the presence of the apse, there is no evidence that the building was ever used as a church. A large capital was found inside the structure that was sculpted on three sides in high relief with scenes of Odysseus and the sea monster Scylla (fig. 139). Running further east, on the south side of the temple precinct there was a double colonnaded portico with shops lining the south.

Further south there was an Odeon that is scarcely visible today and a nicely preserved house outfitted with a bath, mosaics and frescoes. Outside of the Byzantine walls on the south there was a second or third century B.C. theater and further south a small, nicely restored first century A.D. theatron. Further west of these is a large horseshoe shaped stadium built during the Roman period and somewhat to the north of this there was a gymnasium. The city had two gymnasiums, both dated to the second or third century A.D., the second located East of the modern road.

Fig. 139 Magnesia ad Maeandrum Pilaster Capital Relief

A second century Market Basilica was built with a pilaster capital depicting a scene from Homer's Odyssey – the encounter with the sea monster Scylla. Shortly after the discovery, thieves damaged the piece and stole several of the heads.

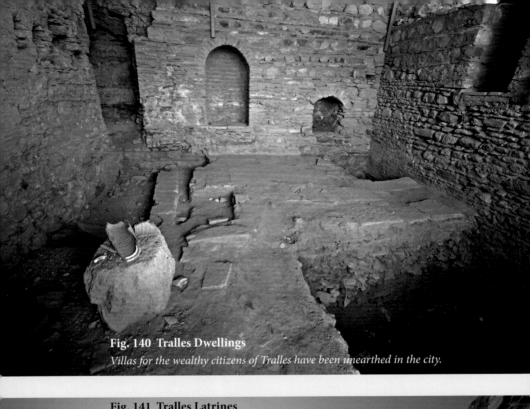

Fig. 140 Tralles Dwellings

Villas for the wealthy citizens of Tralles have been unearthed in the city.

Fig. 141 Tralles Latrines

A large latrine with an open air atrium provided relief in Tralles.

The Ancient History and Archaeology of Tralles (Aydın)

The Ancient History of Tralles

The earliest information we have regarding the founding of the city at Tralles comes from Strabo. However, scholars are skeptical of Strabo's account. The ancient geographer claimed that the city was founded by colonists from Argos in the Peloponnese and Trallians from Thrace. The city took its name from the barbarian Thracian settlers. According to Strabo, the region of the Maeander River was populated by various people including Carians, Lydians, Ionians and Aeolians, so perhaps having a diverse population at the city's inception as Strabo described was not so unusual. During his own time, Strabo declared that the city was wealthy and that many of the Asiarchs (rulers of Asia) came from the city. However, the history of the city is not well known. In 400 B.C. the Spartans unsuccessfully tried to seize the city from the Persians. Later, in 334 B.C. Alexander succeeded in taking the city and he used it as a base for his armies. After Alexander's death in 313, Antigonus captured the city, but upon his death in 301 the city came into the possession of the Seleucids. At this time the city was called Seleucia. After the battle of Magnesia in 189 B.C., Tralles was given to the Pergamene Kingdom, and when the Pergamene Kingdom was dissolved, Tralles became a part of the Roman Province of Asia Minor. Sometime during the Pergamene period the city's name was changed back to Tralles. Strabo adds that the city was ruled by the sons of Cratippus (whom he calls tyrants) during the war with Mithridates VI. During the time of Augustus, the city was destroyed by an earthquake and was rebuilt with the emperor's assistance. At this time the name of the city was changed again to Caesarea, but reverted back to Tralles in the years following Nero.

Christian Beginnings at Tralles

Ignatius' Letter to the Trallians (A.D. 108) notes that the bishop of Tralles Polybius visited Ignatius at Smyrna when he was in route to his martyrdom in Rome. The letter mentions the maturity of the congregation and its resistance to false teaching, suggesting that the emergence of Christianity in Tralles was not a recent development. The origin of the church is sheer speculation, but it is possible that a disciple from Paul's School of Tyrannus (Acts 19:9-10) had a hand in it. Paul trained coworkers at the school "for two years, so that all who lived in Asia heard the word of the Lord." Tralles was less than 50 kilometers from Ephesus and we know that one of those coworkers, Epaphras travelled much further up the Maeander River valley to evangelize Colossae, about 190 kilometers upstream (Col 1:7). To add to the speculation, Paul himself would have taken this route down the Maeander River valley on his third journey to Ephesus. Acts 18:23 indicates that he passed through Galatia and Phrygia "strengthening all the disciples" before arriving at Ephesus. Particular cities were not mentioned, but the passage suggests that Paul was doing evangelistic work along the way.

The Current Remains at Tralles

A Turkish military base currently covers two thirds of the ancient site and is thus, inaccessible. At the northern end of the site, a stadium and theater have been spotted in the past, but today both of these structures are hard to distinguish. Likewise in the north a necropolis and city wall are more evident. At the southern end of the site (east of the military zone) a little more can be seen. Most conspicuous are the three large arches of a Roman bath and gymnasium complex, dating to the late Roman period (fig. 137). New excavations begun in 1996 have shown that an early Roman bath stood here prior to the earthquake in 26 B.C. Sur-

Fig. 142 Metropolis Villa Mosaic

The reception hall of a villa near the theater contains a mosaic of Dionysus, the patron deity of the theater.

rounding the gymnasium and palaestra, these recent excavations have revealed more of the bath complex, in particular the caldarium (the hot water bath). Directly to the east of the gymnasium is what appears to be a two-storied pillared Roman basilica (fig. 138). Northeast of the gymnasium and bath complex, there is a row of eleven late Roman or early Byzantine shops that have been recently excavated (fig. 140). Roofing has been provided for these shops to protect them from the elements. At the eastern end of these shops, a huge latrine from the Roman period has been discovered (fig. 141). South of the gymnasium Jewish lamps were found in a building that may be a synagogue from the early third century A.D.

Metropolis and Nysa

Two sizeable cities located near Ephesus should be considered probable locations where churches were established in the first century. Neither Metropolis nor Nysa are mentioned in the New Testament or early Christian writings and there is currently no evidence of a Jewish presence in these cities. However, since Metropolis was located only twenty kilometers from Ephesus and Nysa was only seventy kilometers from Ephesus on the main route to the east, it is highly probable that these cities were evangelized. The lack of references to these cities in the earliest Christian literature could be an oversight or it could be that churches established in these cities were small and insignificant.

Metropolis (near Torbalı)

The Ancient History of Metropolis

The earliest remains at Metropolis date back to the Neolithic period and a recently discovered hieroglyphic seal (as yet undeciphered) may indicate a Hittite presence at the site during the Bronze Age. Several nearby caves, likewise dating to the Bronze Age, were found to contain the remains of shrines dedicated to an ancient Anatolian fertility goddess. The name of the city itself, Metropolis, reflects the importance given to the Anatolian mother god (Meter Gallesia) and the place was probably given this name because of these shrines.

The city was founded in the late eighth century B.C. upon the slopes of Alaman Dağı and the city flourished during the Hellenistic period. Metropolis became a primary center for the production of wine according to Strabo. It became a part of the Pergamene kingdom up until the kingdom was ceded to the Romans. At the time of the Mithridatic wars, Metropolis was first overtaken by the Pontic king Mithridates VI, but with the approach of Sulla and the evident success of the Romans, Metropolis along with several other cities revolted against Mithridates VI in

Fig. 143 Metropolis Theater and Altars

Three well preserved altars dedicated to Augustus have been recovered in the theater.

85 B.C. According to Appian, Mithridates inflicted punishment upon the rebels and retook the city, only later to be taken by the Romans as Mithridates was forced to withdraw. During the Roman period the city expanded to the area below the slopes and this expansion continued during the Byzantine period.

The Current Remains at Metropolis

The earliest remains at Metropolis are centered upon the hill. Later occupation carried the city to the lower slopes and plains below. An acropolis crowned the top of the hill with Hellenistic defensive walls encircling the site. The primary gate to the acropolis lies on the east. Most significantly, the temple of Ares lies somewhere within the acropolis walls. Temples to Ares, the Greek god of war, are rare in Anatolia. Although the temple is yet to be located, inscriptions found at Metropolis indicate that this temple to Ares was the second to be established in Anatolia, following the temple to Ares at Halicarnassus.

A Hellenistic bouleuterion was constructed midway down the slopes. During the Byzantine period the walls from the acropolis were extended down the slopes and ran directly through the bouleuterion, dividing it in half. A nicely restored late Hellenistic theater can be seen on the lower slopes. During the early Roman period three cylindrical altars were added to the theater and dedicated to Augustus. The theater was also outfitted with four seats for priests, one of which bears Hermes' caduceus. A recently discovered villa contains an excellent mosaic floor with human representations and the scant remains of frescoed walls.

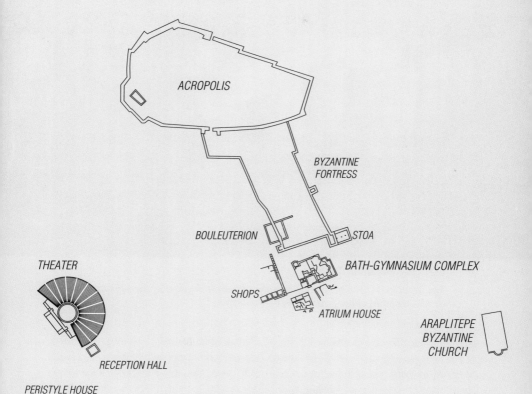

ACROPOLIS

BYZANTINE
FORTRESS

BOULEUTERION

STOA

THEATER

BATH-GYMNASIUM COMPLEX

SHOPS

ATRIUM HOUSE

ARAPLITEPE
BYZANTINE
CHURCH

RECEPTION HALL

PERISTYLE HOUSE

LOWER BATH
(HANYIKIGI)

N

METROPOLIS

Design by **TUTKU TOURS**

Fig. 144 Metropolis Baths

The hypocaust (heating system) is evident beneath the floor of the caldarium (hot water bath) of the gymnasium bath complex.

A second century A.D. Roman bath complex is likewise located on the slopes. This bath evidently contained a section for visitors to the city and had sections for hot (caldarium) and cold (frigidarium) water bathing. Down the slope a latrine was erected and a palaestra has been identified next to the baths. Higher on the slope, directly above the bath is a third century B.C. stoa measuring 70 by 11 meters. The stoa was bisected by a wall running laterally along the length. This stoa was destroyed by an earthquake in 17 A.D.

Nysa (Sultanhisar)

The Ancient History of Nysa

Strabo gives us the best understanding of Nysa. Strabo's mentor Aristodemus lived in Nysa and Strabo himself was educated in the city. Strabo claims that three broth- ers founded three cities in the area and that the cities were combined at some point and the city was known as Athymbra, after one of the brothers. Inscriptions

216

down to the third century B.C. refer to the inhabitants as Athymbrians. Around 200 B.C. the name of the city was changed to Nysa. This was probably a name given to the city to honor one of the Seleucid princesses or queens. Stephanus of Byzantium asserts that the city was founded by the Seleucids and some Seleucid connection is probable, since writings confirm that official Seleucid decrees were conferred upon the city as early as 281 B.C. Evidence from the site indicates that the city was founded no earlier than the third century. By 190 B.C. the city fell under the dominion of the Pergamene kingdom and when the Pergamene kingdom fell in the latter part of the second century, Nysa was given to the Romans.

Nysa was known for producing philosophers and orators, but the primary notoriety of the city came from the nearby Charonium in Acharaca (Salavath) 6 km. to the west. The Charonium was a cave supposedly leading underground to Hades. At the cave there was a Ploutonium, a temple dedicated to the god of the underworld and to Persephone, his wife. This facility was used as a healing site for those with serious illnesses.

The Current Remains at Nysa

Nysa is divided by a ravine created by a stream that descends from Mount Messogis. The western bank of the ravine contains a gymnasium far to the south. A small gymnasium was built at this site in the first century B.C. and was replaced by a larger 70 by 165 meter gymnasium in the third or fourth century A.D. The site is poorly preserved with only one large arch remaining along with a few decorative pieces and a Corinthian column. Moving further north along the ravine, one can see the impressive substructure supports and barrel vaulting on the eastern side of the ravine. Further north are the remains of the stadium. The stadium was constructed straddling the stream and the ravine, with the stream running beneath the stadium. This afforded the opportunity to fill the stadium with water from the stream for naval battles. Unfortunately, the stadium is in quite poor shape.

Further up the bank on the west side of the ravine, are several shops from one of the main thoroughfares through the city and further north of these shops are a nymphaeum, Roman street and a second century library in excellent shape. The library currently stands to a height of two tall stories, but there may have been a third.

Well preserved vaulting to the north of the stadium provided a platform for the theater. This structure was built during the first century B.C. and was supplemented during the second and third centuries A.D. The theater is in excellent shape and had forty-nine rows capable of seating 12,000 people. The stage (or skene) was originally a two storied structure and currently contains several beautiful friezes in high relief with scenes of Dionysus (the patron deity of theater) and of the abduction and return of Persephone.

At least two Roman bridges connected the western part of the city with the eastern city. These are not in good shape, but the piers are evident. The bridge just north of the stadium supported the Decumanus Maximus, the major east-west street. Lower in the ravine, the stream ran through a large one hundred meter tunnel. On the eastern side of the city there were Roman baths and a very nice bouleterion with an entrance of composite construction. Parts of a frieze, matching that from the nearby porticoes of the agora, were miscellaneously placed in the newer entrance. The bouleterion was rectangular in shape with a semicircular interior. The building could hold 600 people and was built in the second century B.C.

Further east is the excellently reconstructed agora from the first century B.C. The agora was surrounded by porticoes. The porticoes on the eastern and northern sides had double rows of Ionian columns, while the western and southern sides had a single row of Doric columns. The northeast corner of the agora was later converted into a basilica. The entire agora measured 114 by 130 meters and the paved Cardo Maximus ran north along the western side of the agora.

Fig. 145 Nysa Theater Friezes

Several reliefs have been restored at the theater in Nysa. They depict scenes of Dionysiac celebrations and the abduction of Persephone by Pluto.

Fig. 146 Nysa Tunnel

A 100 meter long underground passage ran beside the theater and north of the stadium.

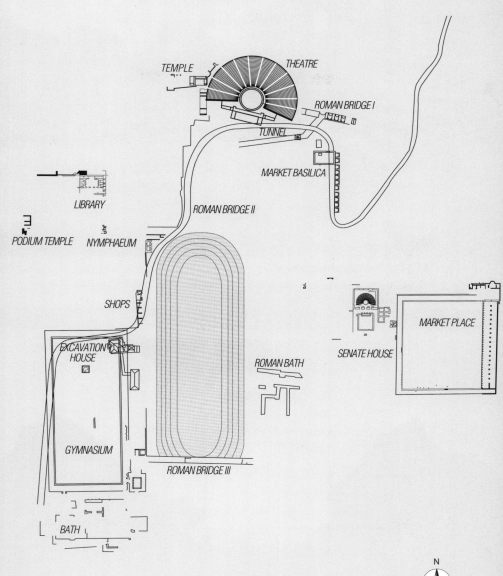

TEMPLE

THEATRE

ROMAN BRIDGE I

TUNNEL

MARKET BASILICA

LIBRARY

ROMAN BRIDGE II

PODIUM TEMPLE   NYMPHAEUM

SHOPS

EXCAVATION
HOUSE

MARKET PLACE

SENATE HOUSE

ROMAN BATH

GYMNASIUM

ROMAN BRIDGE III

BATH

N

NYSA

Design by **TUTKU TOURS**

Fig. 147 Nysa Bouleuterion

Originally built in the first century A.D. the bouleuterion could hold 600 people. The city leaders met here to discuss civic matters.

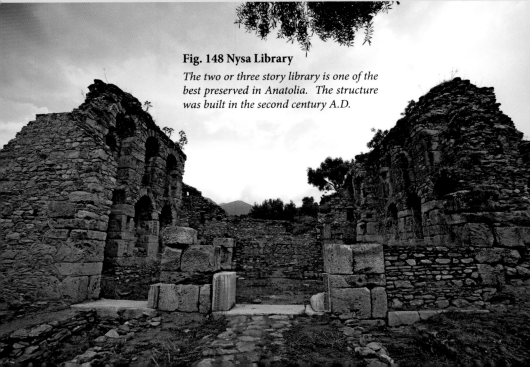

Fig. 148 Nysa Library

The two or three story library is one of the best preserved in Anatolia. The structure was built in the second century A.D.

Pliny the Younger's Trials of Christians

Pliny the Younger's Correspondence with Trajan

Pliny the Younger was appointed governor of Bithynia and Pontus in A.D. 110 during the reign of Trajan. The province of Bithynia abutted the province of Asia Minor and Pliny's term as governor was closely connected to the time and places of Ignatius' letters in Asia Minor. As a newly appointed governor, Pliny was made aware of the growing Christian population in the region and he was somewhat familiar with prior Roman policies as they related to the new religion.

Several letters of Pliny have survived and one of them, *Epistulae* 10. 96, gives us a great deal of insight into how the Roman governors and emperor dealt with Christians at the beginning of the second century. Shortly after taking office in Bithynia Pliny

Fig. 149 Phrygia Christians for Christians Inscriptions

Prior to the time of Constantine, the church went through sporadic but intense periods of persecution. Many funerary steles in Phrygia from the 3rd and early 4th centuries fearlessly proclaimed the faith of the deceased with crosses and "Christians for Christians" inscriptions. Kütahya Archaeological Museum.

ΤΟΝ ΘΕΟΝ ΣΟΙ ΜΗ ΔΙΚΗΣΙΣ

Α ΘΗΝΟΔΟΤΟΣ ΔΟΚΕΙ ΜΕΥΣΤΕ
ΧΝΕΙΤΗΣ

ΓΙΟΝ ΤΟΛΛΟΙΩΝ ...
ΟΣΙΩΤΕΡΟΝ ΑΝΔΡΑ ΝΑΠΙΣ
ΤΟΝ ΟΥΝΟΥ ΜΑ ΤΡΟΦΙΜΟΣ
ΘΕΟΥ ΠΡΟΝΟΙΑΝ ΜΕΓΑΛΗΝ
ΣΧΩΝ ΖΗΣΑΣ ΕΥΣΕΒΩΣ ΚΕ
ΕΝΔΟΞΗ ΜΕΤΑΣΤΑΣ ΕΝΘΑ
ΔΕ ΚΙΤΑΙ ΣΥΝ ΚΟΥΡΙΔΙΗ ΤΕ ΣΥΝΕΥ
ΝΩ ΡΟΥΦΙΝΗ ΤΗ ΣΕΜΝΟΤΑΤΗ ΚΝ ΥΥ
ΦΗ ΤΗ ΣΟΦΗ ΑΕ ΞΑΡΑΡΗ ΑΥΠΕ
ΙΝ Η ΧΑΡΙΝ ΤΕΚΝΑ ΠΑΡΕΣΧΑΝ
ΠΡΩΤΟΣ ΥΙΟΣ ΠΑΤΡΙΚΙΟΣ ΣΥ ΤΗΡ
ΤΗΣ ΧΡΙΣΤΟΥ ΥΠΑΡΧΩΝ Κ ΚΥΡΙ
ΛΟΣ ΚΗ ΟΥ ΓΑΤΕΡΕΣ ΑΥΤΩΝ ΠΑ
ωΙΑ ΚΟΝ ΟΝ Α ΕΘ ΘΟΦΡΟΝΙΣ ΕΣΤ

ΣΑΝ ΣΤΗ ΛΗΝ ΕΚ ΤΩΝ ΕΙΔΙΩΝ ΑΝΑΛΩΜΑ
ΤΩΝ ΧΡΗΣΤΙΑΝΟΙ ΧΡΗΣΤΙΑΝΟΙΣ

was confronted with the problem of Christians who were present within his domain. For the Christians who were seized and brought before him, Pliny followed what he understood to be the procedures and policies of the governors who preceded him in the office. At the same time, he wrote a letter to Trajan in order that the emperor might clarify and confirm (or perhaps correct) the practices that he was following. Among Pliny's collection of letters we also have Trajan's response (*Epistulae* 10.97) which affirmed Pliny's actions.

At the outset of his letter, Pliny acknowledged that he had never participated in the trials of Christians. However, when Christians were dragged before him, Pliny prosecuted them and executed those who were found guilty. It is clear from Pliny's correspondence that there had been an established Roman policy for dealing with Christians. It is not clear how far back in time this policy can be traced but it seems reasonable to assume that the policy took shape during Domitian's reign and continued through Nerva's and Trajan's reigns as emperors. The book of Revelation offers somewhat vague details, often couched in symbolic terminology, that give us a glimpse of what transpired during that time.

Pliny took it for granted that the mere confession of the Christian faith was a crime deserving of death. Pliny even considered whether or not apostate Christians who had given up the faith as many as twenty years earlier should be punished. Moreover, Pliny asked Trajan whether or not young Christian children should be given mercy. All of this reflects a severe and coldhearted posture that had been established toward Christians in the years leading up to the time when Pliny took office.

Through his interrogations Pliny acknowledged that these Christians committed no crimes. The apostates who were questioned maintained that the Christians bound themselves with an oath not to commit crimes, not to steal, not to commit adultery and not to lie. Pliny took this testimony to be true, yet he still believed that Christians should be punished, not because they posed a threat to Roman rule, but simply because of their obstinate refusal to follow the will of the emperor.

Those who had been accused of being Christians, but denied that they ever were,

Fig. 150 Phrygian Christians Remembered in Life and Death
Family members set up this stele for a loved one who "through the providence of God lived piously and was highly honored." The monument was also erected "for the cause of Christ" and for the support of "Christians for Christians." Kütahya Archaeological Museum.

Fig. 151 Phrygia Tombstones

Many of these "Christians for Christians" funerary steles display a cross sur-rounded with a wreath. Some scholars believe they represent the Christian community's protest against the antagonistic secular society. These steles are on display in the Kütahya Archaeological Museum.

had to prove their denial by praying and worshipping images of the gods and the em-peror and by cursing Christ. Those people were released. For those who confessed that they had been Christians, Pliny offered an opportunity to deny their faith. He claimed that he questioned them a second and third time threatening them with death. Pliny was unsure of how to deal with those who renounced their faith. His question was: should they be punished for their past participation in this cult? On the other hand, Pliny had no question about how to deal with those who persisted in the faith. Those Christians were executed.

Through his actions Pliny came to realize the breadth of the problem. He recounted that the disease (as he called it) had spread to persons of all ages, sexes and social classes. He realized that the faith had spread throughout the cities, villages and countryside. Pliny was concerned about the large numbers involved in the faith and wrote to Trajan asking him for advice regarding how he should proceed. Pliny suspended the proceedings against the Christians until he heard back from Trajan.

Trajan's response affirmed Pliny's actions. However, Trajan continued by indicating that Pliny should not aggressively pursue the issue by going about looking for Christians. Nevertheless, Trajan stated that Christians who were denounced and found guilty should be punished as Pliny had done. Trajan also indicated that anyone who abandoned the faith should be given mercy and a pardon.

This correspondence between Pliny and Trajan is important not only for insights into what was happening in Bithynia and Pontus, but these letters also give us a glimpse into what was happening throughout the Roman empire. When Pliny took office in Bithynia in A.D. 109 he was familiar with the Roman practice of persecuting Christians elsewhere in the empire. However, Pliny did not know how this practice was to operate in his domain. By the end of the first century Christianity had sunk deep roots into Asia Minor, Bithynia, Galatia, Cappadocia and Pontus. The first epistle of Peter was addressed to Christians in these regions. With the large number of Christians who represented all levels of society in the province, Pliny was asking Trajan: how far do we go with the intimidation and persecution of these people?

Other letters of Pliny may also refer to the presence of Christians in Bithynia, although the word Christian is lacking in these letters. In *Epistulae* 10.33 Pliny wrote to Trajan asking permission to establish an association for firemen. The city of Nicomedia had suffered a devastating fire which destroyed two public buildings and several private homes while the people stood by helplessly. Pliny requested Trajan's consent to create a small fireman's association not to exceed 150 people, while guaranteeing that the association would not engage in subversive activities. The Romans were cautious of all associations, fearing that these groups might be involved in surreptitious and seditious activity against the empire. Christian gatherings in particular were looked upon with great suspicion. Since the Christians refused to venerate Caesar and refused to participate in the imperial temples they were accused of treason.

Trajan's response (*Epistulae* 10.34) was to refuse Pliny's request to establish an association of firemen. Trajan replied that these cities (referring to Nicomedia and Nicaea) were notorious for creating disturbances through factions like these. Trajan's fear was that they would become a secret brotherhood (*hetaeria*). The Latin term *hetaeria* was used with negative connotations and may be translated "cabals" or "conspirators." The same term was also used in Pliny's above mentioned letter regarding Christians (*Epistulae* 10.96.7). There Pliny claimed that the Christians stopped gathering together after he issued an edict banning the existence of secret brotherhoods (*hetaerias*). Thus, it appears that Trajan's reference to secret brotherhoods in 10.34 was primarily concerned with Christian congregations. It is also possible that the persons who were condemned in yet another letter (*Epistulae* 10.31) and whose sentences were terminated or reduced to lesser punishments were Christians. Pliny stated that they were currently living respectable and peaceable lives.

We have also found several funerary inscriptions from this area that can be dated to the second century which bear testimony of a large Christian community (figs. 149, 150 and 151). These inscriptions were mostly found in northern Phrygia near the borders of Bithynia and Asia Minor. These inscriptions were grave steles that bore the names of the deceased and included sundry details of the person's life. Additionally, however, these inscriptions included the expression "Christians for Christians" and they often included Christian symbols, particularly the cross. Written during the turbulent and precarious times of the Antonine and Severan dynasties these funerary inscriptions were evidence that the sporadic persecutions levied against the Christian communities did not suppress the testimony of the growing church.

The Ancient History and Archaeology of Nicomedia (Izmit)

The Ancient History of Nicomedia

Stephanus of Byzantium relays the myth that the site at the inner recess of the Astakene Gulf was founded by Astakus, the son of Poseidon and the nymph Olbia. The site was named Astakus, after its founder. Other sources indicate that Greek colonists from Megaris founded the site in 711 B.C. Thucydides claimed that a tyrant named Euarchus ruled the city from around 430 to 420 B.C. By the early fifth century B.C., the northwest area of Anatolia had been overrun by Thracians who crossed over the Bosphorus and occupied the region. Herodotus claimed that they were led by Bassaces, the son of Artabanus. They called themselves Strymonians, after the Strymon River from whence they had come. During the fourth century, they fought with the Greek cities on the coast and after Alexander's death, under the leadership of Zipoites, they achieved three victories against Lysimachus. As a consequence, Zipoites proclaimed himself king of Bithynia in 297 B.C. However, as a consequence of the fighting, the city of Astakus was largely destroyed. Pausanias suggested that Zipoites, the father of Nicomedes I refounded a city at the site named Zipoition, which was later changed to Nicomedia. Stabo, Arrian and others however, state that Nicomedes I rebuilt and refounded the damaged city around 264 B.C. and named it after himself.

Nicomedia was founded at the far eastern edge of the Astakene Gulf and possessed an excellent harbor. All roads heading to the Bosphorus from Anatolia passed through Nicomedia, making it a strategic city for both sea and land travel. After the city was reestablished its population was increased by importing people from elsewhere in the area and it immediately became the capital and residence of the Bithynian kings. Stephanus claimed that Nicomedia was also known as Olbia and it has been suggested that the newly founded Nicomedia was formed from the combination of the gulf cities of Olbia and Astakus. Bithynia maintained its independence for most of the second century and in the early years of the first century B.C. until the final Bithynian king Nicomedes IV turned over the kingdom to the Romans in 74 B.C. Rome's Carthaginian arch enemy Hannibal sought refuge in Nicomedia in his final years. The Bithynian king Prusias I welcomed Hannibal and enlisted his aid in a war with the Pergamene kingdom, an ally of Rome's. The Romans intervened and demanded that the Bithynians surrender Hannibal. With the prospect of falling into the hands of the Romans, Hannibal committed suicide in 182 B.C. It is believed that his grave is in Libyssa (modern Gebze), 35 kilometers west of Nicomedia.

During the Roman period the prominent tribes Dia, Hiera, Asklepias and Poseidonias were known to reside in the city. An imperial temple to Augustus was built in Nicomedia in 29 B.C. The city was frequently mentioned in letters of Pliny the Younger, who was governor of Bithynia during the reign of Trajan. The city thrived up through the Byzantine Period. In A.D. 286 the emperor Diocletian made the city his eastern capital during his reign. Constantine used the Nicomedia as his capital until he moved the capital to Byzantium in 330 and renamed it Constantinople.

Fig. 152 Nicomedia Aqueduct
A large aqueduct that transported water to the ancient city of Nicomedia.

The Current Remains at Nicomedia

The large city of Izmit has grown up on top of the ancient city of Nicomedia, thus limiting what can be seen and excavated in the old city. Portions of a city wall can be seen here and there in the city. The vaulted substructures of a poorly preserved theater and a temple to Augustus are also to be seen. A small necropolis is located a short distance to the north of the city in a small park and further north there are the scant remains of an aqueduct (fig. 152). Near the aqueduct there is a small fountain with a Greek inscription and a short distance away there are Hel-lenistic burial mounds (tumuli), possibly of the Bithynian kings. Illegal digs indicate that these underground tombs have been recently entered. Illegal digs destroy a great deal of what can be learned through a scientific excavation, but the problem of illegal digs is ubiquitous throughout Turkey (fig. 153). A very nice museum exists in Izmit near the shore in the center of the city. Several nice indoor displays are overshadowed by an even better collection of antiquities outdoors in the gardens.

The Ancient History and Archaeology of Nicaea (Iznik)

The Ancient History of Nicaea

The mythological origins of Nicaea indicate that Dionysus, the god of Wine, founded this city and named it after his lover Nicaea. Excavations have revealed that the site of Nicaea was first occupied around 2500 B.C. More recently, Strabo claimed that the site was colonized by Bottiae-ans (in ancient Macedonia) as early as the 7th century B.C. and that the place was called Angore. After Alexander's conquests, in 316 B.C. Antigonus Monophthalmus established a city at this place and named it after himself, Antigoneia. Following the battle of Ipsus in 301, Lysimachus gained control of the city and renamed it after his wife, Nicaea. After Lysimachus' death in 281, Nicaea was taken by Nicomedes I and the city functioned as the capital of the kingdom of Bithynia until the capital was moved to Nicomedia in 265. The city was strategically located on trade routes and throughout the third century the town flourished and was often the residence of the kings of Bithynia. When Nicomedes IV died in 74 B.C., he offered Bithynia to the Romans and the Senate promptly made Bithynia a province, naming Nicaea as its capital.

The city prospered throughout the Roman Imperial peri-

Fig .153 Nicomedia Tomb
An illegal dig at a nobleman's tomb in ancient Nicomedia.

od. At that time three main tribes populated the city: the Sebaste, the Aureliane, and the Dionysiae. Augustus significantly added to the city's infrastructure and during the reign of Claudius, Nicaea became the chief city of Bithynia. In A.D. 123 the emperor Hadrian visited the city and Nicaea maintained its prominent position up through the Byzantine period. The emperor Constantine had a palace constructed on the Lake and the first and seventh Ecumenical Councils were held in Nicaea in 325 and 787. The Nicene Creed, one of the first and most important doctrinal statements by the Christian church was formulated at the first Ecumenical council. Here 250 to 318 bishops from across the Mediterranean gathered together in Constantine's palace to discuss, debate and agree upon some of the primary Christian beliefs. After its conquest by the Ottoman Turks, the people of Iznik developed its ceramic tile industry into a world leader, so that in the centuries that followed Iznik tiles were produced to adorn mosques and palaces throughout the world.

Christian Beginnings at Nicaea

The first epistle of Peter is addressed to residents of Pontus, Cappadocia, Galatia, Asia and Bithynia. Although the epistle never explicitly states that Peter visited these regions, early Christian sources claim that he did. The apostles typically wrote their letters to Christian communities that they had personally established or supervised.

If it is accepted that Peter spent time in these regions, where did he go and where were the early Christian communities established? This is largely guesswork. However, based upon the patterns of Christian evangelists, one can posit some educated guesses. The early Christian evangelists typically targeted large and prominent cities within the Roman provinces. Nicaea was the chief city of Bithynia during Peter's lifetime and the city had a network of Roman roads that provided easy access to the city. If Peter traveled from the capital of Galatia, Ankyra, a Roman road led from there directly to Nicaea.

Fig. 154 Nicaea Menorah & Psalm Inscription

An underground pool (perhaps used as a baptistery) in an early church at Nicaea holds an ashlar block that was reused (probably from an earlier synagogue). The piece was inscribed with a menorah and a Greek inscription that quotes Psalm 136:25.

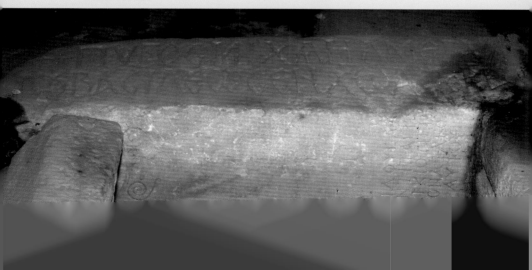

Fig. 155 Nicaea Istanbul Gate

The Istanbul Gate at Nicaea was first constructed in honor of the emperors Vespasian and Titus in the late first century and was reconstructed during the Byzantine period.

The early Christian evangelists also typically visited cities that had synagogues and a Jewish presence. A recently discovered inscription in Nicaea with a menorah and Jewish scripture, strongly suggests a Jewish presence in the city (fig. 154). Unfortunately, written sources tell us very little of the earliest Christian community in Nicaea. The second century apocryphal writing, Acts of Andrew, claims that the Apostle Andrew came to Nicaea where he cast out seven demons, baptized the people of the city and appointed a bishop to oversee the church. Pliny the Younger's correspondence with Trajan in the early second century also gives us some insight into the presence of Christian communities in Bithynia and the governor's and emperor's policy for dealing with them. Pliny's letter indicates that the number of Christians in the province was sizeable and that the faith had spread to the cities, towns and farms and had permeated all steps of society. The choice of Nicaea for the first Ecumenical Council, may be due to the founding of a church here at an early date and probably also testifies to the fact that the Nicaean church was strong and vibrant during the early fourth century.

Fig. 156 Nicaea Lefke Gate

The Lefke Gate guards the eastern side of the city. The decorative gates surrounding Nicaea were probably originally triumphal arches that were later connected with the walls of the city during the Byzantine period.

The Current Remains at Nicaea

The city was laid out in a grid on the eastern shore of Lake Iznik. The walls, which are still standing for the most part at a height of ten to thirteen meters, surround the city for four and a half kilometers and were built during the third century A.D. There were 114 defensive towers and four gates, one in each of the compass directions. The earlier Hellenistic walls have largely disappeared and the later walls reused some of the Hellenistic materials and encompassed a larger city than the Hellenistic one.

The gates of the old city are fascinating. They were originally constructed as triumphal arches by Vespasian and Titus in the late first century A.D. The later walls used these triumphal arches for the entrances into the city. Reconstruction of the walls and the gates themselves has made for an interesting mix of stones. In the north, the Istanbul Gate is a triple gate with one entrance inside of the other (fig. 155). The middle gate is the earliest one and is a Roman structure. A bronze dedication was inset above the middle arch, but it has not survived. The upper portion of the gate is visible and another three meters of the gate are still buried underground. There are two niches on the sides of the gate for statues and below these niches there were smaller pedestrian entrances (still largely buried) flanking a larger middle entrance used for traffic to the city. A relief of cavalry and another of three individuals can be seen in secondary use on the innermost gate. The innermost gate is crowned with two massive theatrical mask reliefs, which may have come from the theater.

On the east side of the city, the Lefke Gate is similar (fig. 156). Like the Istanbul Gate, this one also has three consecutive portals lying a few meters inside of the others. The outside gate is a composite construction with two statue bases built into the wall on either side of the opening. Two marble relief pieces are on the right wall, one of a sacrificial scene and the other of Roman infantry. This outer gate is flanked by two circular towers. Like the Istanbul Gate, the middle gate is the oldest and dates to the Roman period. Its construction was similar to the

middle Istanbul Gate and must have been constructed at the same time. Unlike the Istanbul Gate, this gate has been excavated down to its original ground level, so one can see not only the statue niches but also the pedestrian entrances flanking the center entrance. Above both of the pedestrian entrances an inscription can be found crediting Marcus Plancius Varus for the construction of the arch. During the reign of Vespasian (A.D. 69-79) Varus lived in Nicaea and served as the Proconsul of Bithynia. Outside of the triple gate an aqueduct still stands.

On the south side of the city, the Yenişehir Gate is a double gate. The innermost gate is Roman, but its construction differs from the Istanbul and Lefke Gates. Here there are no statue niches or pedestrian entrances. An inscription indicates that it was constructed (or perhaps reconstructed) in A.D. 268 by Claudius II Gothicus. The outer gate is of later construction and is flanked by two circular towers. The gate that originally stood on the west side of the city facing the lake has been destroyed.

Fig. 157 Nicaea Hagia Sophia Church

The Council of Nicaea, the first of seven ecumenical councils, met in Constantine's palace on the shores of Iznik Lake in 325 A.D. The seventh and last ecumenical council met here in the Hagia Sophia Church in 787.

Fig. 158 Nicaea Hagia Sophia Church

The interior of the Hagia Sophia Church. The church was built by Justinian in the 6th century and has recently been converted into a mosque.

In the southwest quadrant of the city, a Roman theater has been uncovered and is in fairly good shape. The theater was constructed during Pliny the Younger's term as governor of Bithynia in the early second century A.D. It has been suggested that the theater could hold 15,000 people, but the estimate seems too large compared with the capacity estimates of other theaters.

There are several important Byzantine churches in the city. In the very center of town is the Hagia Sophia (fig. 157). In the sixth century Justinian built a church here over an earlier church from the fourth century (fig. 158). Justinian's church was destroyed by an earthquake in the 11th century and the current basilica was constructed afterwards. Because of its location in the center of the city, this church probably covers the earlier Roman gymnasium that Strabo described as being at this point. The seventh Ecumenical Council met at this church in 787.

In the southeast quadrant of the city rests the largely destroyed Koimisis Church variously dated from the 6th to the 9th century. A little to the east of the Church of the Koimisis are the remains of a Byzantine fountain house. Downstairs, a small square pool, which may have functioned as a baptistery, is framed with stones in secondary use. One of the stones, dating anywhere from the fourth to the sixth century A.D., is inscribed with a menorah and the Greek text of Ps. 136:25.

Fig. 159 Nicaea - Ruins from Constantine's Palace

Little remains of the palace where Constantine called together 318 bishops from across the Mediterranean world. It was here that the Nicene Creed was hammered out.

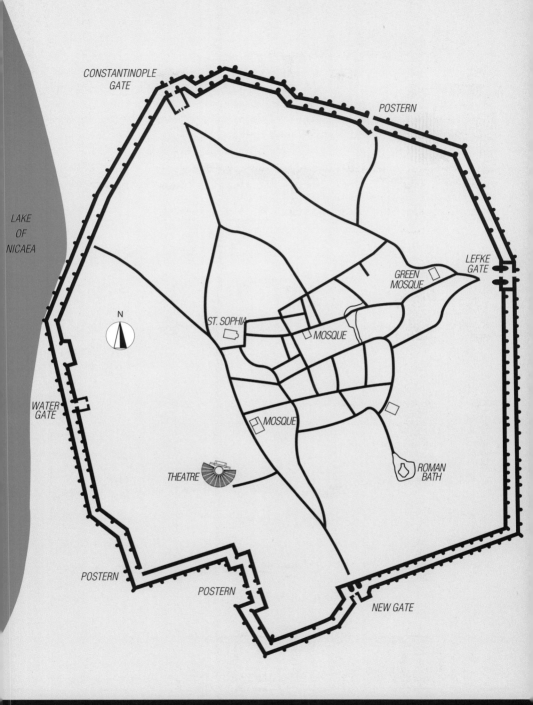

CONSTANTINOPLE
GATE

POSTERN

LAKE
OF
NICAEA

LEFKE
GATE

GREEN
MOSQUE

N

ST. SOPHIA

MOSQUE

WATER
GATE

MOSQUE

THEATRE

ROMAN
BATH

POSTERN

POSTERN

NEW GATE

NICAEA

Design by **TUTKU TOURS**

The lakeside palace of Constantine, where the first Ecumenical Council met, is in ruins. A little of the foundation is all that can be seen along the lake in the southwestern part of Iznik (fig. 159). The Iznik Museum in the northeast quadrant of the city houses many of the artifacts that have been found throughout the city. Five kilometers northeast of Iznik there is a twelve meter obelisk constructed as a burial monument to C. Cassius Philiscus. The obelisk, known as the Beştaş (or Dikilitaş), probably dates to the first century A.D. Seven kilometers north of town in Elbeyli, there is a fifth century underground tomb known as the Yeralti Mezar. The tomb is a family tomb with well preserved frescoes of peacocks and flowers.

Conclusion

The apostle Paul's journeys into ancient Anatolia had widespread consequences for the expansion of the gospel throughout the land. By the end of the first century the Christian faith had spread east to Syria and Mesopotamia, north to Cappadocia, Galatia, Pontus, Paphlagonia, Bithynia and Mysia, and west to Cilicia, Pamphylia, Pisidia, Lycia, Caria, Phrygia and Asia Minor. At the same time, Christianity was quickly emerging in other regions surrounding the Mediterranean Sea. The rapid advance of the Christian faith from one end of the Mediterranean world to the other was a shocking development in the eyes of pagans. This occurred not through force or

Fig. 160 Byzantine Basilica at Anazarbus

A cross flanked with an Alpha / Omega is visible on a Byzantine church in the Roman city of Anazarbus.

Fig.161 Arch of Titus, Rome

The Arch of Titus was erected in A.D. 82 by Emperor Domitian to commemorate the victories of his brother Titus in Judaea. The arch depicts the conquest of Jerusalem and details Jewish slaves who were brought back to Rome.

military conquests, but by the power of God's Spirit working through apostles and disciples who were burdened to carry the message of salvation to a world enshrouded in the darkness of sin and ignorance. In fact, the surprising expansion of the gospel took place in the face of tremendous opposition and persecution. Tertullian, writing at the end of the second century during the reign of Septimius Severus, expressed it this way while writing to Christian opponents: "We are but of yesterday, and we have filled every place among you - cities, islands, fortresses, towns, market-places, the military camps, tribes, town councils, palace, senate, forum. We have left nothing to you but the temples of your gods. . . . For now it is the immense number of Christians which makes your enemies so few, almost all the inhabitants of your various cities being followers of Christ. Yet you choose to call us enemies of the human race" (Apologeticus pro Christianis 37). "Crucify us, torture us, condemn us, grind us to dust . . . as often as we are mown down by you, the more we grow in numbers; the blood of the Christians is the seed" (Apologeticus 50).

The extensive expansion of the gospel was not accomplished through the work of Paul alone, but was facilitated by the work of numerous other apostles who carried the

238

Christian message far and wide throughout the Middle East. Luke's account in the Acts of the Apostles does not tell us enough to give us a good picture of how and by whom this evangelistic work took place. The book of 1 Peter was written to churches in Bithynia, Pontus, Cappadocia, Galatia and Asia (1 Peter 1:1). Although some scholars believe that Peter himself visited these churches, it is not at all clear how these congregations were established. Timothy, a disciple and follower of Paul's seems to have been in Ephesus at the time of Paul's death (1 Timothy 1). His ministry beyond Ephesus is unknown. Trustworthy early Christian writers tell us that the apostle John spent his last years in Ephesus and Asia Minor. From there, he wrote his gospel and letters. No doubt his ministry continued to broaden the expanse of the gospel not only in Asia Minor, but elsewhere as well. The apocalypse (Revelation) was written near the end of the first century in this same region. It addressed serious issues of false teaching and apostasy in the face of intense persecution in congregations throughout Asia Minor. As much as we learn from the Christian scriptures, however, they do not tell the whole story. The gospel found its way into numerous small villages and towns as well as into the larger cities mentioned in the Bible. Likewise, the gospel spread to the countryside as well as the large urban centers.

If we look outside of the scriptures into the writings of the church fathers and into the non-canonical writings, we get a glimpse of what was going on elsewhere. Several Apocryphal Acts of the Apostles described the travels of Andrew, Philip, Bartholomew, Prochorus, Thecla and other disciples in Anatolia. Despite the fact that some of these stories may be legendary, there is enough evidence to indicate that these disciples were heavily involved in the evangelization of Anatolia and elsewhere. The tomb of Philip has been recently discovered in Hierapolis by Italian excavators and the Austrians have recently exposed a cave in Ephesus with Frescoes of Paul and Thecla. Moreover, the presence of a large martyrium at Seleucia ad Calycadnum adds credence to traditions testifying of Thecla's ministry in Anatolia.

Untold stories lost through the centuries will never be recovered to complete the account of early Christian developments in Anatolia. Yet, the passion, toil and the sacrifices of unknown committed Christians have been duly noted in God's chronicles of Christian history. Their labors were crucial for the construction of the church that exists throughout the world today. Some of the most important theologians of the early church thrived in Anatolia and Anatolia remained the center of the Christian world for centuries.

It is no coincidence that all seven of the early ecumenical councils took place in Anatolia. Beginning with the council of Nicaea in A.D. 325 and continuing with councils at Constantinople in A.D. 381, 553 and 680, Ephesus in A.D. 431, Chalcedon in

Fig. 162 Byzantine Church at Cambazli

A well preserved Byzantine basilica lies on the Roman road south of Diocaesarea in Ciilicia at Cambazli. The church was built during the second half of the fifth century.

A.D. 451 and concluding with a second council at Nicaea in A.D. 787 the early church debated theological issues and wrestled with problems that emerged among the congregations. At that time the Christian church realized that the church founded by Jesus Christ was one united church and that issues in one congregation were concerns for all of the congregations worldwide. Even though all of the leaders and scholars of the church did not concur on all of the issues, they nevertheless held to common core beliefs that they considered fundamental to the church.

These foundational beliefs were expressed in the early creeds that have been handed down to us today. Most of our congregations today continue to affirm creeds such as the Apostle's Creed and the Nicene Creed. That sense of a bonded, united and fully integrated church has been somewhat lost today as denominations have carved the church up into segments that often have little communication with one another and share little in common. With separate leadership structures and separate budgets we have lost touch with what it means to be Christ's church. Whereas the earlier church was willing to overlook theological squabbles regarding peripheral issues, today those same issues sometimes become the center of divisions that divide denominations and congregations. Jesus' paramount command to love one another has been subjugated to our desire to be right and for others to see things as we do.

When we examine the early church in Asia Minor, we recognize that these churches were not in competition with one another. Rather they prayed earnestly for one another and shared their financial resources with one another. The leaders of these congregations humbly received instructions from those who were more experienced and from those who were more closely connected with the apostolic tradition. The churches were not separated from one another as "Paul's churches" or "John's churches" and the leadership of each congregation received "the brethren" (leaders and messengers) from other nearby congregations who traveled the roads to share Christ's message with brothers and sisters in other cities, towns and in the countryside. In spite of the lack of transportation as we have it today, we get the sense that these early Christians were compelled to take this message of salvation to others in distant lands. Like their progenitor Paul, they were willing to endure "dangers from rivers, dangers from bandits, dangers from their countrymen, dangers in the city, dangers in the country, dangers at sea and dangers from false brethren" (2 Cor. 11:26).

For millennia prior to the emergence of Christianity in Anatolia and for the centuries following, the region functioned as the chief land bridge between Asia and Europe. Even today numerous caravan serais can be found all over Turkey. Some have been restored and turned into boutique hotels. Almost all trade caravans from the east to the west passed through Anatolia. The Romans facilitated movement through the land

Fig. 163 Phrygian Monastery

This was one of the rock cut Byzantine churches in the cliffs near Doger in ancient Phrygia.

by constructing hundreds of roads in Anatolia and Paul availed himself of these roads during his travels. These roads greatly increased commerce and travel in Anatolia and the early Christians took to the roads to spread the gospel. The combination of an influx of merchants and travelers to Anatolia along with the concern of the church to convey the gospel to lands unreached by earlier disciples lead to a missionary movement that had a broad and far reaching scope. Today, it is common for people to think of Jerusalem and Rome as being the two primary centers of the early Christian faith. However, such people fail to realize that Anatolia (in particular Asia Minor) was the place where the bulk of the missionary work was being done, and the place where the earliest theological issues were resolved.

For the past several hundred years, Turkey has been the neglected biblical land. Although the country is loaded with biblical sites related to the Hebrew scriptures, as well as to the Christian scriptures, few people have ventured into Turkey to examine the remains. Fortunately, things are changing. Turkey is opening to the west and biblical Turkey is increasingly being exposed by archaeologists and scholars. Turkish universities are now training archaeologists and ancient historians in numbers never before seen. As the sites are excavated and new discoveries are revealed, visitors are starting to realize the treasure that still lies underground in Turkey.

Fig. 164 Sarica Monastery

Sarica Monastery in Cappadocia was likely built between the 10th and 13th centuries. The rock cut dwellings, churches, monasteries and underground cities of Cappadocia contain many well preserved frescoes.

    As the crossroads of civilizations Turkey has been a witness to great civilizations that have inhabited the land. From the very beginning, when humans first made the transition from hunter gatherers to domestic life at Gobeklitepe (near Sanliurfa), to the influx of Indo-European travelers (the Hattians and Hurrians), to the Hittites, the Assyrians, the Urartian people, the Persians, the Greeks and the Romans, the land was rich in diverse culture. Indigenous populations, such as the Phrygians, Galatians, Lycians, Lycaonians, Carians and Lydians, with unclear origins inhabited the central, southern and western regions of Anatolia. It was in this disparate land that Christianity found its cradle. As the faith grew Anatolia became more than a transient home for Christians. Anatolia became the epicenter of early Christian theology and Anatolia was the hub for missions in the centuries following the apostles Paul and John. Today, there are few places in Turkey where the cross cannot be found among its ruins.

Glossary

Acropolis The acropolis was a hill around which the city was generally built. The acropolis was often surrounded by a wall and was the area where the people fled if the city was assailed by enemies. Before the Romans established a measure of peace in the Mediterranean world, the older cities were independent of one another and were vulnerable to attacks by others. The acropolis provided security for the citizens. The palace of the king was usually located on the acropolis along with the city's most important temples.

Agora Generally located at the center of the city, the agora was the commercial center of the city. Agoras were large open squares that were surrounded by shops selling a wide variety of goods and services. Most agoras had columns and stoas along the periphery.

Amphitheater The Amphitheater was a circular structure with seats surrounding an arena. The Amphitheater was used for entertainment, including gladiator contests, animal hunts and for the destruction of criminals.

Aqueduct An Aqueduct was a structure that brought water into the city from far away water sources, such as mountain streams, rivers and springs.

Atrium An atrium was an open area located within a building. Atriums were unroofed and were open to the outside air, but were often surrounded by colonnaded buildings or stoas. Many homes of the most wealthy people had atriums.

Basilica	A Basilica was a public building that could serve a variety of functions. Later when Christian structures were erected (after the time of Constantine), the style of the Basilica was adapted by the Christians. An apse (a semicircular enclave) often was constructed at the front of the Basilica.
Baths	Roman baths were an innovation that everyone in the city enjoyed. Water was heated or brought in from local hot springs and was diverted to a room called the Caldarium (the hot water bath). Warm water was channeled to the Tepidarium and cold water was taken to the Frigidarium. Baths sometimes had swimming pools located in the complex. The baths became a place of social gatherings.
Bema	The Bema was a speaker's platform. These were usually located in the agora or forum where political speeches were given or where judicial proceedings took place.
Bouleuterion	The Bouleuterion was a building used for meetings of the town council (the Boule). The bouleuterion had a semicircular shape like a theater, but it was smaller and most of them were roofed. The bouleuterion could also double as an Odeon.
Caldarium	See Baths
Cardo Maximus	The Cardo Maximus was the main street in a Roman city which ran in a northsouth direction.
Cistern	A cistern was a large underground receptacle for the collection of water. Cisterns were plastered to retain the water.
Decumanus Maximus	The Decumanus Maximus was the main street in a Roman city which ran in an east-west direction.
Forum	The Forum was a Roman adaptation of the agora. Like the agora, the Forum was a large open square or rectangular area in the center of the city. However, the Forum was chiefly a political arena, although commercial activity was also often associated with the Forum. The most important political buildings surrounded the Forum.

Frigidarium   See Baths

Gymnasium   A structure used for exercise and education. School children were often taught in the Gymnasium as physical education was coupled together with mental exercises. Gymnasiums usually had a Palaestra and usually had a bath complex associated with the Gymnasium.

Heroon   A Heroon was an honorific tomb located within the city. Most people were buried outside of the city, but notable citizens may be buried within the city in a monumental Heroon.

Hippodrome   Hippodromes were used for chariot races. Shaped like a stadium, the hippodrome was much larger than a stadium, allowing enough room for horses to turn at the ends. The center of the hippodrome had a wall (spina) running most of the length of the structure, separating the two sides of the track.

Insula   The homes of many of the peasants were connected to one another, sharing common walls surrounding a common courtyard. This style of housing is known as insula construction.

Macellum   The macellum was a large building usually with more than one story that housed shops and generally bordered the agora.

Martyrium   A Martyrium was a Christian building that was constructed to commemorate the martyrdom of a notable Christian.

Necropolis   The Necropolis was an ancient cemetery. The Necropolis was always located outside of the city because of the impurity of a corpse. However, as the city grew throughout the years, some tombs where eventually incorporated within the enlarged city.

Neokoros   A Neokoros was an honor conferred upon a city whereupon the city was permitted to construct a temple to the emperor. The city became the guardian of the imperial temple and cities throughout the Mediterranean world competed for this honor.

Nymphaeum The Nymphaeum was a decorative fountain. The Nymphaeum was generally fed with water flowing from an aqueduct and many of these fountains were multi-storied and contained statues and other decorative features.

Odeon An Odeon was a building shaped like a small theater and was used chiefly for musical performances. It was usually roofed and in many cities the bouleuterion doubled as an Odeon.

Palaestra The Palaestra was an open air exercise area where athletes could run, jump, throw and wrestle. The Palaestra was the part of the gymnasium where physical exercise took place.

Prytanaeum The most important civic building which contained the sacred hearth and eternal fire. The Prytanaeum was where city officials would entertain dignitaries from other cities and the fire represented the life and vitality of the community.

Sarcophagus A sarcophagus was a large stone carved tomb with a lid. These could be plain or could be elaborately decorated.

Stele A stele was a flat stone or column with a relief carving or inscription. Steles were commonly used as grave markers (known as funerary stele) or as commemorative pieces for public display.

Stadium Stadiums were large oblong structures surrounded by seats. Stadiums with an open ended horseshoe shape were uncommon. Stadiums were primarily used for the Greek athletic competitions.

Stoa The Stoa was a colonnaded and roofed structure that generally lined city streets and surrounded agoras. The Stoa provided protection from the sun and rain and was a favorite place for philosophers and debates.

Temple   Temple were built for a wide variety of deities. Generally a city had one chief patron deity, but temples to numerous other deities were common in most cities and towns.

Temple Features:
Cella – The inner chamber of the temple
Doric Columns – Columns without decorative capitals
Ionic Columns – Columns with capitals that resemble a scroll lying on top
Corinthian Columns – Columns with capitals surrounded by acanthus leaves
Peripteral Temple – A temple surrounded by columns
Dipteral Temple – A temple surrounded by two rows of columns
Pseudodipteral Temple – A temple with one row of columns double spaced from the cella

Tepidatium   See Baths

Theater   Theaters were structures that were primarily used for theatrical productions. The plays were a very popular form of entertainment in the ancient cities. The theater was a semicircular building with seats ascending around an orchestra where the actors originally performed. Later, a stage (or skene) was erected upon which the plays were conducted. Public meetings could also be held in the theater.

Ancient Archaeological Periods

Prior to 3300 B.C.	**Stone Age**	Time when people primarily used stone tools
	Subdivisions Paleolithic Neolithic Chalcolithic	
3300 – 1200 B.C.	**Bronze Age**	Use of bronze tools, implements and weapons
	Subdivisions Early Bronze Age Middle Bronze Age Late Bronze Age	
1200 – 586 B.C.	**Iron Age**	Use of iron tools, implements and weapons
	Subdivisions Early Iron Age Late Iron Age	
550 – 332 B.C.	**Persian Period**	Eastern Mediterranean dominated by Persians
332- 37 B.C.	**Hellenistic Period**	Eastern Mediterranean dominated by Greeks
37 B.C. – A.D. 324	**Roman Period**	Mediterranean World dominated by Romans
A.D. 324 – 1068	**Byzantine Period**	Byzantine (Christians) control Anatolia
A.D. 638 – 1099	**Early Muslim Period**	Muslims rulers control most of the eastern Mediterranean
A.D. 1037 – 1194	**Selçuk Period**	Selçuk Turks control Anatolia and most of the Middle East
A.D. 1099 – 1291	**Crusader Period**	Crusaders attempt to reclaim eastern Mediterranean
A.D. 1291 – 1453	**Late Muslim Period**	Muslim control of the eastern Mediterranean
A.D. 1453 – 1923	**Ottoman Period**	Ottoman Empire controls eastern Mediterranean

Asia Minor Historical Time Line

Prior to 1200 B.C.	Limited colonization of Anatolia by the Mycenaeans
1200 – 550 B.C.	Greek settlers migrate across the Aegean Sea to Anatolia ("East")
1000 B.C.	Independent cities establish Leagues for mutual trade and protection Aeolian League – Northern Aegean Coast of Anatolia Ionian League – Central Aegean Coast of Anatolia Dorian League – Southern Aegean Coast of Anatolia
550-332 B.C.	The Persian (Achaemenian) Empire spreads west controlling Asia Minor Many local Persian governors (Satraps) appointed from the native Anatolian population and Greek culture predominates
499 – 495 B.C.	Ionian Revolt against the Persians
478 – 404 B.C.	Delian League established to resist Persian control. Headed by Athens.
332 B.C.	Alexander the Great's conquests pushes the Persians out of Asia Minor
323 B.C.	Upon Alexander's death Anatolia is divided among his generals The Diodochi (Alexander's successors) war with one another over Anatolia Seleucid Empire – based in Syria Ptolemaic Empire – based in Egypt Antigonid Empire – based in Macedonia Lysimachus Empire- based in Thrace
301 B.C.	Battle of Ipsus. Antigonus I defeated and Antigonids pushed out of Asia Minor
281 B.C.	Battle of Corupedium. Lysimachus defeated and killed.
270-190 B.C.	Asia Minor controlled largely by Seleucids, with limited Ptolemaic possessions
189 B.C.	Battle of Magnesia ad Sipylum. Romans crushed Seleucid forces and ceded control of Asia Minor to the Pergamene Kingdom.
133 B.C.	The Pergamene Kingdom dissolved and Asia Minor given to the Romans
89-63 B.C.	Mithridatic Wars. Mithridates VI, king of Pontus fights Romans for Asia Minor and is ultimately defeated
27 B.C. – A.D. 14	Augustus (Gaius Julius Caesar Octavianus) begins Roman imperial rule
A.D. 14 – 37	Tiberias (Tiberias Claudius Nero Caesar) rules over Roman Empire.
A.D. 27 – 30	Public ministry of Jesus of Nazareth
A.D. 33	Saul (Paul) has Damascus Road experience & embraces Jesus as Christ
A.D. 37 – 41	Caligula (Gaius Caesar Germanicus) rules over Roman Empire
A.D. 41 – 54	Claudius (Tiberias Claudius Nero Germanicus) rules over Roman Empire
A.D. 46 – 47	Apostle Paul's first mission

A.D. 47	Jerusalem Council – debate with Judaizers regarding issues of circumcision & Torah observance for Christians
A.D. 48 – 52	Apostle Paul's second mission
A.D. 50's	Apostle Peter's possible mission to Pontus, Cappadocia, Galatia, Asia Minor and Bithynia
A.D. 53 – 58	Apostle Paul's third mission
A.D. 54 – 68	Nero (Claudius Nero Caesar) rules over Roman Empire
A.D. 58 – 60	Paul imprisoned at Caesarea, Palestine
A.D. 60 – 62	Paul imprisoned at Rome, writes letters to Ephesus and Colossae
A.D. 64 – 65	Paul imprisoned 2nd time at Rome, writes letters to Timothy
A.D. 60 – 65	Peter in Rome writes 1 & 2 Peter to churches in Pontus, Cappadocia, Galatia, Asia Minor and Bithynia
A.D. 66 – 73	Jewish War with Rome, destruction of Jerusalem
A.D. 68 – 69	Galba, Otho, Vitellius each briefly rule over the Roman Empire
A.D. 69 – 79	Vespasian (Titus Flavius Vespasianus) rules over Roman Empire
A.D. 60's or 70's	Apostle John moves to Ephesus
A.D. 79 – 81	Titus (Titus Flavius Vespasianus) rules over Roman Empire
A.D. 81 – 96	Domitian (Titus Flavius Domitianus) rules over Roman Empire
A.D. 80's – 90's	John writes letters 1, 2, 3 John
A.D. 94	John writes apocalypse (Revelation) & letters to seven churches of Asia Minor
A.D. 96 – 98	Nerva (Marcus Cocceius Nerva) rules over Roman Empire
A.D. 98 – 117	Trajan (Marcus UlpiusNerva Traianus) rules over Roman Empire
A.D. 109	Ignatius travels through Asia Minor, writes letters and is martyred in Rome
A.D. 109 – 112	Pliny the Younger appointed governor of Bithynia and Pontus
A.D. 112	Pliny the Younger writes to Emperor Trajan regarding treatment of Christians
A.D. 117 – 138	Hadrian (Publius Aelius Traianus Hadrianus) rules over Roman Empire

• Many of these dates are disputed. This timeline follows the most commonly recognized dates for the listed historical events and follows the traditional authorship and dates for the Christian writings and traditions.

• Yellow background is used to highlight the reign of the Roman emperors.

• Blue background is used to highlight the events associated with the Bible.

Bibliography

Important Commentaries on the New Testament

Acts

Barrett, C.K. *Critical and Exegetical Commentary on the Acts of the Apostles*. 3 vols. ICC. Edinburgh: T&T Clark, 1994-98.

Bauckham, Richard, ed. *Palestinian Setting*. Vol. 4 in The Book of Acts in Its First Century Setting. Grand Rapids: Eerdmans, 1995.

Bock, Darrell L. *Acts*, Baker Exegetical Commentary on the New Testament. Baker, 2007.

Bruce, F.F. *The Acts of the Apostles: The Greek Text with Introduction and Commentary*. Grand Rapids: Eerdmans, 1951.

_____. *Commentary on the Book of the Acts*. NICNT. Rev. Ed. Grand Rapids: Eerdmans, 1990.

Conzelmann, Hans. *Acts of the Apostles*. Hermeneia. Philadelphia: Fortress, 1987.

Fitzmyer, Joseph A. *Acts of the Apostles*. New York: Doubleday, 1998.

Gill, David W.J. and Conrad Gempf, eds. *The Book of Acts in Its Graeco-Roman Setting*. Vol. 2 in The Book of Acts in Its First Century Setting. Grand Rapids: Eerdmans, 1994.

Haenchen, Ernst. *The Acts of the Apostles: A Commentary*. Philadelphia: Westminster, 1971.

Keener, Craig S. *Acts: An Exegetical Commentary*. Vols 1-4. Grand Rapids: Baker Academic, 2012-2015.

Lake, Kirsopp and Cadbury, Henry J. *The Acts of the Apostles*. Vol. 4 of The Beginnings of Christianity. Grand Rapids: Baker, 1979.

Levinskaya, Irina. *Diaspora Setting*. Vol. 5 in The Book of Acts in Its First Century Setting. Grand Rapids: Eerdmans, 1996.

Marshall, I. Howard. *The Acts of the Apostles.* TNTC. Grand Rapids: Eerdmans, 1980.

Neil, William. *The Acts of the Apostles.* NCBC. Grand Rapids: Eerdmans, 1973.

Peterson, David G. *The Acts of the Apostles.* Pillar New Testament Commentary. Grand Rapids: Eerdmans, 2009.

Rackham, R.B. *The Acts of the Apostles, An Exposition.* London: Methuen, 1901.

Rapske, Brian. *Paul in Roman Custody.* Vol. 3 in The Book of Acts in Its First Century Setting. Grand Rapids: Eerdmans, 1994.

Winter, Bruce W. and Clarke, Andrew D., eds. *The Book of Acts in Its Ancient Literary Setting.* Vol. 1 in The Book of Acts in Its First Century Setting. Grand Rapids: Eerdmans, 1993.

Witherington, Ben, III. *The Acts of the Apostles: A Socio-Rhetorical Commentary.* Grand Rapids: Eerdmans, 1997.

Ephesians

Abbott, T.K. *Epistles to the Ephesians and to the Colossians.* International Critical Commentary. Edinburgh: T.&T. Clark, 1897.

Arnold, Clinton E. *Ephesians.* Zondervan Exegetical Commentary on the New Testament. Grand Rapids: Zondervan, 2010.

Barth, Markus. *Ephesians 1-3*, *Ephesians 4-6*. Anchor Bible, vols. 34, 34A. Garden City, NY: Doubleday, 1974.

Best, Ernest. *Ephesians.* International Critical Commentary. Edinburgh: T. & T. Clark, 1998.

Bruce, F. F. *Epistles to the Colossians, to Philemon and to the Ephesians.* NICNT. Grand Rapids: Eerdmans, 1984.

Eadie, John. *Commentary on the Greek Text of the Epistle of Paul to the Ephesians.* Edinburgh: T.&T. Clark, 1883.

Foulkes, Francis. *The Letter of Paul to the Ephesians.* Tyndale N. T. Commentary. Grand Rapids: Eerdmans, 1989.

Fowl, Stephen E. *Ephesians: A Commentary.* New Testament Library. Louisville: Westminster / John Knox, 2012.

Hoehner, Harold W. *Ephesians: An Exegetical Commentary.* Grand Rapids: Baker, 2002.

Lincoln, Andrew T. *Ephesians.* Word Biblical Commentary. Waco, TX: Word, 1990.

O'Brien, Peter T. *Ephesians.* Pillar N.T. Commentaries. Grand Rapids: Eerdmans, 1999.

Robinson, J. Armitage. *Commentary on Ephesians.* Grand Rapids: Kregel, 1904.

Thielman, Frank. *Ephesians.* Baker Exegetical Commentary. Grand Rapids: Baker, 2010.

Westcott, Brooke Foss. *Saint Paul's Epistle to the Ephesians.* Grand Rapids: Baker, 1906.

Colossians

Abbott, T. K. A *Critical and Exegetical Commentary on the Epistles to the Ephesians and to the Colossians*. International Critical Commentary series. Edinburgh: T. and T. Clark, 1897.

Barth, Markus., and Helmut. Blanke. *Colossians: a New Translation with Introduction and Commentary*. New York, London: Doubleday, 1994.

Bruce, F. F. and E. K. Simpson. *Commentary on the Epistles to the Ephesians and to the Colossians*. NICNT. Grand Rapids: Eerdmans, 1968.

———. *The Epistles to the Colossians, to Philemon, and to the Ephesians*. NICNT. Grand Rapids, Eerdmans, 1984.

Carson, Herbert M. *The Epistles of Paul to the Colossians and Philemon*. TNTC. Grand Rapids: Eerdmans, 1978.

Dunn, James D. G. *The Epistles to the Colossians and to Philemon: A Commentary on the Greek Text*. NIGTC. Grand Rapids: Eerdmans, 1996.

Eadie, John. *Commentary on the Epistle to the Colossians*. Grand Rapids: Zondervan, 1856.

Hendricksen, William. *New Testament Commentary: Exposition of Philippians and Exposition of Colossians and Philemon*. Grand Rapids: Baker, 1979.

Lightfoot, J. B. *Saint Paul's Epistles to the Colossians and to Philemon*. London: Macmillan, 1892.

Lohse, Eduard. *Colossians and Philemon*. Hermeneia. Philadelphia: Fortress, 1971.

Martin, Ralph P. *Colossians and Philemon*. NCBC. London: Marshall, Morgan, and Scott, 1973.

Moo, Douglas J. *The Letters to the Colossians and to Philemon*. Pillar N.T. Commentaries. Eerdmans, 2007.

Moule, C. F. D. *The Epistles of Paul the Apostle to the Colossians and to Philemon*. CGTC. Cambridge: Cambridge Univ., 1962.

O'Brien, Peter T. *Colossians, Philemon*. Word Biblical Commentary. Vol. 44. Waco: Word, 1982.

Pokorny, P. *Colossians: A Commentary*. Peabody, MA: Hendrickson, 1991.

Schweizer, Eduard. *The Letter to the Colossians*. London: SPCK, 1982.

Witherington, Ben III. *The Letters to Philemon, the Colossians, and the Ephesians: A Socio-Rhetorical Commentary on the Captivity Epistles*. Grand Rapids: Eerdmans, 2007.

Wright, N. T. *The Epistles of Paul to the Colossians and to Philemon*. TNTC. Grand Rapids: Eerdmans, 1986.

1-2 Timothy

Bernard, J. H. *The Pastoral Epistles*. Grand Rapids: Baker, 1899.

Dibelius, Martin and Conzelmann, Hans. *The Pastoral Epistles*. Philadelphia: Fortress, 1972.

Fee, Gordon D. *1 and 2 Timothy, Titus*. NIBC. Peabody, MA: Hendrickson, 1988.

Guthrie, D. *The Pastoral Epistles*. Rev. Ed. TNTC. Grand Rapids: Eerdmans, 1990.

Hanson, A. T. *The Pastoral Epistles*. NCBC. Grand Rapids: Eerdmans, 1982.

Johnson, Luke T. *First and Second Timothy*. Anchor Bible. New York: Doubleday, 2000.

Kelly, J. N. D. *A Commentary on the Pastoral Epistles*. Grand Rapids: Baker, 1963.

Knight III, George W. *Commentary on the Pastoral Epistles*. NIGNT. Grand Rapids: Eerdmans, 1992.

Marshall, I. Howard. *A Critical and Exegetical Commentary on the Pastoral Epistles*. Edinburgh: T&T Clark, 1999.

Mounce, William D. *The Pastoral Epistles*, Word Biblical Commentary. Nashville: Nelson, 2004.

Towner, Philip H., *The Letters to Timothy and Titus*, Eerdmans 2004.

Quinn, Jerome D. and Wacker, William C. *The First and Second Letters to Timothy*. Grand Rapids: Eerdmans, 2000.

1-3 John

Brooke, Alan. *A Critical and Exegetical Commentary on the Johannine Epistles*. ICC. Edinburgh: T&T Clark, 1912.

Brown, Raymond. *The Epistles of John*. Anchor Bible 30. Garden City, NY: Doubleday, 1982.

Bultmann, Rudolf. *The Johannine Epistles*. Hermeneia. Philadelphia: Fortress, 1973.

Dodd, Charles Harold. *The Johannine Epistles*. 2nd Ed. London: Hodder & Stoughton, 1947.

Houlden, J. L. *A Commentary on the Johannine Epistles*. New York: Harper & Row, 1973.

Marshall, I. Howard. *The Epistles of John*. NICNT. Grand Rapids: Eerdmans, 1978.

Schnackenburg, Rudolf. *The Johannine Epistles: Introduction and Commentary*. New York: Crossroad, 1992.

Smalley, Stephen S. *1,2, 3 John*. Word Biblical Commentary 51. Waco, TX: Word, 1984.

Stott, John R. W. *The Epistles of John*. TNTC 19. Grand Rapids: Eerdmans, 1964.

Strecker, Georg. *The Johannine Letters*. Hermeneia Commentary. Minneapolis: Fortress, 1996.

Westcott, Brooke Foss. *The Epistles of St. John.* 2nd Ed. London: Macmillan, 1886.

Yarbrough, Robert W. *1-3 John.* Baker Exegetical Commentary on the New Test. Grand Rapids: Baker, 2008.

Revelation

Aune, David. *Revelation 1-5, 6-16, 17-22.* Word Biblical Commentary, 52a, 52b, 52c. Dallas: Word, 1997-1998.

Beale, G. K. *Revelation.* New International Greek Testament Commentary. Grand Rapids: Eerdmans, 2000.

Beasley-Murray, G. R. *The Book of Revelation.* New Century Bible Commentary. Grand Rapids: Eerdmans, 1974.

Beckwith, Isbon T. *The Apocalypse of John.* Grand Rapids: Baker, 1919.

Caird, G. B. *The Revelation of St. John the Divine.* Harper's N.T. Commentaries. New York: Harper & Row, 1966.

Charles, R. H. *Critical and Exegetical Commentary on the Revelation of St. John.* ICC. Edinburgh: T&T Clark, 1920.

Duff, Paul B. *Who Rides the Beast? Prophetic Rivalry and the Rhetoric of Crisis in the Churches of the Apocalypse.* Oxford: Oxford Univ., 2001.

Ford, J. Massyngberde. *Revelation.* The Anchor Bible, 38. Garden City, NY: Doubleday, 1975.

Friesen, Steven J. *Imperial Cults and the Apocalypse of John.* New York: Oxford, 2001.

Hemer, Colin J. *The Letters to the Seven Churches of Asia in Their Local Setting.* Grand Rapids: Eerdmans, 1986.

Ladd, George Eldon. *A Commentary on the Revelation of John.* Grand Rapids: Eerdmans, 1972.

Mounce, Robert H. *The Book of Revelation.* Rev. Ed. NICNT. Grand Rapids: Eerdmans, 1999.

Morris, Leon. *Revelation.* Rev. Ed. Tyndale New Testament Commentaries. Grand Rapids: Eerdmans, 1988.

Osborne, Grant. *Revelation.* Exegetical Commentary on the New Testament, Grand Rapids: Baker, 2002.

Thompson, Leonard L. *The book of Revelation: Apocalypse and Empire.* New York: Oxford Univ., 1989.

General Historical and Archaeological Resources

Broughton, T. R. S. "Roman Asia Minor." In Tenny Frank, *An Economic Survey of Ancient Rome*, vol IV. Baltimore: Johns Hopkins,1938, 499-918.

Cohen, Getzel M. *The Hellenistic Settlements in Europe, the Islands, and Asia Minor.* Berkeley, CA: Univ. California, 1995.

Coulton, J. J. "Roman Aqueducts in Asia Minor." In Sarah Macready and F. H. Thompson, eds. *Roman Architecture in the Greek World.* London: Thames and Hudson,1987, 72-84.

Dignas, Beate. *Economy of the Sacred in Hellenistic and Roman Asia Minor.* Oxford: Oxford Univ., 2002.

Dmitriev, Sviatoslav. *City Government in Hellenistic and Roman Asia Minor.* Oxford: Oxford Univ, 2005.

Foss, Clive. "Archaeology and the 'Twenty Cities' of Byzantine Asia," *American Journal of Archaeology.* 81 (1977), 469-486.

French, David H. "The Roman Road System of Asia Minor." *ANRW* II. 7. 2 (1980), 698-729.

Friesen, S.J. "Revelation, Realia and Religion: Archaeology in the Interpretation of the Apocalypse." *Harvard Theological Review* 88 (1995), 291-314.

Harland, Philip A. "Honoring the Emperor or Assailing the Beast: Participation in Civic Life among Associations (Jewish, Christian and Other) in Asia Minor and the Apocalypse of John." *Journal for the Study of the New Testament* 77 (2000), 99-121.

Haxley, G.L. *The Early Ionians.* London, 1966.

Jones, Arnold H. M. *The Cities of the Eastern Roman Provinces.* Oxford: Oxford Univ., 1971.

Kearsley, R.A. *Greeks and Romans in Imperial Asia.* Inschriften Griechischer Städte aus Kleinasien 59). Bonn, 2001.

Macro, Anthony D. "The Cities of Asia Minor under the Roman Imperium." *ANRW* II.7.2 (1980), 659-697.

Magie, David. *Roman Rule in Asia Minor to the End of the Third Century after Christ.* Princeton: Princeton Univ., 1950.

Mitchell, Stephen. *Anatolia: Land, Men and Gods in Asia Minor.* I. Oxford: Clarendon, 1995.

Parke, H. W. *The Oracles of Apollo in Asia Minor.* London, 1985.

Ramsay, William M. *The Cities of Saint Paul and Their Influence on His Life and Thought: The Cities of Eastern Asia Minor.* London: Hodder and Stoughton, 1907.

_____. *The Historical Geography of Asia Minor.* London: John Murray, 1890.

_____. *The Letters to the Seven Churches and Their Place in the Plan of the Apocalypse.* London: Hodder and Stoughton, 1904.

Sato, Noboru. "Athens, Persia, Clazomenae, Erythrae: An Analysis of International Relationships in Asia Minor at the Beginning of the Fourth Century BCE." *Bulletin of the Institute of Classical Studies* 49 (2006), 23-38.

Archaeological and Historical Resources for the Cities of Asia Minor

Alexandria Troas

Cook, J. M. "Cities in and around the Troad." *Annual of the British School at Athens* 83 (1988), 7-19.

_____. *The Troad. An Archaeological and Topographical Study.* Oxford: Clarendon Press, 1973.

Görkay, Kutalmış. "A Podium Temple in Alexandria Troas: 1997 Campaign, Preliminary Report." *Asia Minor Studien.* Band 33. *Die Troas. Neue Forschungen III.* Bonn: Rudolf Habelt, 1999, 5-26.

Hemer, Colin J. "Alexandria Troas." *Tyndate Bulletin* 26 (1975), 79-112.

Jones, A. H. M. *Cities of the Eastern Roman Provinces.* Oxford: Oxford Univ., 1937, 42.

Leaf, W. "The Military Geography of the Troad." *Geographical Journal* 47 (1916), 401-416.

_____. "Some Problems of the Troad." *Annual of the British School at Athens* 21 (1915), 16-30.

Öztaner, Hakan. "The Nymphaeum at Alexandria Troas." *Asia Minor Studien.* Band 33. *Die Troas. Neue Forschungen III.* Bonn: Rudolf Habelt, 1999, 27-36.

Sayce, A. H. "Notes from Journeys in the Troad and Lydia." *Journal of Hellenic Studies* 1 (1880), 75-93.

Smith, A. C. G. "The Gymnasium at Alexandria Troas: Evidence for an Ouline Reconstruction." *Anatolian Studies* 29 (1979), 23-50.

Taşlıklıoğlu, Z. and P. Frisch. "Inscriptions from the Troad." *Zeitschrift für Papyrologie und Epigraphik* 19 (1975), 219-224.

Winter, F. E. "Notes on Neandria." *American Journal of Archaeology* 89 (1985), 680-683.

Aphrodisias

Bean, George E. "Aphrodisias." *Turkey Beyond the Maeander.* London: John Murray, 1980, 188-198.

Chaniotis, A. "New Inscriptions from Aphrodisias (1995-2001)," *AJA* 108 (2004), 377-416.

258

_____. "The Jews of Aphrodisias: New Evidence and Old Problems." *Scripta Classica Israelica* 21 (2002), 209-242.

Erim, Kenan T. "Aphrodisias, Awakened City of Ancient Art." *National Geographic Magazine* 141.6 (1972), 766-791

_____. "Two Inscriptions from Aphrodisias." *Papers of the British School at Rome* 37 (1969), 92-95.

_____ and C. Roueche. "Sculptors from Aphrodisias: Some New Inscriptions." *Papers of the British School at Rome* 50 (1982), 102-15.

_____ and C. Roueche, eds. *Recent Work at Aphrodisias, 1986-1988.* Aphrodisias Papers 1: Recent Work on Architecture and Sculpture. Ann Arbor, MI: Journal of Roman Archaeology Supplemental Series, 1990, 9-36.

_____ and R.R.R. Smith, eds. *Introduction to the Excavation of the Theatre.* Aphrodisias Papers 2: The Theatre, a Sculptor's Workshop, Philosophers, and Coin-types. Ann Arbor, MI: Journal of Roman Archaeology Supplemental Series, 1991, 7-8.

_____. "The School of Aphrodisias." *Archaeology* 20.1 (1967),18-27.

Freely, John. "Aphrodisias" *The Western Mediterranean Coast of Turkey.* Istanbul: SEV Matbaacılık ve Yayıncılık, 1997, 18-37.

Jones, C.P. and R.R. Smith. "Two Inscribed Monuments of Aphrodisias." *AA* (1994), 455-72.

Parrish, David, ed. *Urbanism in Western Asia Minor: New Studies on Aphrodisias, Ephesos, Hierapolis, Pergamon, Perge and Xanthos.* JRA Suppl. 45. Portsmouth: JRA, 2001.

Reynolds, Joyce M. *Aphrodisias and Rome.* London: Society for the Promotion of Roman Studies, 1982.

_____. "New Evidence for the Imperial Cult in Julio-Claudian Aphrodisias." *Zeitschrift für Papyrologie und Epigraphik,* 43 (1981), 317-327.

_____. "Ruler-cult at Aphrodisias in the late Republic and under the Julio-Claudian Emperors." In A. Small, ed., *Subject and Ruler: the Cult of the Ruling Power in Classical Antiquity,* Journal of Roman Archaeology Supplemental Series 17 (1996), 41-50.

_____ and Robert Tannenbaum. *Jews and God Fearers at Aphrodisias.* Cambridge: Cambridge Philological Society, 1987.

Roueche, C. *Aphrodisias in Late Antiquity.* London, 1989.

Smith, R.R.R. "The Imperial Reliefs from the Sebasteion at Aphrodisias." *Journal of Roman Studies,* 77 (1987), 88-138.

Van der Horst, P.W. "Jews and Christians in Aphrodisias in the Light of Their Relations in Other Cities in Asia Minor." *Nederlands Theologisch Tÿdschrift,* 43 (1989), 106-121.

Assos

Arslan, Nurettin and Beate Böhlendorf-Arslan. *Assos Living in the Rocks: An Archaeological Guide.* İstanbul: Homer Kitabevi, 2010.

Clarke, Joseph T., Francis H. Bacon and Robert Koldewey. *Investigations at Assos.* Cambridge: Archaeological Institute of America, 1902.

Chroust, Anton-Hermann. "Aristotle's Sojourn in Assos." *Historia: Zeitschrift für Alte Geschichte.* 21 (1972), 170-176.

Congdon, L. O. K. "The Assos Journals of Francis H. Bacon." *Archaeology* 27 (1974), 83-95.

Norton, Richard. "Two Reliefs from Assos." *American Journal of Archaeology* 1, no. 6 (1897): 507-514.

Uluarslan, Hüseyin. *Assos Behramkale.* Çanakkale: Okullar Pazarı, 1998.

Wescoat, Bonna D. "Designing the Temple of Athena at Assos: Some Evidence from the Capitals." *American Journal of Archaeology* 91 (1987), 553-568.

Colossae

Bean, George E. "Laodiceia and Colossae." *Turkey Beyond the Maeander.* London: John Murray, 1980, 213-224.

Cadwallader, Alan H. and Michael Trainor, eds. *Colossae in Space and Time: Linking to an Ancient City.* Göttingen: Vandenhoeck & Ruprecht, 2011.

Cadwallader, A. H. "Revisiting Calder on Colossae." *AS* 56 (2006), 103-111.

Freely, John. "Colossae" *The Western Mediterranean Coast of Turkey.* Istanbul: SEV Matbaacılık ve Yayıncılık, 1997, 47-48.

Macdonald, D.J. "The Homonoia of Colossae and Aphrodisias," *Jahrbuch für Numismatik und Geldgeschichte* 33 (1983), 25-27.

Reicke, B. "The Historical Setting of Colossians," *Review and Expositor* 70 (1973), 429-38.

Sappington, Thomas J. *Revelation and Redemption at Colossae.* JSNTSupp 53. Sheffield: JSOT Press, 1991.

Ephesus

Arnold, Irene R. "Festivals of Ephesus," *American Journal of Archaeology* 76 (1972), 17-22.

Bammer, Anton. "A Peripteros of the Geometric Period in the Artemision of Ephesus." *Anatolian Studies* 40 (1990), 137-160.

_____. "Recent Excavations at the Altar of Artemis in Ephesus." *Archaeology* 27 (1974), 202-205.

Biguzzi, Giancario. "Ephesus, Its Artemision, Its Temple to the Flavian Emperors, and Idolatry in Revelation." *Novum Testamentum* 40 (1998), 276-290.

Bowie, E. L. "The 'Temple of Hadrian' at Ephesus." *Zeitschrift für Papyrologie und Epigraphik* 8 (1971): 137-141.

Erdemgil, Selahattin, A. Evren, Ö. Özeren and D. Tüz. *The Terrace Houses in Ephesus.* Istanbul: Hitit Color, 2000.

Freely, John. "Ionia II Ephesus" *The Aegean Coast of Turkey.* Istanbul: SEV Matbaacılık ve Yayıncılık, 2000, 176-228.

Friesen, Steven F. *Twice Neokoros. Ephesus, Asia and the Cult of the Imperial Family.* Leiden: Brill, 1993.

George, Michele. "Domestic Architecture and Household Relations. Pompei and Roman Ephesos." *JSNT* 27 (2004), 7-25.

Grant, Robert M. "The Description of Pul in the *Acts of Paul and Thecla.*" *Vigiliae Christianae* 36 (1982), 1-4.

Habicht, Christian. "New Evidence on the Province of Asia." *The Journal of Roman Studies* 65 (1975): 64-91.

Harland, Philip. "Honors and Worship: Emperors, Imperial Cults and Associations at Ephesus (First to Third Centuries C.E.)." *Studies in Religion / Sciences Religieuses* 25 (1996), 319-334.

Henderson, Arthur. "The Hellenistic Temple of Artemis at Ephesus." *Journal of the Royal Institute of British Architects* 22 (1915), 130-34.

_____. "The Temple of Diana at Ephesus." *Journal of the Royal Institute of British Architects* 41 (1933), 767-71.

Knibbe, Dieter. "Emperor Worship at Ephesus." *ANRW* I.18.3 (1990), 1659-60.

Koester, Helmut, ed. *Ephesos: Metropolis of Asia. An Interdisciplinary Approach to its Archaeology, Religion and Culture.* HTS 41. Cambridge, MA: Harvard Univ., 2004.

Krinzinger, Friedrich, ed. *Ephesos: Architecture, Monuments, Sculpture.* Istanbul: Ertuğ and Kocabıyık 2007.

Lethaby, W. R. "The Earlier Temple of Artemis at Ephesus." *The Journal of Hellenic Studies* 37 (1917): 1-16.

Murphy-O'Connor, Jerome. *St. Paul's Ephesus: Texts and Archaeology.* Collegeville, MN: Liturgical, 2008.

Murray, A. S. "Remains of Archaic Temple of Artemis at Ephesus." *The Journal of Hellenic Studies* 10 (1889): 1-10.

Oster, Richard. "The Ephesian Artemis as an Opponent of Early Christianity." *Jahrbuch für Antike und Christentum* 19 (1976), 24-44.

_____. "Ephesus as a Religious Center under the Principate, I. Paganism before Constantine." *ANRW* II.18.3 (1990), 1661-1728.

Parrish, David. "Architectural Function and Decorative Programs in the Terrace Houses at Ephesos." *Topoi* 7 (1997), 579-633.

_____, ed. *Urbanism in Western Asia Minor: New Studies on Aphrodisias, Ephesos, Hierapolis, Pergamon, Perge and Xanthos.* JRA Suppl. 45. Portsmouth: JRA, 2001.

Plommer, H. "St. John's Church, Ephesus." *Anatolian Studies* 12 (1962), 119-129.

Rogers, Guy M. *The Sacred Identity of Ephesos: Foundation Myths of a Roman City.* London: Routledge, 1991.

_____. *The Mysteries of Artemis of Ephesos: Cult, Polis and Change in the Graeco-Roman World.* New Haven, CT: Yale Univ., 2012.

Scherrer, Peter, ed. *Ephesus: The New Guide.* Rev. ed. Istanbul: Ege Yayınları, 2000.

Strelan, Rick. *Paul, Artemis and the Jews in Ephesus.* BZNW 80. New York: Walter de Gruyter, 1996.

Trebilco, Paul. *The Early Christians in Ephesus from Paul to Ignatius.* Grand Rapids: Eerdmans, 2007.

Winter, Erich. "Towards a Chronology of the Later Artemision at Ephesus." *AJA* 84 (1980), 241.

Wiplinger, Gilbert and Gudrun Wlach. *Ephesus: 100 Years of Austrian Research.* Vienna: Böhlau, 1996.

Hierapolis

Bean, George E. "Hierapolis." *Turkey Beyond the Maeander.* London: John Murray, 1980, 199-212.

D'Andria, Francesco. "Conversion, Crucifixion and Celebration: St. Philip's Martyrium at Hierapolis Draws Thousands over the Centuries." *Biblical Archaeology Review* 37.4 (2011), 34-46, 70.

_____. "Hierapolis of Phrygia: Its Evolution in Hellenistic and Roman Times." In D. Parrish (ed.), *Urbanism in Western Asia Minor.* Journal Roman Archaeology, Supplement 45. Portsmouth, RI: JRA, 2001, 96-115.

_____. *Hierapolis of Phrygia (Pamukkale): An Archaeological Guide.* Istanbul: Ege Yayınları, 2003.

_____. "Hierapolis of Phrygia". In W. Radt, *Stadtgrabungen und Stadtforschung im westlichen Kleinasien*, in *Byzas*, 3 (2006), 113-124.

Freely, John. "Hierapolis" *The Western Mediterranean Coast of Turkey.* Istanbul: SEV Matbaacılık ve Yayıncılık, 1997, 37-47.

Parrish, David, ed. *Urbanism in Western Asia Minor: New Studies on Aphrodisias, Ephesos, Hierapolis, Pergamon, Perge and Xanthos.* JRA Suppl. 45. Portsmouth: JRA, 2001.

Ritti, T. *An Epigraphic Guide to Hierapolis (Pamukkale).* Istanbul: Ege Yayınları, 2006.

Vanhaverbeke & Waelkens. "The Northwestern Necropolis of Hierapolis (Phrygia). The Chronological and Topographical Distribution of the Travertine Sarcophagi and Their Way of Production." In: D. De Bernardi Ferrero (ed.): *Hieraplis IV. Scavi e Ricerche. Saggi in onore di Paolo Verzone.* Rome: G. Bretschneider, 2002.

Laodicea

Bean, George E. "Laodiceia and Colossae." *Turkey Beyond the Maeander*. London: John Murray, 1980, 213-224.

Freely, John. "Laodicea" *The Western Mediterranean Coast of Turkey*. Istanbul: SEV Matbaacılık ve Yayıncılık, 1997, 48-52.

Johnson, Sherman E. "Laodicea and Its Neighbors," *BA* 13 (1950), 1-18.

Mitchell, Stephen. "Italian and Turkish Archaeological Work in the Lycus Valley around Laodicea and Hierapolis." *JRA* 14 (2001), 632-34.

Şimşek, Celal and B. Yener. "An Ivory Relief of Saint Thekla." *Adalya* 12 (2010), 321-334.

Şimşek, Celal. "Ancient City Laodicea and Travertine." Proceedings of 1st International Symposium on Travertine. Ankara: 2005, 361.

_____. "A Menorah with a Cross Carved on a Column of Nymphaeum A at Laodicea ad Lycum." *Journal of Roman Archaeology* 19 (2006), 343-346.

_____ and Mustafa Büykolanci. "The Water Springs of Laodicea and Its Distribution Systems." *Adalya* 9 (2006), 83-104.

Magnesia Ad Maeandrum

Austin, Michel M. "The Founding of Artemis Leukophryene at Magnesia on the Maeander." *The Hellenistic World from Alexander to the Roman Conquest: A Selection of Ancient Sources in Translation*. 2nd ed. Cambridge: Cambridge Univ., 2006, 174, 189-90.

Bagnall, Roger S. and Peter Derow, eds. "Magnesia on the Maeander and Artemis Leukophryene." *The Hellenistic Period: Historical Sources in Translation*. Oxford: Blackwell, 2004, 247-252.

Bean, George E. "Magnesia on the Maeander." *Aegean Turkey: An Archaeological Guide*. London: Ernest Benn, 1966, 246-251.

Bingöl, Orhan. *Magnesia on the Meander: The City of Artemis with White Eyebrows. An Archaeological Guide*. Istanbul: Homer Kitabevi, 2007.

_____. *Theatron: Magnesia on the Meander*. Istanbul: Homer Kitabevi, 2005.

Dusanic, S. "The Ktisis Magnesias. Philip V and the Panhellenic Leukophryene." *Epigraphica* 45 (1983), 11-48.

Errington, Malcolm R. "The Peace Treaty between Miletus and Magnesia." *Chiron* 19 (1989), 279-288.

Freely, John. "Magnesia ad Maeandrum" *The Western Mediterranean Coast of Turkey*. Istanbul: SEV Matbaacılık ve Yayıncılık, 1997, 1-8.

Kiel, Machiel. "Magnesia on the Maeander. From Hellenistic polis to Byzantine castle and to Emirate and Ottoman Marketplace." *Proceeding to the Second Intern. Congress of Ottoman Archeology*. Zaghouan: Fondation Temimi pour la echerche Scientifique et l'information, 1998, 101-114.

Piejko, Francis. "Decree of Antioch in Persis accepting Magnesian "Asylia" *Rivista Storica dell'Antichita* 17 (1987), 179-184.

_____. "Response of an Unknown City to Magnesia Concerning Her Asylia" *Rivista Storica dell'Antichita* 17 (1987), 185-188.

Metropolis

Aybek, Serdar. "Hellenistic and Roman Sculpture of Metropolis." Unpublished D.Phil. Dissertation. Ankara: Ankara University, 2004.

_____, Aygün Ekin Meriç and Ali Kazım Öz. *Metropolis: A Mother God City in Ionia. An Archaeological Guide*. Istanbul: Homer Kitabevi, 2009.

Ekin Meriç, Ayğun. "The Cult Cave of the Mother Goddess in Metropolis." Unpublished D. Phil. Dissertation. İzmir: Dokuz Eylül University, 2008.

Ersoy, A. "The Metropolis Stoa in the Light of the Hellenistic Western Anatolian Stoas." Unpublished D. Phil. Dissertation. İzmir: Ege University, 1988.

Freely, John. *The Aegean Coast of Turkey*. Istanbul: Sev Matbaacılık Ve Yayıncılık, 2003.

Gürler, B. "The Hellenistic Pottery from Metropolis." Unpublished D. Phil. Dissertation. İzmir: Ege University, 1994.

Köymen, C. "The Architectural Evaluation of Metropolis Ares Temple in the Light of Findings." Unpublished M. Phil. Thesis. İzmir: Dokuz Eylül University, 2004.

Meriç, Recep. "Pre-Bronze Age Settlements of West-Central Anatolia." *Anatolica* 19 (1993), 143-150.

Miletus

Bayhan, S. *Priene, Miletus, Didyma*. Istanbul, 1997.

Bean, George E. "Miletus." *Aegean Turkey: An Archaeological Guide*. London: Ernest Benn, 1966, 219-230.

Fontenrose, J. *Didyma: Apollos Oracle, Cult and Companions*. Berkeley, 1988.

Goedecken, K.B. "A Contribution to the Early History of Miletus: The Settlement in Mycenaean Times and Its Connections Overseas." In E.B. French and K.A. Wardle (eds.), *Problems in Greek Prehistory*. Bristol, 1988.

Gorman, Vanessa B. *Miletos: The Ornament of Ionia. A History of the City to 400 B.C.E.* Ann Arbor: Univ. of Michigan, 2001.

Herda, Alexander. "On the Lion Harbour and Other Harbours in Miletos: Recent Historical, Archaeological, Sedimentological, and Geophysical Research." *Proceedings of the Danish Institue at Athens* 7 (2013), 49-103.

Parke, H. W. "The Temple of Apollo at Didyma: The Building and Its Function." *JHS* 106 (1986), 121-131.

Schiering, W. "The Connections between the Oldest Settlement at Miletus and Crete." In R. Haegg and N. Marinatos (eds.), *The Minoan Thalassocracy: Myth and Reality.* Goeteborg, 1983.

Nicaea

Akbaygil, I., H. İnalcık and O. Aslanapa, eds. *Iznik Throughout History.* Istanbul: Türkiye İş Bankası, 2003.

Corsten, T. "The Role and Status of the Indigenous Population in Bithynia." In T.B. Nielsen (ed.), *Rome and the Black Sea Region: Domination, Romanisation, Resistance.* Aarhus: 2006, 85-92.

Harris, B.F. "Bithynia: Roman Sovereignty and the Survival of Hellenism." In W. Hasse and W. H. Temporini (eds.). *ANR* II, 7.2 (1980), 857-901.

Levick, B. "Pliny in Bithynia and What Followed." *Greece and Rome* 26 (1979), 119-131.

Nicols, J. "Patrons of Provinces in the Early Principate. The Case of Bithynia." *Zeitschrift für Papyrologie und Epigraphik* 80 (1990), 101-108.

Rabbel, W., H. Stümpel, Ş. Bariş, R. Pašteka, and P. Niewöhner. "A Newly Discovered Byzantine Church in Iznik/Nicaea," in: M. Şahin (ed.), *Uluslararsı İznik I. Konsil Senato Sarayının Lokalizasyonu Çalıştayı* Bursa, 2011, 105-127.

Storey, J.S. "Bithynia: History and Administration to the Time of Pliny the Younger." M.A. Thesis at Univ. Alberta. 1998.

Nicomedia

Çalık-Ross, A. *Ancient Izmit: Nicomedia.* Istanbul: 2007.

Corsten, T. "The Role and Status of the Indigenous Population in Bithynia." In T.B. Nielsen (ed.), *Rome and the Black Sea Region: Domination, Romanisation, Resistance.* Aarhus: 2006, 85-92.

Güney, Hale. "The Mint of Nicomedia (İzmit) and Civic Coins during the Roman Period." *Marmara Studies Symposium Proceedings* 27 (2008), 41-51.

_____. "The Resources and Economy of Roman Nicomedia." Ph.D. dissertation at Univ. of Exeter. 2012.

Harris, B.F. "Bithynia: Roman Sovereignty and the Survival of Hellenism." In W. Hasse and W. H. Temporini (eds.). *ANR* II, 7.2 (1980), 857-901.

Levick, B. "Pliny in Bithynia and What Followed." *Greece and Rome* 26 (1979), 119-131.

Marshall, A.J. "Pompey's Organization of Bithynia-Pontus: Two Neglected Texts." *Journal of Hellenic Studies* 58 (1968), 103-109.

Nicols, J. "Patrons of Provinces in the Early Principate. The Case of Bithynia." *Zeitschrift für Papyrologie und Epigraphik* 80 (1990), 101-108.

Storey, J.S. "Bithynia: History and Administration to the Time of Pliny the Younger." M.A. Thesis at Univ. Alberta. 1998.

Summerer, L. "Greeks and Natives on the Southern Black Sea Coast in Antiquity." In G. Erkut and S. Mitchell (eds.), *The Black Sea: Past, Present and Future.* London: British Institue at Ankara, 2007, 27-36.

Tsetskhladze, G.R. "Greek Penetration of the Black Sea." In G.R. Tsetskhladze and F. De Angelis (eds.) *The Archaeology of Greek Colonisation: Essays Dedicated to Sir John Boardman.* Oxford: 1994, 111-136.

Ward-Perkins, J.B. "The Marble Trade and Its Organisation. Evidence from Nicomedia." *Memoirs of the American Academy in Rome.* 36 (1980), 325-338.

_____. "Nicomedia and the Marble Trade." *Papers of the British School at Rome.* 48 (1980), 23-69.

Nysa

Bean, George E. " Nysa and Acharaca." *Turkey beyond the Maeander.* London: John Murray, 1980, 177-187.

Freely, John. *The Aegean Coast of Turkey.* Istanbul: Sev Matbaacılık Ve Yayıncılık, 2003.

_____. *The Western Interior of Turkey.* Istanbul: Sev Matbaacılık Ve Yayıncılık, 1998.

İdil, Vedat. "A Bust of Athena - Minerva from the Theatre at Nysa on the Meander." *Patronvs: Coşkun Özgünel'e 65. Yaş Armağanı. Festschrift für Coşkun Özgünel zum 65. Geburtstag.* Öztepe, Erhan and Musa Kadıoğlu (eds.). Istanbul: Homer Kitabevi, 2007.

Magie, David. *Roman Rule in Asia Minor to the End of the Third Century after Christ.* Princeton: Princeton Univ., 1950, 989-991.

Pergamon

Bean, George E. "Pergamum." *Aegean Turkey: An Archaeological Guide.* London: Ernest Benn, 1966, 68-94.

Cimok, Fatih. *Pergamum.* Istanbul: A. Turizm Yayinlari, 2001.

Evans, Richard. *A History of Pergamum: Beyond Hellenistic Kingship.* New York: Bloomsbury, 2012.

Freely, John. "Mysia: Pergamum" *The Aegean Coast of Turkey.* Istanbul: SEV Matbaacılık ve Yayıncılık, 2000, 27-59.

Hansen, Esther. V. *The Attalids of Pergamon.* 2nd ed. New York: Cornell Univ., 1971.

Koester, Helmut, ed. *Pergamon Citadel of the Gods: Archaeological Record, Literary Description, and Religious Development.* HTS 46. Harrisburg: Trinity Press International, 1998.

Kuttner, Ann. "Republican Rome Looks at Pergamon." *Harvard Studies in Classical Philology* 97 (1995): 157-178.

Lawall, Mark L. "Early Excavations at Pergamon and the Chronology of Rhodian Amphora Stamps." *Hesperia* 71, no. 3 (2002): 295-324.

Mattern, S.P. *Galen and the Rhetoric of Healing.* Baltimore: Johns Hopkins Univ., 2008.

Parrish, David, ed. *Urbanism in Western Asia Minor: New Studies on Aphrodisias, Ephesos, Hierapolis, Pergamon, Perge and Xanthos.* JRA Suppl. 45. Portsmouth: JRA, 2001.

Radt, Wolfgang. *Pergamon: Archaeological Guide.* 3rd ed. Istanbul: Turkiye Turing ve Otomobil Kurumu, 1984.

Romano, David G. "The Stadium of Eumenes II at Pergamon." *American Journal of Archaeology* 86 (1982), 586-589.

Thonemann, Peter. *Attalid Asia Minor: Money, International Relations, and the State.* Oxford: Oxford Univ. Press, 2013.

Philadelphia

Burrell, Barbara. "Iphigeneia in Philadelphia." *Classical Quarterly* 24 (2005), 223-256.

Freely, John. "Philadelphia" *The Western Mediterranean Coast of Turkey.* Istanbul: SEV Matbaacılık ve Yayıncılık, 1997, 52-56.

Malay, H. "The Sanctuary of Meter Phileis Near Philadelphia." *Epigraphica Anatolica* 6 (1985), 111-26.

Sardis

Bean, George E. "Sardis." *Aegean Turkey: An Archaeological Guide.* London: Ernest Benn, 1966, 259-270.

Buckler, W.H. and D. Robinson. *Sardis VII. 1: The Greek and Latin Inscriptions 1.* Leiden: Brill, 1932.

Freely, John. "Sardis" *The Aegean Coast of Turkey.* Istanbul: SEV Matbaacılık ve Yayıncılık, 2000, 115-131.

Gadbery, Laura M. "Archaeological Exploration of Sardis." *Harvard University Art Museums Bulletin* 3, no. 2 (1995): 54-59.

_____. "Archaeological Exploration of Sardis." *Harvard University Art Museums Bulletin* 4, no. 3 (1996): 49-53.

_____. "Archaeological Exploration of Sardis." *Harvard University Art Museums Bulletin* 5, no. 3 (1997): 47-50.

_____. "Archaeological Exploration of Sardis." *Harvard University Art Museums Bulletin* 6, no. 1 (1998): 51-54.

Gombosi, Elizabeth. "Archaeological Exploration of Sardis." *Annual Report (Harvard Art*

Museum) (2001): 54-58.

Gombosi, Elizabeth. "Archaeological Exploration of Sardis." *Annual Report (Harvard Art Museum)* (2002): 59-62.

Gombosi, Elizabeth. "Archaeological Exploration of Sardis." *Annual Report (Harvard Art Museum)* (2003): 65-69.

Greenwalt, Crawford H. Jr., Marcus L. Rautman. "The Sardis Campaigns of 1994 and 1995." *American Journal of Archaeology* 102, no. 3 (1998): 469-505.

Hanfmann, George M. A. *Sardis from Prehistory to Roman Times: Results of the Archaeological Exploration of Sardis 1958-1975.* Cambridge, MA: Harvard Univ., 1983.

_____ and Jane C. Waldbaum. *A Survey of Sardis and the Major Monuments Outside the City Walls.* Archaeological Exploration of Sardis. Cambridge, MA: Harvard Univ., 1975.

Piejko, Francis. "The Settlement of Sardis after the Fall of Achaeus." *American Journal of Philology* 108 (1987), 707-728.

Ramage, Nancy, H. "Two New Attic Cups and the Siege of Sardis." *American Journal of Archaeology* 90, no. 4 (1986): 419-424.

Ratté, Christopher, Thomas N. Howe and Clive Foss. "An Early Imperial Pseudodipteral Temple at Sardis." *American Journal of Archaeology* 90, no. 1 (1986): 45-68.

Ratté, Christopher. "Anthemion Stelae from Sardis." *American Journal of Archaeology* 98, no. 4 (1994): 593-607.

Seager, Andrew R. "The Building History of the Sardis Synagogue." *American Journal of Archaeology* 76, no. 4 (1972): 425-435.

Shear, Theodore L. "A Roman Chamber-Tomb at Sardis." *American Journal of Archaeology* 31, no. 1 (1927): 19-25.

Waldbaum, J.C. and G.M.A. Hanfmann. *A Survey of Sardis and Major Monuments Outside the City Walls.* Cambridge Report 1. Cambridge: Cambridge Univ., 1975.

Yegul, Fikret K. "The Marble Court of Sardis and Historical Reconstruction." *Journal of Field Archaeology* 3, no. 2 (1976): 169-194.

Smyrna

Ameling, Walter. "The Christian *lapsi* in Smyrna, 250 A.D. (*Martyrium Pionii* 12-14)." *Vigiliae Christianae* 62 (2008), 133-160.

Anderson, J. K. "Old Smyrna: The Corinthian Pottery." *The Annual of the British School at Athens* 54 (1959): 138-151.

Bagnall, Roger S. "Informal Writing in a Public Place: The Graffiti of Smyrna." In *Everyday Writing in the Graeco-Roman East*, ed. Roger Bagnall. Berkeley: Univ. California, 2010, 7-26.

Bean, George E. "Smyrna." *Aegean Turkey: An Archaeological Guide.* London: Ernest Benn, 1966, 41-52.

Boardman, John. "Old Smyrna: The Attic Pottery." *The Annual of the British School at Athens* 54 (1959): 152-181.

Cadoux, Cecil John. *Ancient Smyrna: A History of the City from the Earliest Times to 324 A.D.* Oxford: Blackwell, 1938.

Cook, J. M. "On the Date of Alyattes' Sack of Smyrna." *Annual of the British School at Athens* 80 (1985), 25-28.

_____, R.V. Nicholls and D. M. Pyle. *Old Smyrna Excavations: The Temples of Athena.* British School at Athens Supplementary Volume 30. London: British School at Athens, 1998.

Doğer, Ersin. *Smyrna of İzmir: From Paleolithic Age to Turkish Conquest.* İzmir: İletişim Kitabevi, 2006.

Ersoy, Akın. "Smyrna: Izmir's Past Glories, Naughty Graffiti and a Mystery Woman Called 1308." *World Archaeology* 52 (2012), 16-20.

Freely, John. "İzmir" *The Aegean Coast of Turkey.* Istanbul: SEV Matbaacılık ve Yayıncılık, 2000, 81-100.

Hasluck, F. W. "The 'Tomb of S. Polycarp' and the Topography of Ancient Smyrna." *The Annual of the British School at Athens* 20 (1914): 80-93.

Jeffery, L. H. "Old Smyrna: Inscriptions on Sherds and Small Objects." *The Annual of the British School at Athens* 59 (1964): 39-49.

Lewis, R. G. "Sulla and Smyrna." *Classical Quarterly* 41 (1991), 126-129.

Nicholls, R. V. "Site-Plan of Old Smyrna." *The Annual of the British School at Athens* 54 (1959).

_____. "Old Smyrna: The Iron Age Fortifications and Associated Remains on the City Perimeter." *The Annual of the British School at Athens* 54 (1959): 35-137.

Tataki, Argyro B. "Nemesis, Nemeseis, and the Gladiatorial Games at Smyrna." *Mnemosyne* 62 (2009), 639-648.

Thyatira

Forbes, Clarence A. "Ancient Athletic Guilds." *Classical Philology* 50 (1955), 238-252.

Freely, John. "Thyatira" *The Aegean Coast of Turkey.* Istanbul: SEV Matbaacılık ve Yayıncılık, 2000, 109-110.

Carter, Michael. "Gladiatorial Combat with 'Sharp' Weapons (τοῖς ὀξέσισιδήροις)." *Zeitschrift für Papyrologie und Epigraphik.* 155 (2006), 161-175.

Hicks, E. L. "Inscriptions from Thyatira." *The Classical Review* 3, no. 3 (1889): 136-138.

Jones, C. "A Decree of Thyatira in Lydia." *Chiron* 29 (1999), 1-21.

Meinardus, Otto F. "The Christian Remains of the Seven Churches of the Apocalypse." *Biblical Archaeologist* 37 (1974), 69-82.

Pleket, H. W. "Olympic Benefactors." *Zeitschrift für Papyrologie und Epigraphic* 20 (1976), 1-18.

Tralles

Bean, George E. "Tralles and Nysa." *Turkey Beyond the Maeander*. London: John Murray, 1980, 177-187.

Freely, John. "Tralles" *The Western Mediterranean Coast of Turkey*. Istanbul: SEV Matbaacılık ve Yayıncılık, 1997, 8-10.

Hansen, William. *Phlegon of Tralles' Book of Marvels*. Exeter: Univ. of Exeter, 1997.

Jones, Christopher P. "An Inscription Seen by Agathias." *Zeitschrift für Papyroligie und Epigraphik* 179 (2011), 107-115.

Moyer, Ian S. "Thessalos of Tralles and Cultural Exchange." In *Prayer, Magic, and the Stars in the Ancient and Late Antique World*, eds. by S. Noegel, J. Walker and B. Wheeler. University Park: Pennsylvania State Univ., 2003, 39-56.

Piekjo, Francis. "Letter of Eumenes II to Tralles Concerning Inviolability and Tax Exemption for a Temple after 188 B.C." *Chiron* 18 (1988), 55-69.

Saraçoğlu, Aslı. "Hellenistic and Roman Unguentaria from the Necropolis of Tralleis." *Anadolu* 37 (2011), 1-42.

THE CRADLE OF THE CIVILIZATION

New Discoveries

THE NEOLITHIC IN TURKEY

NEW EXCAVATIONS & NEW RESEARCH

Edited by:
MEHMET ÖZDOĞAN
NEZİH BAŞGELEN
PETER KUNIHOLM

THE EUPHRATES BASIN

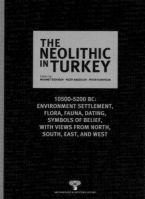

THE NEOLITHIC IN TURKEY

Edited by:
MEHMET ÖZDOĞAN - NEZİH BAŞGELEN - PETER KUNIHOLM

**10500-5200 BC:
ENVIRONMENT SETTLEMENT,
FLORA, FAUNA, DATING,
SYMBOLS OF BELIEF,
WITH VIEWS FROM NORTH,
SOUTH, EAST, AND WEST**

ARCHAEOLOGY & ART PUBLICATIONS

THE NEOLITHIC IN TURKEY

NEW EXCAVATIONS & NEW RESEARCH

Edited by:
MEHMET ÖZDOĞAN
NEZİH BAŞGELEN
PETER KUNIHOLM

THE TIGRIS BASIN

THE NEOLITHIC IN TURKEY

NEW EXCAVATIONS & NEW RESEARCH

Edited by:
MEHMET ÖZDOĞAN
NEZİH BAŞGELEN
PETER KUNIHOLM

**NORTHWESTERN TURKEY
AND ISTANBUL**

THE NEOLITHIC IN TURKEY

NEW EXCAVATIONS & NEW RESEARCH

Edited by:
MEHMET ÖZDOĞAN
NEZİH BAŞGELEN
PETER KUNIHOLM

CENTRAL TURKEY

THE NEOLITHIC IN TURKEY

NEW EXCAVATIONS & NEW RESEARCH

Edited by:
MEHMET ÖZDOĞAN
NEZİH BAŞGELEN
PETER KUNIHOLM

WESTERN TURKEY

ARCHAEOLOGY & ART
PUBLICATIONS

www.arkeolojisanat.com

THE NEOLITHIC IN TURKEY

NEW EXCAVATIONS & NEW RESEARCH

Edited by:
MEHMET ÖZDOĞAN
NEZİH BAŞGELEN
PETER KUNIHOLM

ARCHAEOLOGY & ART PUBLICATIONS

www.arkeolojisanat.com / info@arkeolojisanat.com